The B

THE BISHOPS

Trevor Beeson

scm press

British Library Cataloguing in Publication data

A catalogue record of this book is available
from the British Library

0 334 02916 3

First published in 2002 by SCM Press
9-17 St Albans Place, London N1 0NX
www.scm-canterburypress.co.uk

This paperback edition published in 2003

SCM Press is a division of
SCM-Canterbury Press Ltd

Typeset by Regent Typesetting, London
Printed and bound in Great Britain by
Biddles Ltd, *www.biddles.co.uk*

Contents

Acknowledgements

This book was floating about in my mind for several years but it was not until I had read Noel Annan's illuminating and hugely entertaining volume *The Dons*, published in 1999 shortly before his death, that I saw how best the bishops might be handled. I cannot offer anything even approaching his erudition and wit, but an acknowledgement of his influence is due.

John Bowden, editor of SCM Press for more than thirty years and a greatly valued friend, gave enthusiastic encouragement when I embarked on this enterprise, and his successor Alex Wright helped me over the final hurdle. I am grateful to them both.

Esmé Parker once again, and with great speed, used her secretarial skill to turn the faint and much-corrected output of my ancient manual typewriter into something the editors could read, and her husband John dealt with the technical mysteries of computers and disks now inseparable from modern authorship. My warmest thanks to them, and also to Fiona Mather for her diligent and invariably successful quest for the many books required by my research.

TB

Introduction

The purpose of this book is twofold. It provides brief portraits of forty-eight bishops who were in office from about the time of the 1832 Reform Bill, when the Church of England as well as the nation as a whole entered a period of continuous change, until the final years of the twentieth century. The bishops have been chosen to illustrate the remarkably rich variety of personality and talent to be found among those who exercised leadership in the Church during that time, and it may be doubted whether any other era in English history was so fortunate. The main part of this book will, it is hoped, be of interest to a readership much wider than that which normally turns to a book about the Church.

There is however another, more urgent, purpose. Whereas the bishops portrayed in these pages can be categorized in one or more dynamic roles, virtually all of today's bishops fall into the single category of pastoral-manager, with the strongest emphasis on manager. Few bishops would choose such a role, but the development of the Church's life in the twentieth century has, in common with that of many other institutions, made strong management essential and, because of the nature of the Church's leadership, the responsibility for too many aspects of this has fallen on the bishops. They now need to be liberated from a role which has become a denial of the true purpose of their sacred office and a serious hindrance to the Church's mission in the twenty-first century.

Bishops have never been popular – at least not in Western Europe. Individual bishops have often been admired, many have been loved in their dioceses, but taken as a whole – as a bench – they have aroused at best suspicion and at worst downright hostility. During the 1830s their palaces were attacked by mobs and their effigies publicly burned. A dead cat was thrown into the Bishop of London's carriage. Today they are seen by most people as relics from the past whose opinions need not be taken seriously and whose chief task is to manage the affairs of churches which are in numerical decline and whose influence in society is no longer significant. Even in the General Synod they are not trusted, as the Bishop of Birmingham, Mark Santer, pointed out in an address to his diocesan synod in 1990.

There is no reason why bishops and the church they lead should be popular. The founder of the faith they exist to promote enjoyed a brief spell of popularity, but for the most part was despised and rejected, and his life was ended by public execution on the national scrap heap outside the city walls of Jerusalem. In an increasingly secularized society, in which Christian beliefs and values no longer command universal support, it would hardly be surprising if bishops who are faithful to Jesus Christ were unpopular. All they stand for directly challenges much of what is commonly regarded as essential to human welfare and necessary to human progress. They are a sign of contradiction, and Archbishop Janani Luwun of Uganda and Archbishop Oscar Romero of El Salvador were powerful late twentieth-century reminders that some modern bishops are still called to martyrdom.

But the long-standing and widespread unpopularity of bishops in the West has nothing to do with courageous witness against the forces of evil in society. On the contrary, it has more to do with the fact that for many centuries the bishops were closely identified with those elements in society which exercise power in an arbitrary and unjust manner, to their own great benefit and to the serious disadvantage of the common people. The anti-episcopal actions of the 1830s did not arise from the bishops' defence of the Nicene Creed, but from the fact that, almost to a man, they opposed in the House of Lords the Great Reform Act which offered the prospect of justice and liberty to the masses.

Without entering into the debate as to whether the conversion of Constantine to the Christian faith in the fourth century was, in effect, the conversion of the Church to the acceptance of state control, or whether the symphony of church and state which resulted from Pope Leo III's crowning of Charlemagne as Holy Roman Emperor in AD 800 involved a fatal compromise of Christian principles, it cannot be disputed that throughout the Middle Ages the price paid by the bishops of Western Europe for their high place in society was submission to the authority of the principalities and powers. The Pope could not appoint a bishop without royal consent and, once appointed, the bishop was free only to conform to the royal will. During the years of the sixteenth- and seventeenth-century Reformation in England the extent of this subordination was demonstrated with painful clarity in the dismissal, the imprisonment and sometimes the execution of bishops who did not accept changes that were as much political as religious. And also in the readiness of most to change their allegiances to meet royal demands.

The bishops lost their high political positions during Cromwell's Commonwealth and, following the Restoration of the Monarchy in the 1660s and the advance of the Enlightenment, steps were taken to exclude them from secular office in the state. Nonetheless they retained their seats in the House of Lords and for another two centuries exerted considerable influence through their speeches and votes in Parliament's Upper House. This influence required the Prime Ministers to take careful account of the political views of those whom they nominated for appointment to bishoprics and, once appointed, the bishops were well aware that their duties included spending six months in London every year in order to support the government in a House of Lords which still had considerable power. Only when the House of Commons began to exercise democratic authority did the political allegiance of bishops become less significant.

The effect of episcopal involvement in state affairs extending over a thousand years was inevitably to create a wide gulf between the bishops and the Church, and between the bishops and society as a whole. The leaders of the community committed to following in the footsteps of the poor man of Nazareth whose mother declared that he had 'put down the mighty from the seat and exalted the humble and meek' lived in great castles and palaces, received massive incomes and occupied the highest positions in society. It was a hugely privileged role and, in theory, should have enabled them to exert strong Christian influence over national affairs, but most were essentially conformists who used religion to defend the status quo. Neither were they, with some notable exceptions, men of any distinction and during the eighteenth century their lack of leadership over a largely somnolent church constituted a dark period in the Church of England's history.

Change came with the general renewal of English society and political advance that attended the passing of the Reform Bill in 1832. Prime Ministers, while not unaware of the need for episcopal support in the House of Lords, began to seek out able men for bishoprics and on some occasions were prepared to accord priority to ability. Gladstone became the first Prime Minister to have an ecclesiastical adviser. Queen Victoria also perceived the need for both church and society to have strong spiritual leadership and from about 1840 onwards the Church of England was led by a number of bishops who, in any age, would be regarded as outstanding in intellect and in administration. The place of the Church in society and the size of episcopal stipends combined to make a bishopric an attractive proposition for those who felt drawn to exercise leadership at the highest level. A number of these moved to the episcopate from headmasterships of the new flourishing public schools.

But, viewed historically, this turned out to be a false dawn. The number of outstanding bishops was small, and the awakening of the Church came too late for it to engage fully or creatively with the huge changes taking place in English society during the nineteenth century. The rapid development of industrial/urban communities left the bishops floundering. Some made valiant efforts to build new churches and deploy more clergy in the expanding towns and cities, but they were constrained by a vision of church and society so limited that their chief aim was to reproduce the parochial system which for the previous 1,000 years had been the bulwark of agrarian societies. It would no longer suffice and although there was a mini-religious revival in the 1870s and 1880s the alienation of the working classes from any sort of religious commitment continued inexorably throughout the century. The twentieth century was to see this alienation spread to the middle classes with serious effects on church attendance.

The gulf between the Church of England and the working classes was widened by the failure of the bishops as a whole to recognize the gross injustices that accompanied the development of the towns and cities and the impoverishment of the countryside. The anti-episcopal riots that resulted from the voting at the time of the Reform Bill caused considerable alarm and prompted some bishops to a greater awareness of the Christian imperative to have compassion on the poor and needy. They instructed their clergy to exercise a special concern for the poorest among their parishioners. But in no sense did they align themselves with the infant but rapidly growing forces that demanded radical social change, emphasizing justice rather than charity. Indeed, the presence of these forces and the noise of revolution in continental Europe encouraged even the most socially conscious bishops to look backwards rather than ahead, believing it to be both desirable and possible for English society to return to the integrated and caring forms of the pre-industrial era.

Equally serious was the failure of the bishops to accept the implications of the scientific revolution which gathered pace throughout the nineteenth century. This was symbolized by the confrontation between Bishop Samuel Wilberforce, among the most able of the bishops, and T. H. Huxley at Oxford in 1860. There was no meeting of minds between the exponents of religion and the pioneers of science and the ramifications of this were experienced not only in the Church's hostility to scientists but also in its treatment of those who sought to apply modern scholarship to the Bible. By the end of the century therefore, the bishops were well on the way to being discredited – politically and intellectually – and inevitably the influence of the Church continued to wane. The parochial clergy were seriously impoverished by agricultural distress.

One effect of this was a serious reduction in the number of able men seeking Holy Orders and providing a strong cadre from which bishops could be chosen. There were in any case other opportunities of serving society and making money. Fellows of Oxford and Cambridge colleges were no longer required to be ordained, neither were headmasters in an increasing number of public schools. Nonetheless, many Oxbridge colleges continued to give admission preference to ordination candidates, even when these were of poor intellectual quality, and, since bishops were still chosen overwhelmingly from members of the older universities, the effect on the Church's leadership was noticeable. Bishop Hensley Henson wrote to the Bishop of Limerick in 1925,

> The extent of the decline in social importance which has befallen the clergy during the last century is difficult to appreciate and almost impossible to overstate. It has been marked with a continual lowering of their intellectual equipment until it would really seem impossible that we can fall lower.

Two years later an exasperated Dick Sheppard wrote in his *Impatience of a Parson* – a small volume which aroused much anger among the Church's leaders –

> Frankly, I doubt if any Bishop on the present Bench is capable of really leading the Church on the road of sacrifice. The Church needs a bigger man than any of its present Bishops.

Which is not to say that the twentieth century did not produce some great bishops, but as in the previous century they were not in the majority and, with the notable exception of William Temple, the best of them were less able than the best of their nineteenth-century predecessors.

Remarkably, and depressingly, the Church of England continued for most of the twentieth century to restrict its choice of leaders to those educated in the socially elite educational institutions. As late as 1958 no fewer than 38 of the 43 diocesan bishops had been to either Oxford or Cambridge. Eighteen of these had been to the leading public schools – Eton, Winchester, St Paul's, Westminster, Rugby, Repton and the like – while the rest had been to minor public schools and well-known grammar schools. All these schools had, prior to 1939, encouraged their pupils to devote their lives to the service of the community, rather than to the making of money. Inasmuch as the overwhelming majority of public school and Oxbridge students were at that time from middle- and upper-class families, the bishops were virtually all from privileged backgrounds, thus reinforcing the Church of England's identification with the prosperous and usually conservative minority in society. The choice of cathedral deans displayed a similar bias. Some able non-public-school, non-Oxbridge men were undoubtedly passed over, though it is impossible to tell how many or to assess what difference to the leadership of the Church the elevation of such men might have made.

By the end of the twentieth century however, the social background of the diocesan bishops had undergone a noticeable change. The number of diocesan bishops who had attended major public schools was reduced from eighteen to four, with none from Eton, Winchester or Rugby. Twenty-eight had been to grammar schools and one, none other than the Archbishop of Canterbury, to a humble secondary modern school. Twenty-six went on to Oxford or Cambridge, five to London University, four to Leeds, two to Lampeter and one each to Exeter, Lancaster, Edinburgh, Nottingham, Belfast and Karachi. Sadly, it is impossible to say that, in consequence, the calibre of the episcopal bench as a whole has been strengthened. On the contrary, the Church of England entered the twenty-first century with an alarming lack of bishops of widely acknowledged ability. The reasons for this are not simple.

After the questioning years of the 1960s, the ordained ministry of the Church ceased to be an attractive or compelling vocation for many of the most able young men of the succeeding decades. The image of the Church as an outdated, deeply conservative and increasingly irrelevant institution made them unwilling to enter its full-time service. They had better things to do. To this dynamic rejection of ordination there was added in the 1980s and 1990s an increasingly secular world view in which the making of money was seen as more laudable than most forms of public service. Thus education, the social services, the armed forces, the police, medicine and nursing joined the Church in experiencing an acute shortage of leaders capable of responding to very challenging situations. The widening of the fields of recruitment has not solved this acute problem, though it may have mitigated a more catastrophic outcome in all these spheres of service.

This is not to say that the present bishops are lacking in gifts or other than deeply devoted to their high calling. Never have they been more busy and rarely has their task been more difficult. Throughout the twentieth century it was acknowledged, whenever the primacy fell vacant, that the Archbishopric of Canterbury was an impossible job which nonetheless someone needed to undertake. In 1998 Archbishop Carey spent three weeks presiding over the Lambeth Conference, visited 30 countries, delivered 140 sermons, speeches and addresses, made more than 50 broadcasts, contributed ten articles to journals and books, spent many hours in the House of Lords and on other state affairs, gave innumerable interviews and dealt with a mountain of letters, emails and faxes. His car was equipped with a telephone and a computer to enable such work to be uninterrupted by journeys, and it was reported that he rose at 6.30 am or earlier, rarely went to bed before midnight and took one weekend off every six weeks. Like Dr Johnson's dog, walking on its hind legs, it was no marvel that Dr Carey's leadership was uncertain but rather that he managed to accomplish anything at all. A review committee, headed by a former Foreign Secretary, Lord Hurd, has made proposals for change in the demands made of archbishops, and these await consideration.

The pressure on other diocesan bishops is obviously less great but remains destructive. This is due partly to the ever-increasing demands made on the leaders of an institution in decline, and partly to a changed understanding of the nature of the institution in which episcopal ministry is exercised. The first creates serious management problems. Until 1939 the Bishop of Durham had no telephone in his episcopal palace, and although he complained about the difficulty of obtaining domestic staff nonetheless maintained a substantial household. He devoted a good deal of time to study and writing, and often occupied his place in the House of Lords. He knew the clergy of his diocese well and, being an outstandingly fine and often controversial preacher, his visits to parishes were awaited expectantly.

This expectancy was heightened by their infrequency. The parish clergy did not for the most part welcome an episcopal visit except for confirmation and other events requiring the bishop's presence. They felt secure in their role and greatly valued their independence. Part of the attraction of the ordained ministry was that it offered a sphere of personal service and little accountability, except to God. The clergyman was self-employed; if he was lucky his income was derived from a local landholding, rather than from central church funds. In any case a life freehold offered absolute security of office and income, unless he committed a very grave offence. Few parishes were wealthy but a private income, financial support from the big houses, a few fund-raising events and modest Sunday collections provided sufficient money to meet the small annual budget. Emergency repairs to an ancient church building required a special appeal, usually responded to by most people in rural parishes and by sufficient in the rest, but little was spent on routine conservation.

In this relatively relaxed atmosphere few noticed how relentlessly the Church's assets of money, membership and ordained manpower were ebbing away, and the 1939–45 world war was needed to awaken the Church to the danger of the financial situation in which it was now engulfed. In spite of considerable and largely successful efforts to obtain higher returns from the Church's new centralized capital, local congregations have been required to find money to pay a significant part of their parson's stipend and the whole of his pension. The cost of training ordination candidates, and of other elements of the central bureaucracy in Westminster, has made unprecedented demands on the parishes. Thus today's bishop cannot ignore money and much of his time is spent managing an institution in which money has become the most powerful influence over action. In June 2001 Truro diocese announced that one-third of its stipendiary clergy posts were to be cut to meet rising costs, and in the following month Wakefield diocese announced a reduction of 25 clergy and lay posts in order to meet a deficit of £700,000. In these circumstances, and faced by a decline in the size of congregations and the marginalization of the Church generally, it is hardly surprising that the morale of many of the clergy is at a low ebb and that they feel uncertain of their role. No longer do they feel secure. Indeed, a London University report in August 2001 indicated that a high proportion of those ministering in urban areas live in fear of physical assault by beggars and other social misfits. No longer are they the confident kings of their own castles.

Hence the requirement of bishops to exercise a more intensive and time-consuming pastoral role among their clergy. They are expected to be out and about in their dioceses, sharing in the worship offered in the parish churches, available for interviews and counselling, and open to requests for help by telephone and email from the rectories and vicarages, few of which are now without a computer. The bishop's chaplain, often a bright young priest who acted as a general factotum, has been replaced by a lay assistant, with good administrative skill, and at least two secretaries who are needed to deal with overfull diaries and a mountain of paper. In April 2000 the Bishop of St Albans reported that he received more than 10,000 letters every year, besides an even larger number of emails, faxes and telephone calls.

Until 1870 there were no suffragan bishops in England, the office having been allowed to lapse at the end of the sixteenth century. In that year two were appointed to assist in the Dioceses of Canterbury and Lincoln; by the end of the century there were nineteen more; by 1950 there were 40 of them and in 2000 they outnumbered the diocesan bishops, having reached a total of 66. The role of suffragan bishop can be a very satisfying one for someone who has strong pastoral gifts. Although he must share to some extent in the administration of a diocese, his responsibilities are considerably less than those of a diocesan bishop and he has therefore much greater freedom to engage in pastoral work among the clergy. On the other hand, he and those to whom he ministers are aware that he does not carry ultimate responsibility, even in those dioceses where an area system is in operation, and a priest who has enjoyed unbridled responsibility for the leadership of a major parish often feels frustrated after spending a few years in a subordinate episcopal role.

This, not infrequently, makes him yearn for appointment to a diocese of his own, and the chances of his being so appointed are now fairly high. A General Synod report *Working with the Spirit: Choosing*

Diocesan Bishops (2001) indicated that, of the nineteen diocesan bishops appointed during the five years 1996–2000, fourteen were suffragans, two were diocesans who had previously been suffragans, and even the professor appointed had once been a suffragan. At first sight this might appear to be a sensible policy inasmuch as the current demands of a diocesan bishopric are believed to require previous episcopal experience. In hierarchical organizations promotion normally follows a similar course, but the Church does not necessarily benefit from adoption of a secular model. Suffragan bishops are chosen by diocesans largely for a subordinate pastoral role. The priest so chosen is not necessarily required to have outstanding intellectual gifts, wide vision or the ability to pioneer new expression of ministry and mission. Some diocesan bishops are careful not to choose suffragans more able than themselves. Thus his elevation to a diocesan bishopric is unlikely to bring much insight or inspiration either to his diocese or to the bench of bishops as a whole. It is also necessary to recognize that in the past some translations from suffragan to diocesan sees have been made in order to solve problems arising from the incompatibility of outlook or temperament experienced in dioceses where a new diocesan bishop has inherited a suffragan appointed by his predecessor. All in all therefore the elevation of suffragans has served to reinforce the concept of the bishop's role as primarily that of a pastoral administrator rather than that of a pioneer visionary leader – a concept which this book aims to challenge.

2

The aristocrats and the courtiers

During the eighteenth century it became common for one of the younger sons of noble families to become a parson. This offered a useful but not too demanding occupation, some sort of income which could if necessary be augmented by family money, and usually a fine rectory in ample grounds that would enable its occupant to live the life of a country gentleman. The family's own living was the natural sphere for his ministry and if he tired of this or entertained ambitions friends of the family with patronage at their disposal could be relied on to look after his interests. Some were excellent parish priests, many played a prominent part in local affairs, and a number who had good political contacts became deans or bishops. This tradition continued into the nineteenth century, during the first three-quarters of which one-half of the bishops of England and Wales were of patrician background.

Lord Robert John Eden was Bishop of Bath and Wells from 1854 to 1869 and he was followed there by Lord Arthur Charles Hervey, son of the fifth Earl and first Marquess of Bristol, who reigned until 1894. Lord John Thomas Pelham, the fourth son of the Earl of Chichester and a fervent evangelical, was at Norwich from 1857 to 1893 and was generally thought to be a very good bishop who, it was said, 'applied a gentle but effective stimulus to the dormant energies of the Honorary Canons and Rural Deans'. Lord Alwyn Compton, a son of the Marquess of Northampton, also did well at Ely where he was Bishop from 1886 to 1906. Before this the Prime Minister, W. E. Gladstone, had suggested him for the Deanery of Windsor but Queen Victoria, demonstrating that she was not to be influenced by aristocratic birth, refused to accept him.

Edward Stuart Talbot

She was however pleased to accept the nomination to the episcopal bench of Edward Stuart Talbot, Bishop successively of Rochester, Southwark and Winchester during the years 1895 to 1923. There was plenty of blue blood in his veins – he belonged to one of the oldest English families – and he was also a man of unusual ability. He was born in 1844, his father being a son of Earl Talbot and his mother a daughter of James Archibald Stuart Wortley-Mackenzie, Lord Warncliffe. His father having died young, his mother, who was a friend of Lady Lyttleton and Mrs Gladstone, sent him to Charterhouse as a day boy, but his time there was cut short by ill-health. This did not however affect his performance at Christ Church, Oxford, where he took firsts in classics, law and modern history and on the strength of this was appointed a tutor.

In 1870, when still only 25, he was appointed first Warden of the newly-founded Keble College, Oxford. It proved to be a brilliant choice. Talbot belonged to the Tractarian tradition of the founders and shared their aim that the college should provide students of limited means with a university education in a community that wholeheartedly embraced the faith and practices of the Church of England. During a period when most of the Oxford colleges were busy ridding themselves of church influence the new foundation was often ridiculed but Talbot stayed for eighteen years and put the college on its feet. He could hardly have foreseen that 100 years after his departure the Warden of Keble would be a lay-woman. He left to everyone's surprise to become Vicar of Leeds. This was a major piece of responsibility, but the contrast between Talbot's background and the mores of a Northern industrial city could not have been greater. A working-class ministry was however well within the Tractarian tradition and Talbot was not the first aristocrat to display concern for the poor. Asked about his political allegiance he replied, 'Conservative, but with a bad conscience.' In Leeds Talbot had more dealings with the leaders of civic life than with the inhabitants of the back street, who were ministered to by a large team of curates. Nonetheless he made good use of the experience and there was great sorrow in the city when his appointment as Bishop of Rochester was announced in 1895.

Plans were already being made for the division of the third largest diocese in the Church of England and Talbot saw these through to completion, bravely electing to become the first Bishop of Southwark when this new see covering the whole of South London was created in 1905. He was already living within the new diocese and one of his first tasks was to turn the former priory church of St Saviour and St Mary Overie, near London Bridge railway station, into a modest cathedral. After much demanding work among people largely alienated from the Church he was in 1911 translated to Winchester. This was a natural move inasmuch as he was now aged 67 and in need of what had a century earlier been known as one of 'the bishoprics of ease'. Moreover he was by now a highly regarded figure in the Church, for whom a senior bishopric would be appropriate, and his background enabled him without difficulty to discharge the duties of the Prelate of the Order of the Garter.

As a High Church bishop he was always treated with suspicion by Winchester's evangelical clergy and the Ritualists were also upset when he felt obliged to call them to liturgical order. Like some other men of brilliant mind, Talbot often had difficulty in expressing himself attractively and with clarity, and his communication problem sometimes led to overlong sermons and speeches. But he was nonetheless an adornment of the episcopal bench and he left the Church of England a rich legacy in his sons – Edward, who became Superior of the Community of the Resurrection, and Neville, who became Bishop of Pretoria. Another son, Gilbert, was killed in the 1914–18 war and Toc H was founded in his memory.

William Cecil

Easily the most extraordinary episcopal appointment of the twentieth century was that of Lord Rupert Ernest William Gascoyne Cecil to the Bishopric of Exeter in 1916. A scion of the great house of Cecil and second son of the third Marquess of Salisbury, the nineteenth-century Prime Minister, he was totally unsuited by aptitude and experience for a bishopric, and his eccentricity sometimes seemed to take him into the realm of madness. Stories of his strange behaviour were legion and greatly relished. What lay behind his appointment to Exeter, made by H. H. Asquith during the darkest days of the 1914–18 war, is impossible to ascertain. Had it occurred in the eighteenth century, when aristocratic influence was everything, it would have occasioned no great surprise, but by 1916 the Church of England, in common with most other institutions, was valuing efficiency and in a rapidly changing world could no longer take old allegiances for granted. One possible, though sadly cynical, explanation relates to the income of the see of Exeter which amounted to £4,200 per annum but was reduced by one third to pay a pension to his predecessor who lived until 1931. Only someone of substantial private means, such as Cecil, could afford to become Bishop of Exeter, and in the event he was in office for twenty years until his death in 1936.

He was born in Hatfield House in 1863 and had an unhappy time at Eton, where he was bullied and, with good reasons, regarded as a queer fish. Thus he acquired the nickname 'Fish' which, among family and friends, stuck for the remainder of his life. His face was also said to resemble a fish, though in later life this was disguised by a long, flowing beard. At University College, Oxford, he greatly enjoyed himself, but was often in trouble with the college authorities and left with an undistinguished third in law. At this point he thought of joining the Royal Navy but pulled back when he contemplated the discipline and salt pork. He then spent a few months working in the slums of London's East End before becoming a curate at Great Yarmouth. Soon afterwards he married Lady Florence ('Fluffy') Bootle-Wilbraham, a daughter of the Earl Lathom, by whom he had four sons, three of whom were killed in the 1914–18 war, and three daughters, one of whom died when she was only eighteen. His curacy lasted little more than twelve months, for in 1888 his father appointed him Rector of Hatfield, with a fine church and rectory alongside the magnificent family seat.

Cecil was unwilling, however, to live in the grand rectory because it was too far from the village, and he persuaded his father to build him something more modest nearer the homes of his parishioners. Nonetheless he enjoyed a comfortable enough life on his stipend and private income which, in today's money, totalled about £45,000 per annum. For the next 28 years he exercised a simple, pastoral ministry, concentrating on the Sunday services and visiting the people in their homes, and eschewing the clubs, missions and parish magazines which had been started in most parishes during the Victorian era. He took great care over the services – simplifying them and sometimes complaining 'The Bible is an awkward book' – and visited in the evenings in order to meet the men. But although he worked hard and was greatly loved, the response was disappointing. 'There is a terrible slackness and torpidity about religion in Hatfield,' he wrote in 1912. 'There is hardly any enthusiasm . . . Alas, what a confession of failure after 24 years.' Earlier, in 1908, Bishop Edward Stuart Talbot of Southwark had invited him to move to a slum parish in South London but he declined on the grounds that the souls of country people were just as important as those of the towns, and that in any case he regarded Hatfield as his life's work. He became Rural Dean of Hatfield, an Honorary Canon of St Albans Abbey and a chaplain to King Edward VII. But then came the totally unexpected offer of the Bishopric of Exeter and, although he did not wish to go, he was eventually persuaded to accept. He took with him an interest in China, which had started when he attended a Pan-Anglican Congress held in London in 1908. This led to several oriental visits, an unsuccessful attempt to establish a Christian university there and a book, *Changing China* (1910), which he wrote with the aid of his wife.

'Love in a mist' they called Cecil in Exeter and it was always said with affection, for his administrative ineptitude and autocratic unwillingness to take advice were matched by a most loving personality. Indeed, the ever-generous W. R. Matthews, who became Dean of Exeter in Cecil's time, described him as 'A great Christian and a great Bishop.' But

Matthews's wife had a shock when she went to have tea with the bishop and his wife on the day before her husband's installation. Soon after her arrival Cecil threw some powdered copper sulphate on the fire to turn the flames bright green. 'Nice colour' he remarked, and when the crumpets appeared two rats came out of holes in the floor. These were tossed pieces of crumpet and Mrs Matthews was assured that rats were intelligent and could be friendly. He refused to live in the grand episcopal palace at Exeter, choosing instead a more modest house some two miles out of the city and retaining only an office in the palace. A bicycle, painted orange to avoid confusion of ownership, was his normal means of transport between the two, but the distinctive colour was not foolproof. On one occasion he rode off on a black model belonging to a lady and, having discovered his mistake, returned to Exeter, apologized to its owner, raised his hat and immediately mounted the same machine and pedalled home. Travelling further afield in the diocese, he generally used the train and had many adventures. Finding himself on one such journey without a ticket, the inspector assured him that the honesty of the Bishop of Exeter was not in doubt. 'But I need a ticket to know where I am going,' was Cecil's plaintive reply. Frequently he would telephone his wife to ask 'Where am I?' and, having safely arrived in a parish, anything could happen. Detached from an outdoor procession and lost, he enquired of an astonished villager, 'Which way did hounds go?' Robing in the church vestry before a service, he held his handkerchief between his teeth, but neglected to return it to his pocket and moved in procession to the altar with it still dangling from his mouth. Yet his support of the parish clergy and concern for the welfare of them and their families was beyond all praise. But in his enthusiasm to increase the amount of pastoral care available to them he crossed swords with the cathedral over a proposal that the office of dean should be abolished and its duties transferred to the bishop. The stipend thus saved would be used to pay a suffragan bishop and the canons would be required to work in the diocese as archdeacons. Unsurprisingly the proposal came to nothing and was remembered only as 'one of Love in a Mist's madcap ideas'.

He rarely went to the House of Lords, except when on duty for saying the Prayers, though he was a strong supporter of the trades unions and in 1926 backed the striking coal-miners. The Convocation of Canterbury and the Church Assembly bored him, and he opposed the 1928 Revised Prayer Book. Earlier he was among the bishops who opposed the appointment of Hensley Henson to the Bishopric of Hereford, but this did not stand in the way of a strong and enduring friendship with Henson. W. R. Matthews, who later moved from Exeter to become Dean of St Paul's, likened Cecil to Bishop Winnington-Ingram of London in as much as 'both were capable of saying some very silly things, but they could sometimes speak like prophets and make one feel that they were closer to God than most men'. He summed him up in verse:

William Exon

A shaggy head, a woolly mind,
The Cecil temper – and behind?
Ah yes ! I wonder what you'd find?
A humble soul, perplext and kind.

These were not bad qualities in a Christian bishop, but hardly sufficient on their own to meet the demands made on episcopal leadership in the twentieth century.

Charles Sumner

Ministering alongside the aristocratic bishops there were always some who owed their position to close association with the Royal Family and the Court. These were rarely of noble birth. Some came from clerical families, others from the merchant class, and often enough it was only by chance that they moved into royal circles and made an impression favourable enough to secure appointment to a bishopric.

Charles Richard Sumner, Bishop of Llandaff 1826–28, then of Winchester, 1828–68, was the son of a Warwickshire rector and owed all his appointments, apart from a Hampshire curacy, to King George IV. Born in Kenilworth in 1790, he went to Eton and on to King's College, Cambridge, with a scholarship. During his final year at Eton, however, he had written what turned out to be a sensational novel, with the intriguing title *The White Nun; or the Black Hog of Dromore*. He sold the manuscript to an Eton bookseller for £5 and on its publication the anonymous author was said to be 'A Young Gentleman of Note'. By this time Sumner was at Cambridge but it did not take the Eton authorities long to decode 'Note' or to identify the novelist and he was superannuated from his King's scholarship.

Trinity College, Cambridge, then took him on and after two years awarded him a scholarship. He was ordained in 1814 and immediately went with Lord Mount-Charles (another Trinity man) and young Lord Francis Conyngham through Flanders and along the Rhine to Geneva. On his return to England he became a curate at Highclere in North Hampshire where he remained for five years, augmenting his meagre stipend by taking in pupils from rich families. Among these was Lord

Albert Conyngham the brother of Lord Francis, whose mother chanced to be the mistress of King George IV. Through her influence Sumner was invited to dine with the King at Brighton in 1821 and created such a good impression that, after three hours of conversation, the King offered him a Canonry of Windsor. But the Prime Minister, Lord Liverpool, while recognizing that the King had a legitimate special interest in the Windsor canonries, objected to Sumner's appointment on the grounds that he had not been consulted, and went so far as to threaten resignation. After much huffing and puffing a deal was struck, by which the canonry went to one Dr James Stonier Clarke and Sumner assumed all his previous appointments. These included Historiographer to the Crown and Librarian to the King, to which was added Domestic Chaplain to the King at Windsor – a post which gave him a fine house in the castle precincts. His income was further augmented by appointment as Vicar of St Helen's, Abingdon, to which he devoted six months of the year.

This was only a start. A year later the King appointed him to a Canonry of Worcester and in the following year made him one of his Chaplains-in-Ordinary and Deputy Clerk of the Closet. By now he was an important member of the Court, but this did not make him entirely compliant, for on one occasion he refused Holy Communion to the King because he had lost his temper and dismissed a servant. Preferments continued to come thick and fast. In 1824 Sumner was offered the new Bishopric of Jamaica, but the King refused to sanction his acceptance on the grounds that he wanted him to be at his bedside when he died. By way of compensation he was given a lucrative Canonry of Canterbury and, at the King's command, a Cambridge doctorate in divinity. In 1826 – now aged 36 – he was made Bishop of Llandaff and, since the income of this Welsh see was meagre, he was also appointed Dean of St Paul's. Many other bishops held dual appointments at that time. The king's expectation that his protégé would remain in and around the Court was however frustrated. Although Llandaff had no episcopal palace, Sumner rented a house and, breaking with recent precedent, took up residence in his diocese. Moreover he soon made his presence felt by carrying out a visitation, having first required the clergy to complete articles of enquiry about their parishes. The answers revealed that in Glamorganshire 62 of the 107 parishes lacked a parsonage and therefore a resident priest, while in Monmouthshire 72 of the 127 parishes were without a parsonage.

But before Sumner could do anything about this he was translated to Winchester, again on the orders of the King, who said he had determined that the see should be filled by a gentleman. The annual income of the see was £50,000 (£1.4 million in today's money), making its occupant one of the richest men in the country. So Sumner remained for the next 40 years and made a good start by electing to be enthroned in person in his cathedral – the first bishop to do so for over 300 years, the others having always sent a proxy to carry out the formalities. The citizens of Winchester were astonished and delighted, and according to his biographer son they were 'most cordial in their welcome. A short distance from the town some 50 tradesmen met him on horseback and, with a band of music at their heads preceded him into the city . . . The bells from the cathedral and various churches of the town struck up merry peals, and the whole scene was one of much enthusiasm.' The bishop, then only 37, was said to be 'a strikingly handsome man – the very embodiment of "the beauty of holiness" '. The city did not however have many opportunities to behold his beauty since, apart from a few brief return visits, most of his time was spent at the episcopal residences in London's St James's Square and Farnham Castle, in Surrey. Nonetheless he was Winchester's first nineteenth-century reforming bishop. In his first visitation charge in 1829 – the last such charge had been delivered in 1788 – he warned the clergy that he was against absenteeism and expected them to work. The rural deaneries were to be revived. Decaying church buildings must be repaired and many new churches built to meet the needs of a population which since 1800 had increased by 38 per cent in Hampshire and 65 per cent in Surrey. The diocese at that time extended from the Thames to the English Channel and then, as now, included the Channel Islands. Sumner was the first ever Bishop of Winchester to visit these islands and went every four years, sometimes in violent storms and always in a ship provided by the government.

Sumner was a Tory and an evangelical. He opposed the 1832 Reform Bill and was generally against social change, though he ensured that the pay and working conditions of the agricultural labourers employed on his own estates were improved. A stream of poor, hungry and elderly came to Farnham Castle for gifts of food and clothing. He was always fiercely opposed to Roman Catholicism and strongly, but unsuccessfully protested against the restoration of the Catholic hierarchy in 1850. It was all the more surprising, therefore, that he voted for the 1829 Catholic Relief Bill and the King was so incensed by this that he more or less excluded him from the Court and it was the Bishop of Chichester who was summoned to the royal deathbed. Sunday Observance was another of his special concerns. Fiercely opposed to the Tractarian movement Sumner steadfastly refused to appoint anyone other than evangelicals to parishes in his own gift and to cathedral canonries. Since he was in office for so long this had a marked effect on the life of the diocese and on the witness of the cathedral. The only exception he ever made to his 'evangelicals only' policy was to appoint his cousin the

High Churchman Samuel Wilberforce to the Archdeaconry of Surrey and curiously enough it was Wilberforce who eventually succeeded him. The establishing of the Ecclesiastical Commissioners in 1835 was anathema to him and he fought all attempts by the Commissioners to deprive him of patronage outside Winchester diocese.

During his long reign at Winchester 201 new churches were built and another 119 rebuilt; 210 new parishes were created, many schools were built and nearly every parish was provided with a parsonage. The total cost of this was in excess of £2 million (almost £50 million in today's money), and the amount of money raised for overseas missionary societies was increased from £70 to £4,000 per annum (well over £100,000 in today's money). And Sumner himself was very generous in his personal contributions to church projects. In 1868 he suffered a stroke which made it impossible for him to carry out his duties but at that time there was no provision for a bishop to resign or to be granted a pension. A Bishops' Resignation Act was rushed through Parliament in 1869 to remedy this and, the income of the see of Winchester having been reduced to £7,000, £2,000 of this was allocated to Sumner's pension. He was permitted to remain in Farnham Castle until his death in 1874.

Cosmo Gordon Lang

Although he was not born into the English Establishment – he was the son of a Church of Scotland minister – Cosmo Gordon Lang was closer to the Royal Family than any other cleric of his time. He had a meteoric rise in the ranks of the Church of England. The association with the Royal Family began, surprisingly, when he was Vicar of Portsea – a parish which covered most of Portsmouth and was populated by sailors, shipyard workers and other artisans. It was not the place for encounters with the mighty, but just across the water, on the Isle of Wight, Queen Victoria was often in residence at Osborne House, and on the strength of Lang's Oxford connections she invited him across to preach and to tell her about his work among the poor.

He made a considerable impression, for he was good looking, had a beautiful voice, was an unusually gifted preacher and had a somewhat unctuous manner. He was immediately appointed one of the Queen's chaplains and commanded to preach at Osborne twice a year. These visits, which occupied whole weekends, included what Lang recorded in his journal as 'long and intimate talks with the Queen and other members of the Royal Family'. Later he wrote, 'I shall ever regard these visits to the great Queen as among the highest privileges of my life.' He also enjoyed visits to Sandringham as the guest of the Prince of Wales – the future King Edward VII. But his association with the Royal Family was destined to cause him much trouble and severely damage his reputation. Although he was not called to minister to the Queen on her deathbed, he conducted a service on board the Royal Yacht which brought her body from the Isle of Wight to Portsmouth. At the end of this service he was deeply moved by the sight of the new king and the German Kaiser, her grandson, kneeling side-by-side at the bier. Thirteen years later, when Archbishop of York, Lang recalled this occasion at a meeting at which, in the highly charged atmosphere of the early days of the 1914–18 war, there was much angry denunciation of all things German. Hoping to cool things, but quite miscalculating the mood of the moment, he described the sight of the kneeling kings as 'a sacred memory'.

This only added fuel to the fire and for some time afterwards he was subjected to much public denunciation and abuse. Outwardly he seemed unperturbed, but he was a lonely man and sensitive to the opinions of others, not least those of King George V and Queen Mary, who for a time cooled to him. In 1916 he suddenly lost all his dark hair and was reduced to a small fringe of white hair above his ears. This transformed his appearance so that he became unrecognizable, even to many of his friends. Wartime visits to the Grand Fleet and to the army in France did something to restore his public reputation but his 1914 indiscretion was long remembered. So also was the broadcast he made in 1936 following the abdication of King Edward VIII. Although he had never got on well with the new king, who rightly discerned that the Archbishop of Canterbury did not approve of his life-style, he was not, contrary to much opinion at the time, involved in the negotiations which led to the abdication. When the deed was done, however, he felt it to be his duty to address the nation in a radio broadcast that was heard by millions in Britain and in other parts of the world. Its main thrust was contained in this passage:

What pathos, nay what tragedy, surrounds the central figure of these swiftly moving scenes! On the 11th day of December, 248 years ago, King James II fled from Whitehall. By a strange coincidence, on the 11th day of December last week King Edward VIII, after speaking his last words to his people, left Windsor Castle, the scene of all the splendid traditions of his ancestors and his Throne, and went out to exile. In the darkness he left these shores.

Seldom, if ever, has any British Sovereign come to the Throne with greater natural gifts for his kingship. Seldom, if ever, has any Sovereign been welcomed by a more enthusiastic loyalty. From God he had received a high and sacred trust. Yet by his own will he has abdicated – he has surrendered the trust. With characteristic frankness he has told us his motive. It was a craving for private happiness. Strange and sad it must be that for such a motive, however strongly it pressed upon his heart, he should have disappointed hopes so high and abandoned a trust so great. Even more strange and sad it is that he should have sought happiness in a manner inconsistent with the Christian principles of marriage, and within a social circle whose standards and ways of life are alien to all the best instincts and traditions of his people. Let those who belong to this circle know that today they stand rebuked by the judgement of the nation which had loved King Edward. I have shrunk from saying these words. But I have felt compelled for the sake of sincerity and truth to say them.

Yet for one who has known him since childhood, who has felt his charm and admired his gifts, these words cannot be the last. How can we forget the high hopes and promise of his youth; his most genuine care for the poor, the suffering of the unemployed; his years of eager service both at home and across the seas? it is the remembrance of these things that wrings from our hearts the cry – 'The pity of it, Oh, the pity of it!' To the infinite mercy and protecting care of God we commit him now, wherever he may be.

This was pure Lang – the orator, the romantic historian, the relisher of drama, the Christian of uncompromising principle and, it has to be said, the man who never lacked the courage to say what he believed to be true. The Prime Minister, Stanley Baldwin, complimented him on having 'spoken for Christian England' and in Court circles and some other privileged places the broadcast was warmly applauded. But others were much less happy with Lang's effort, and the popular newspapers, sensing a widespread revulsion against moralizing and kicking a man who was down, roundly denounced him. Soon however Lang was preoccupied with the coronation of King George VI, the ceremonial side of which he masterminded and presented with enormous dramatic skill. And in the teeth of much opposition, he allowed the service to be broadcast and some parts of it to be filmed. But his reputation never recovered from the disastrous Abdication broadcast.

Lang was born in an Aberdeenshire manse in 1864. He went to Glasgow University when he was only fourteen and, after graduating there, visited Cambridge, where he was overwhelmed by the beauty of King's College and asked the porter how he might become a member of the college. This was duly arranged, though not by the porter, but Lang then changed his mind and went instead to Balliol College, Oxford. Besides his academic work he was President of the Oxford Union, a founder (significantly) of the Oxford University Dramatic Society, and undergraduate secretary of Toynbee Hall. His heavy involvement in this piece of social work led the Master of Balliol, the legendary Benjamin Jowett, to tell him, 'Your business is not to reform the East End of London but to get a first class in the school of *literae humaniores*.' In the event he got a disappointing second, but made up for this by taking a first in modern history. He then went to London to train for the Bar, with a view to using this as a route to politics, but in 1888 he was elected, at his second attempt, as a fellow of All Souls – a college that became an important part of his long life. Ordination soon followed and in 1890 he became a curate at Leeds Parish Church under Edward Stuart Talbot, and threw himself into the work of the parish – visiting, teaching, preaching fine sermons and running youth clubs. He had a particular empathy with young men which remained for the rest of his life.

After three years of this however he was in demand for work elsewhere and was invited to become Dean of Divinity at Magdalen College, Oxford. A year after moving into residence he took on the additional responsibility of Vicar of St Mary the Virgin, the university church, the life of which was at a low ebb but quickly revived under Lang's leadership. His love affair with St Mary's was however only a brief one, for in 1896 he accepted the challenge of Portsea. The history of that parish, under Lang and then under Cyril Garbett, has entered the annals of the Church of England as evidence of what could be achieved in tough working-class communities at the end of the nineteenth century. The resources were considerable. A parish church of cathedral-like proportions, seating 2,000, had recently been erected, and each of five districts, with its own church, was served by a senior and a junior curate. The 14–16 curates lived austerely in community with the vicar, who required them to address him as 'Sir' and to book an appointment if they wished to see him. Among them were so many Oxford and Cambridge cricket Blues that they were said to be capable of fielding a team to take on the Australians. This was never tested, but they defeated a Channel Fleet XI and some of the strongest army teams. Their work among the poor of Portsmouth was no less impressive and at the parish church 400 men assembled for a Sunday afternoon Bible Class, while as many as 2,000 attended Evensong to hear Lang preach.

In March 1901, not long after Queen Victoria's death, Lang was mystified to receive a telegram from the Prime Minister's private secretary which read – 'Announcement of your appointment will be in the Press on Monday.' Enquiry revealed that a letter offering him the Suffragan Bishopric of Stepney, combined with a Canonry of St Paul's, had been misdirected and ended up in the Dead Letter Office. Downing Street assumed that its recipient would accept, which he did. The confusion was not yet ended, however, for at Lang's installation at St Paul's the aged and forgetful dean insisted on naming the new canon as Charles Gore. The validity of the proceedings was fortunately never challenged. During the next eight years Lang continued and developed Winnington-Ingram's notable episcopal work in London's East End, though he was never the sort to walk in populist ways. Since much was later to be made of his snobbery and delight in the company of duchesses, it must be recorded that during his Stepney days he influenced towards ordination Dick Sheppard, who became a legendary Vicar of St Martin-in-the-Fields, and was also responsible for the return to faith of George Lansbury, a social reformer and future Leader of the Labour Party.

Lang's translation from a suffragan bishopric to the Archbishopric of York in 1909, on the nomination of H. H. Asquith, inevitably caused many eyebrows to be raised. An early visit to Windsor Castle led Queen Alexandra to remark that she had not previously thought herself old enough to be the mother of an archbishop. King Edward VII charged him to 'keep the parties in the Church together and to prevent the clergy from wearing moustaches'. During the post-war era he remained a lonely figure and, in spite of his undoubted gifts, lived under the shadow of the Archbishop of Canterbury, Randall Davidson, who was almost old enough to be his father and had by this time become the dominant figure in the Church. Lang was treated as a member of Davidson's family and often stayed at Lambeth Palace. His appointment to York came when he was too young to make a significant impact on the life of the Church, and by the time he succeeded Davidson at Canterbury in 1928 it was too late for him to guide the Church in new directions. He was also unfortunate to get off to the worst possible start in the senior archbishopric, for almost immediately after his enthronement he became seriously ill and three years passed before he was fully fit again. He strengthened relations between the Anglican and Eastern Orthodox Churches, and set up a Church of England Council for Foreign Relations to maintain contact with these and other Churches. Full communion with the Old Catholic Church was achieved in 1931. These were significant advances but little other new ground was broken during Lang's tenure of the primacy. The problems arising from Parliament's rejection of the 1928 Prayer Book were allowed to drift, which was a disappointment to Dick Sheppard and other reformers who had always hoped that he would one day provide the Church with the dynamic leadership it so urgently needed. But he was essentially a cautious administrator and certainly no prophet. He enjoyed a close relationship with King George VI and Queen Elizabeth which began long before they reached the throne. On the day following the abdication he received a long letter from the new consort which concluded, 'For the first time and with great affection, Elizabeth R.'

In the Diocese of Canterbury he devoted more time than most archbishops had done to pastoral work in the parishes, where the clergy held him in high regard, but also with a degree of fear because he was very conscious of his high office and never relaxed. During his archiepiscopal years he travelled only once, and then fiercely protesting, on a train, and never set foot in a shop. Sir William Orpen, who painted his portrait when he was at York, began the first sitting by asking, 'I see seven Archbishops, which of them am I to paint?' It was a perceptive question, for Lang was a highly complex personality and some said that it was almost possible to hear a click of change from one characteristic to another. Orpen chose to paint the least attractive of the seven and there is a story, hopefully not true, that when Lang showed the painting to Hensley Henson of Durham and commented, 'They say it portrays me as proud, prelatical and pompous' – the response was, 'To which of these epithets does your Grace take exception?' The verdict of Archbishop Söderblom of Sweden was kinder : 'That is what the devil meant him to be, but thanks be to God it is not so.' He retired in 1942 to make way for William Temple and until his death in 1945 occupied a royal grace-and-favour residence at Kew. His last official act as archbishop was to conduct the confirmation of Princess Elizabeth, the future queen, at Windsor.

Robin Woods

Lang was apparently very surprised to be offered the Archbishopric of Canterbury by a Prime Minister, Stanley Baldwin, who was smoking a pipe. It seems fair to assume therefore that he would have been deeply shocked by the circumstances in which Robin Woods discussed with his sovereign a proposal that he should move from the Deanery of Windsor to the Bishopric of Worcester, which he occupied from 1971 to 1981. In his autobiography Woods explained how he felt uncertain about this and how

> To clarify matters I went to Balmoral at the invitation of the Queen. The understanding with which I was greeted and the warmth of the welcome in a sense made it all the more difficult to consider leaving such a rewarding position in the Royal Household. But over some long talks and wholly delightful excursions on to the moors in chase of either grouse or deer I left with a much clearer picture of where our future should lie.

That it lay at Worcester may have been a disappointment for in a revealing letter from one of his sons, reproduced in the autobiography, there is an indication that the real dilemma in the decanal mind was not so much the pain of leaving Windsor as the agony of accepting a fairly unimportant diocese like Worcester, when he was hoping for London or Winchester. This was unrealistic, since he was not equipped for national leadership in the Church.

His introduction to the Royal Household came early, for his father, Edward Woods, who later became Bishop of Lichfield, was Lord High Almoner and a greatly valued friend of King George VI. From 1917 to 1981 there was never a time when a member of the Woods family was not occupying an English bishopric. Robin Woods's appointment as Dean of Windsor owed much to the fact that when the post fell vacant in 1962, following the death of the aged Bishop Hamilton, the Queen – prompted no doubt by the Duke of Edinburgh – decided that St George's Chapel and its surrounding buildings should be opened to wider use in the service of the Church. New blood was needed and Woods conveniently combined regal style with considerable experience of the Church's attempts to engage with industrial society. This led to the setting up of St George's House as a conference centre, designed to encourage dialogue between theologians and the captains of industry, and to provide a kind of staff college for clergy at the mid-point of their ministry.

The publicity attending the opening of the house suggested that the project was a combination of a long-standing Windsor tradition of clerical/lay partnership involving the Canons of Windsor and the Knights of the Order of the Garter. This, unsurprisingly, led some seasoned observers to wonder if the true nature of the gulf between the Church and an increasingly secularized society had been fully grasped. Once established, the house was handed over to lay leadership leaving Woods free to concentrate on his chief role, that of Domestic Chaplain to the Queen.

Like his predecessors, at least from Queen Victoria's time, he provided an alternative source of information and advice on Crown appointments and other church matters, so that the Queen was not entirely reliant on 10 Downing Street and Lambeth Palace. A close friendship developed with the Queen and the Duke of Edinburgh, who was much involved in the St George's House project, and this became a family affair as the Woods's children were of the same ages as Prince Charles and Princess Anne. When the royal children went away to boarding school Woods sometimes visited them at weekends and later, after attending a dinner to discuss the future education of Prince Charles, he was despatched to Cambridge to assess the potential of six colleges for this purpose. He recommended Trinity College because he felt that its Master, R. A. Butler – a former Deputy Prime Minister – would know best how to handle the heir to the throne. He enjoyed dancing with the Queen at Windsor balls.

Woods was born in 1914 at Lausanne, where his father was serving as chaplain to the English-speaking community and recovering from tuberculosis. He went from a minor public school to Trinity College, Cambridge, where he took a third in English. After preparing for Holy Orders at Westcott House, Cambridge, he started his ministry unusually as Missionary Secretary of the Student Christian Movement. On the outbreak of war in 1939 he was put in charge of the movement's work in the Midland universities, where he remained until enlisting as an army chaplain in 1942. These years with the SCM had a lasting impact upon him. He developed a concern for Christian unity and for the Church's involvement in social issues, which enabled him later to make a valuable contribution in these spheres and also enabled him to resist the most dangerous temptations of the royal courtier.

Woods had an interesting and sometimes exciting war as chaplain of the senior brigade of the Indian Army, which had British officers and was involved in the gruelling task of driving the Germans out of Italy. He was Mentioned in Despatches and, as the end of the war came in sight, was promoted to Deputy Assistant Chaplain General with the task of establishing a Chaplains' School and Moral Leadership Centre in Northern Italy. A tall man, possessed of assumed authority and the confidence that comes from an upper-middle-class upbringing, he was very much at home in the army and recognized as an effective leader. On demobilization he was given the more humdrum responsibility of the parish of South Wigston, on the outskirts of Leicester, where for five years he ran a very lively church and became involved in pioneering industrial mission work in the city. He was said to be 'good with men'.

In 1951, however, he left to become Archdeacon of Singapore and Vicar of St Andrew's Cathedral, Singapore. Again he exercised a vigorous ministry forming new congregations in the developing areas of Singapore, raising money for the building of a cathedral hall, and overseeing the work of the Anglican Church in Malaya and Indonesia. He was also involved in a consultation that led to Singapore's independence. On his return to England in 1958 the Bishop of Sheffield, Leslie Hunter, appointed him Archdeacon of Sheffield and Rector of the coal-mining parish of Tankersley. He took a lot of pastoral responsibility from the bishop's shoulders and, on the strength of his Leicester experience, was made chairman of the Sheffield Industrial Mission. The mission was then at its strongest and most influential and Woods offered understanding and support to its mercurial Senior Chaplain, Ted Wickham, though he was himself more at home with the managers than with the men on the shop floor.

At Worcester he enjoyed living in Hartlebury Castle and was a hard-working pastoral bishop who got to know the 300 parishes and their

clergy, and maintained his long-standing concern for ecumenical collaboration and social affairs. A difficult problem arose when a general
shortage and maldistribution of Church of England clergy required him
to reduce the number of priests serving in the diocese from 260 to 185,
but he achieved this without undermining the morale of the remaining
clergy and most of the parishes. While at Windsor he had been secretary of the ill-fated Anglican–Methodist Unity Commission, to which he
devoted a great deal of time, and he was bitterly disappointed when its
proposals were finally rejected by the Church of England.

He was chairman of the Birmingham Manpower Services Commission concerned with the implications of industrial change for the work-
force. Most Wednesdays were spent in London, attending the House
of Lords, where he was a member of a Select Committee on Unemployment. During his Windsor years he was a member of a government commission concerned with the future of the public schools and when he
became a bishop he deplored the fact that 'whereas Oxford, Cambridge
and London had satisfied most of the needs of the Church of England up
to 1939, from the peace of 1945 onwards the privileged and professional
families clearly became disillusioned about the Church, so their sons did
not even begin to contemplate entering the ministry. No longer were the
public schools the seedbed of the ministry . . . to the great detriment of
the Church both at home and overseas.'

Meanwhile his links with the Royal Family were maintained. He was
invited to parties at Buckingham Palace, the Prince of Wales stayed at
Hartlebury Castle, and after the Queen and the Duke of Edinburgh had
departed from a private lunch following their attendance at Worcester's
13th centenary celebrations Woods noted, 'All of us who remained
sat down with a sense of enormous pleasure and contentment.' Most
unusually for a cleric, he was rewarded with two knighthoods – a KCVO
for his work at Windsor and a KCMG for his work as Prelate of the
Order of St Michael and St George. A suggestion that his autobiography
should be titled *The Queen and I* was rejected.

There is no-one very grand among today's bishops – not even an
Honourable – and this for the simple reason that the aristocracy has
for several decades failed to produced more than a handful of clergy.
The last to make a mark on the Church were the Honourable Oliver
William Twisleton-Wykeham Fiennes, the younger son of the 20th Baron
Saye and Sele, who was Dean of Lincoln 1969–89, and the Honourable
Hugh Dickinson, the grandson of Baron Dickinson, who was Dean of
Salisbury 1986–96 – both good appointments as it turned out. Neither is

there any longer a place for high-born courtiers. The Lord High Almoner is the son of a war RAF Pilot Officer; the Clerk of the Closet was a grammar school boy, as was the Dean of Windsor; the Prelate of the Order of the Garter is the son of a cathedral musician; and the Dean of Westminster has a Salvation Army background. Not since Archbishop Geoffrey Fisher has there been a close relationship between the Archbishop of Canterbury and the Royal Family.

All of which is a result of the decline in the Church of England's position as a pillar of the Establishment and of wider changes in the ranking of Britain's social and economic hierarchies. Yet the Establishment remains. Bishops continue to be appointed in the name of the Crown. They continue to pay homage to the Queen on their appointment and grace many a royal occasion in their dioceses. And, although the present Queen does not seek to emulate her great-great-grandmother's involvement in the choice of bishops, she is no less of a churchwoman who seeks to uphold Christian values and is by no means indifferent as to how the Church is faring.

The Church of England is the only Established church in the Anglican Communion and were its life to be started from scratch in the twenty-first century no-one would dream of initiating the present church–state arrangement. But, far from starting from scratch, the Church of England has a long history involving a partnership with the state which cannot easily be disentagled. The question today is whether the level of secularization among the indigenous population on the one hand, and the presence in Britain of substantial communities which embrace non-Christian faiths on the other, make the the Establishment of the Church of England not only inappropriate but actually undesirable.

My own view is that there remains sufficient residual Christianity in England and enough attachment to the Church of England by a wide spectrum of the population to make the retention of the church–state link desirable for at least a little longer. If Parliament, reflecting the opinion of the majority of the electorate, ever demands that the link be broken there would be no reason for the Church to attempt resistance. It does not need to be propped up by the state and might conceivably flourish better if it no longer appeared to be closely identified with the high and the mighty. But no such demand from Parliament seems likely within the foreseeable future. Indeed, Prime Minister Tony Blair has stated quite firmly that he wishes the Establishment to remain and any politician seeking to create a more integrated and caring society needs all the support he can get. The Church also now sees its Established role in terms of service, rather than of privilege. Under normal political and social conditions therefore it seems reasonable to expect the Establishment in its present form to remain for at least another fifty years.

Adjustments are however needed. The latest proposals for the reform of the House of Lords envisage a reduction in the number of bishops allocated seats in the House of Lords and the appointment of leaders of other churches to the second chamber. This is clearly right and it is also very desirable that on all state occasions when a church presence is deemed appropriate this should be of an ecumenical character. Since the Church's control of episcopal appointments is now virtually complete it is doubtful whether the residual involvement of the Crown needs to be eliminated, though the requirement of homage to the sovereign and the royal demand that a Dean and Chapter elect a nominated bishop should be abolished.

More urgent and more complicated than this, however, is agreement on the form that future coronations should take. Splendid and moving though the coronation of the present Queen was in 1953, it is inconceivable that this could ever be repeated, so great have been the changes in society during the last fifty years. The bishops and peers who surrounded the Queen in Westminster Abbey were not representative of the religious, political and social life of the nation then, and they certainly are not now. Other elements in society, including representatives of other religious faiths, will need to be involved, and this may well require the return to an earlier tradition under which the coronation ceremonies were divided between Westminster Hall and the Abbey. None of which can be separated from a re-examination of the role of the monarchy itself.

3

The scholars

From the second century onwards bishops were seen as guardians of the Christian faith. It was their task to ensure that the faith was preserved in the purity of its original form and neither distorted nor diluted by heresy. The danger of the infant Church succumbing to Gnosticism and other heresies was real enough and the presence of a bishop whose spiritual ancestry could be traced to an early date was regarded as a guarantee of his church's orthodoxy. This did not preclude the expression of the faith in the thought forms and languages of the prevailing Greek and Latin cultures, but in every case the resulting doctrine was authenticated by comparison with 'the faith once delivered to the saints'. The councils of the Church, held during the first five centuries of its life, were concerned largely with this issue and the Creeds were formulated as statements of official orthodox doctrine. This required bishops to have some theological skill, both for their own preaching and, most of all, for the robust defence of the faith. Their attendance at councils and synods convened to deal with doctrinal matters, some of these involving great subtlety of thought, also called for a degree of theological sophistication. Among the early bishops were men of outstanding intellect and learning whose writings were immensely influential and are still studied by those who take Christian theology seriously.

As the Church grew in size and influence the maintaining of so high an intellectual standard among its leaders became less easy and less important. The sacerdotal aspect of the episcopal office was more strongly emphasized. Pastoral gifts became increasingly valued, while the deepening relationship between church and state called for skills of diplomacy and statesmanship. Nonetheless godly learning was never entirely neglected and the Church continued to have its scholar bishops, some of whom enjoyed a European reputation.

At the sixteenth-century Reformation the Church of England declared and later defended its ecclesiastical integrity by appealing to Scripture, Tradition and Sound Learning. It sought by means of the developing scholarship of the time to get behind the mediaeval religious accretions to the pure faith revealed in Scripture and taught by the Fathers of the primitive Church. Once again, therefore, there was a need for learned bishops who were capable of handling historical evidence and of defending what later became known as Anglicanism against assaults from Rome and Geneva. The Reformation saw also the revival of the prophetic element in the Church's life, expressed in preaching, and this in turn required an ordained ministry with sufficient intellectual equipment for the exposition of Scripture. Thus the Ordinal attached to the Book of Common Prayer of 1549 began the Form of Consecrating of an Archbishop or Bishop with the presentation of the bishop-elect by two other bishops, who said:

> Most reverend Father in God, we present unto you this godly and well learned man to be consecrated Bishop.

This was retained in subsequent revisions of the Ordinal until the Alternative Service Book of 1980 when the words 'godly and well learned' were transferred to a new ceremony in which the archbishop presented the bishop-elect to the people:

> Those who have authority to do so have chosen N as a man of godly life and sound learning.

'Well learned' and 'sound learning' have never been defined and are not quite the same thing, but during the sixteenth and seventeenth centuries the Church of England's episcopal bench was occupied by a remarkable number of outstanding scholars whose work provided the foundations of a distinct Anglican theology. A few able theologians were also appointed during the early years of the eighteenth century, but other considerations – royal or political favour – dominated as that century advanced.

The revival of church life in the early part of the nineteenth century, which owed much to the survival of the scholarly High Church tradition associated with Archbishop Laud, and then to the Oxford Movement, saw the emergence of another crop of brilliant episcopal scholars. Their appointments were due to several Prime Ministers who valued learning, and in a letter to Archbishop Randall Davidson in 1911 the then Prime Minister, H. H. Asquith, pointed out that in 1895 no fewer than thirteen of the thirty diocesan bishops had previously been professors, dons or headmasters. He regretted that this number was now reduced to five.

Connop Thirlwall

Connop Thirlwall was appointed Bishop of St David's in 1839 and for the next 34 years was the most able academic mind on the episcopal bench. Three years earlier it was suggested that he ought to become Bishop of Norwich, but the Prime Minister, Lord Melbourne, would not hear of this and his later offer of St David's as a consolation prize was strongly opposed by the Archbishop of Canterbury, William Howley. The problem about Thirlwall was that he had spent some time in Germany and become interested in the new, critical approach to the Bible. What is more, he had published, albeit anonymously, an English translation of the liberal Friedrich Schleiermacher's *A Critical Essay on the Gospel of St Luke* (1825), adding an introduction of his own and appending an essay on the state of the current controversy about Gospel origins. This made him highly suspect in conservative quarters. But as a scholar his chief claim to fame lay in the authorship of a monumental *History of Greece* which was published in eight volumes between 1835 and 1847 and led the field until well into the twentieth century.

Born in 1797 at Cottingham, Hull, where his father was the vicar, Thirlwall was extraordinarily precocious as a child. He learned Latin when he was only three and a year later read Greek with, it was said, 'an easy fluency which astonished all who heard him'. At Trinity College, Cambridge, he carried all before him, became a fellow of the college and in 1825 was called to the Bar. At this point he was resisting suggestions that he should be ordained, but on his return from studying theology in Germany he became an assistant tutor at Trinity and accepted ordination. He was a good teacher, very active in college life, and for a short time held the living of Over, near Cambridge, but all this ended suddenly in 1834 following his publication of a pamphlet in which he argued for the admission of Dissenters to the university and the abolition of compulsory chapel for undergraduates. The Master of the college demanded his resignation.

Soon afterwards Lord Brougham came to Thirlwall's rescue with the offer of the rich living of Kirkby Underdale in Yorkshire. He ministered there for the next six years with some energy, though he seems to have spent most of his time in his study – as many as sixteen hours a day – working on the *History of Greece*, most of which he had completed by the time he moved to the Bishopric of St Davids. Publication took much longer.

Life in the small, remote village where the bishops lived suited him well. He enjoyed rural pursuits, quickly taught himself Welsh and tried valiantly to revive church life in the diocese. During his 34 years there

183 churches were restored, many new parsonages and schools were built, and he spent £40,000 of his own money on various charities (over £1 million in today's money). He was also hospitable and often entertained his clergy, yet he was never popular. No-one doubted his immense intellectual capacity, but there was something about his personality that gave the impression of being critical and cold. It was said that he was more capable of managing the peacocks on his terrace than the clergy of his diocese, and when complaints were made to the Archbishop of Canterbury about his lack of pastoral skill he ceased inviting parish clergy to the palace and dealt with them only through the archdeacons.

The long distance between St Davids and London also reduced his usefulness in the wider life of the Church, though he was diligent in attending Convocation and the House of Lords, in both places making his presence felt from time to time. His liberal spirit led him in 1842 to plead for the toleration of the Tractarian movement, but he had little time for Dr Pusey, whom he described as 'a painful enigma'. In 1847 he refused to sign a letter of protest against the appointment of the liberal theologian R. D. Hampden to the Bishopric of Hereford, in the following year he voted in the House of Lords for the removal of the disabilities suffered by the Jews in English life, and in 1853 he supported the liberal F. D. Maurice when he was dismissed from his teaching post at King's College, London. Ten years later he was the only member of the bench of bishops to dissent from a Canterbury Convocation resolution condemning Bishop Colenso's supposedly heretical *Commentary of the Epistle to the Romans*. He was also one of the few bishops who refused to inhibit Colenso from preaching in his diocese. On the other hand he joined in the episcopal censure of *Essays and Reviews* (1860), believing this to contain opinions contrary to the Christian faith.

Appointment to a bishopric marked for Thirlwall the end of his contribution to scholarship but this may not have been unrelated to the completion of his magnum opus on the history of Greece. He continued to spend a good deal of time in his library, which he called 'The Chaos', and the eleven visitation charges which he delivered at three-yearly intervals were models of their kind, combining deep learning with the practical needs of the diocese and its parishes. He also served as chairman of the committee responsible for the Old Testament translation in the Revised Version of the Bible project, but resigned from this towards the end of his life when the bishops decreed that scholars who did not believe in the divinity of Christ were to be excluded from the project. He believed that scholarship, rather than faith, should be the sole criterion for involvement. There were no more books from his pen and he resigned from the bishopric, blind and partially paralysed, a year before his death in 1875.

Joseph Barber Lightfoot

On the face of it there was madness in sending Joseph Barber Lightfoot from Cambridge to the Bishopric of Durham in 1879. He had one of the finest minds in Europe and his life's work appeared to be confined to a pioneering approach to the Pauline Letters and the Apostolic Fathers. He had no small talk, was given to long periods of silence, and lacked the social graces which oil the wheels of leadership. Greek and Latin were his favourite languages, though he was also fluent in Hebrew, French, German, Spanish and Italian, and had a working knowledge of Arabic, Syrian, Ethiopian and the Coptic dialect. The diocese to which he went was grappling with the devastating effect of the Industrial Revolution. A large section of its population worked in the always dehumanizing and often dangerous coal mines. Shipbuilding on the Tyne, Wear and Tees was creating large urban communities with poor housing, deep poverty and negligible welfare provisions. The Church of England had lagged far behind in the offering of Christian ministry, leaving the initiative to the Methodists who had already built hundreds of chapels in the pit villages and established preaching posts in the towns.

It is hardly surprising that Lightfoot himself questioned his suitability for such a task, but in response to the urging of his friends he accepted the challenge and in the short space of ten years established himself as one of the Church of England's greatest bishops. Besides his massive gifts of learning, he turned out to have strong administrative skill and considerable money-raising capacity. On his arrival in the North-East he wasted little time. Durham diocese then extended from the Tees to the Scottish border and a scheme for creating a new Diocese of Newcastle, to cover Northumberland, was immediately implemented. In the following year the first Diocesan Conference of clergy and laity was held and a Board of Education established. Soon after this a church building appeal was launched and within four years £224,000 had been raised and spent on new churches, vicarages and schools. By the end of his episcopate 45 churches had been built. The laity were drawn into active ministry as readers and evangelists, and Lightfoot, who had noted the significant place of women in the churches of the Apostolic age, ordained a number of deaconesses. He took a personal interest in the ministry to seamen at the ports and welcomed the growth of the co-operative movement. All this enabled the diocese to make up much lost ground, though – as elsewhere in nineteenth-century industrial England – the effort came too late to halt the alienation of the working classes.

Lightfoot was born in Liverpool in 1828. As a child frail health prevented his attending school and he was educated at home, but following the death of his accountant father in 1843 the family moved to Birmingham, where young 'Joe' was deemed well enough to attend King Edward VI School. There he came under the influence of the headmaster, Prince Lee, whose pupils at that time included Brooke Foss Westcott, who notably followed Lightfoot at Durham, and Edward White Benson, who became Archbishop of Canterbury. Lee himself became a rather unsatisfactory Bishop of Manchester, but his gifts as a teacher of classics were unrivalled and Lightfoot went to Trinity College, Cambridge, where he graduated as Senior Classic and as a mathematics Wrangler. On the strength of this he was elected to a fellowship and in 1854 was ordained by Prince Lee.

Seven years later he was appointed Hulsean Professor of Divinity at Cambridge and his lectures on the New Testament attracted such large numbers that they had to be given in the hall of Trinity. When the Regius Chair of Divinity fell vacant in 1870 there was a general expectation that Lightfoot would succeed to it, but he deliberately stood aside to leave the way clear for Westcott – his former tutor and three years his senior. There were in any case many other things to keep him occupied. In 1870 he joined the company of scholars made responsible for a Revised Version of the Bible and during the next ten years played an influential part (requiring attendance 40 days a year) in the new translation of the New Testament. Appointment to a Canonry of St Paul's came in 1871 and, while retaining his Cambridge chair, he played an active part in the general revival of the cathedral's life. Never an eloquent preacher, his sermons in St Paul's nonetheless attracted large crowds. Later at Durham he was apt to preach the same Easter Day sermon in the cathedral, and on being asked by a member of the congregation about the reason for this he replied that he had not changed his mind on the subject since the previous year.

Meanwhile, substantial books were being written. Commentaries on *St Paul's Letters to the Galatians* (1865), *Philippians* (1868) and *Colossians with Philemon* (1875) combined extraordinary erudition with lucid exposition and to the second he appended a substantial dissertation on the origins of the Christian ministry in which he argued, controversially but in the end convincingly, that the office of bishop had emerged because of need, rather than by direct succession from the Apostles. Alongside all this Lightfoot was engaged in major work on the Apostolic Fathers, who lived in the age immediately succeeding the New Testament era, and a ground-breaking volume on St Clement of Rome published in 1869.

Two years later, when still only 39, he declined the Bishopric of Lichfield, but in 1879 became the first bishop since John Cosin (1660) to go to Durham without having first held another see. And, in spite of his initial hesitations, he greatly enjoyed his years as a bishop. He was not much to look at; indeed, a heavy low slung jaw and a cast in one eye made him seem ugly. Once, when standing on a Scottish railway station, an American woman enquired of him: 'I am told that the Bishop of Durham will be on this train. Can you tell me if that tall, handsome man is he?' 'No, ma'am,' replied Lightfoot, 'the Bishop of Durham is short and plain.' But he soon became a much admired figure in Durham and, although he did not have much to say to the coal miners, they found him easy to talk to and his combination of wisdom and tolerance evoked the loyalty and affection of the clergy.

He never married and at Auckland Castle he lived in the company of six or eight Oxbridge graduates who came to him for ordination training. He treated them like sons and, following their ordinations, they served in some of the toughest Durham parishes. In the space of ten years he ordained 323 men, and eventually 60 per cent of the clergy in the diocese were graduates. He stayed up late at night to complete a two-volume study of two more Apostolic Fathers – St Ignatius and St Polycarp – and celebrated this by financing out of his own pocket a fine new church in Sunderland dedicated in honour of St Ignatius. Articles from his pen continued to appear in learned journals, and for several years a major preoccupation was an extensive revision of his St Clement of Rome, on which he was working until three days before his death in December 1889.

During the previous year he had begun to feel the strain of the ceaseless round of confirmations – there was no suffragan bishop – and after spending most of July much involved in the work of the Lambeth Conference complained that this 'broke me down hopelessly'. A serious heart condition was diagnosed and although he returned to Durham after a long convalescence his days were now numbered.

Mandell Creighton

Although Mandell Creighton, in common with Lightfoot, was on the episcopal bench for only ten years – Peterborough 1891–97, London 1897–1901 – he was in many ways the most interesting of the Victorian bishops. A man of brilliant mind – Lord Rosebery, a former Liberal Prime Minister, said that he was 'perhaps the most alert and universal intelligence that existed in this island at the time of his death' – he was nonetheless always ready to seek the advice of others. And besides his academic successes at Cambridge, where he was the first Dixie Professor of Ecclesiastical History, he was for nine years the much loved rector of a remote, tough parish in Northumberland. Moreover he was an outstandingly good speaker of epigrammatic style and his after-dinner speeches were spiced with humorous anecdotes, of which he seemed to have an endless supply.

It is far from certain however that he was really cut out to be a bishop in the closing years of the nineteenth century, and that an episcopal ministry was the best use of his gifts. Soon after his appointment to Peterborough he said, with characteristic candour, 'A bishopric is to me, after the flesh, a terrible nuisance. But how is a man to refuse the responsibilities of this branch of service?' It was only with difficulty that he managed to complete, during his time at Peterborough, the fifth volume of his great *History of the Papacy from 1378 to 1527*, and apart from his Hulsean Lectures on *Persecution and Tolerance* (1895) and some volumes of sermons he published no more. He was hugely successful as Bishop of Peterborough, but following his translation to London the strains and stresses of an impossibly large and demanding diocese took their toll and in the end claimed his life at the early age of 58. London diocese had at that time 800 parish priests and over twice as many curates. The number of candidates at each of the quarterly ordinations ranged from 40 to 80 and endless time was occupied with interviews. During 1897 he gave no fewer than 294 sermons and addresses, and since he would not employ a secretary virtually all his letters, apart from a few dictated to a chaplain, were handwritten. In these circumstances it was surprising that he was able to continue for so long and in his final illness, caused by a stomach ulcer, he seemed to lose all desire to live.

Creighton was born in Carlisle in 1843 and as a child lived over his father's furniture shop. He attended the cathedral school, then Durham Grammar School, before going to Merton College, Oxford, as a scholar. Having secured a double first in classics, he then took, after six months of further study, a second in law and modern history. By now he was a High Churchman and a political Liberal. In 1866 he was elected as a fellow of Merton, he lectured on ecclesiastical, Italian and Byzantine history, played a full part in college life and was ordained in 1870. Two years later he married Louise von Glohn, whose father was Estonian. They met when attending a lecture given by John Ruskin and were engaged three weeks later. It proved to be a very happy marriage enriched by many shared interests, including Italian art. Eventually Louise became, in the words of David L. Edwards, 'the most formidable bishop's wife in England' and after her husband's death wrote a classic two-volume biography.

In 1875 Creighton felt attracted to parish work and needed to get away from his Oxford responsibilities in order to write the major history of the Renaissance papacy on which he had recently embarked. The well-endowed college living of Embleton on the Northumberland coast fell conveniently vacant, though it was no sinecure as the population of the village consisted of unruly quarrymen and their families, and the parish boundaries embraced several smaller communities scattered over a wide area. Nonetheless he was very happy there. He threw himself into pastoral work and the general life of the neighbourhood, and was involved in the creation of the new Diocese of Newcastle. He also completed the first two volumes of his History and several other books on historical subjects.

On the strength of this academic work he was elected in 1884 to the new chair of ecclesiastical history at Cambridge, where he proved to be an eloquent lecturer and, it was said, transformed the teaching of history in the university. As at Oxford, he admitted women to his lectures, and he demonstrated his concern for the education of women by serving on the council of Newham College, though he opposed their admission to degrees and was always against women being granted the franchise. During vacations he lived at Worcester where he held a canonry of the cathedral, to which he had been appointed by W. E. Gladstone. He took this seriously and became much involved in the life of the cathedral and the city, but eventually it claimed more time than he could spare from academic life and in 1891 he was pleased to be offered a Canonry of Windsor, with its lighter responsibilities. Before he could be installed, however, came the offer of the Bishopric of Peterborough, which at that time included Leicestershire as well as Northamptonshire and Rutland.

It was a time of considerable social and economic change in the diocese and Creighton, who resided in Leicester for a time every year in order to make his presence felt there and to reduce the burden of travelling to distant parishes, counselled the clergy to live disciplined lives. Morning and Evening Prayer were to be said daily, they were to visit the parish schools regularly and be ready to stand for parish and district councils – 'Nothing that makes for good should be unimportant in the eyes of God's minister.' Lectures for the clergy covered social and political matters as well as theology and biblical criticism. A reading list in the diocesan calendar suggested 215 titles on a wide variety of subjects, including novels, of which he was himself an avid reader. When a Boot and Shoe strike brought poverty and bitterness to the diocese in 1895 he played an influential part behind the scenes in the securing of a settlement.

A tall, thin, wiry figure, he had worn a long beard since his undergraduate days and was never other than well dressed. He was essentially a man of liberal mind who declared himself to be 'almost crazy for liberty', and his conversation was sparkling and witty. Certainly he lacked the earnestness of the late Victorian era, but there was a serious and sometimes stern side of his that could not lightly be dismissed.

Frederick Temple, whom he succeeded as Bishop of London, said, 'For sheer cleverness Creighton beats any man I know,' but there was ambiguity in this description.

When Edward White Benson died in 1896 there was some talk of Creighton succeeding him at Canterbury, but in the event the primacy went to Frederick Temple. In some ways Canterbury would have been easier for him than London proved to be, for in addition to the massive pastoral and administrative load, which he attempted to carry as if he were still in Peterborough, there was an intense ritual controversy to grapple with. Temple, his predecessor, had tended to ignore Protestant complaints against what they claimed to be Romish practices, but their clamour became too great for Creighton to refuse action, distasteful though this was to him. He would never take legal action against any priest, however, preferring to discuss the issues with the parties involved in any dispute. 'If a man wishes to make a smell, let him do so,' was his response to a complaint about the use of incense. This informal, conciliatory approach proved to be remarkably successful and by the time his episcopate ended there were no more than three parishes in London that remained out of line. But it all took an enormous amount of time.

Less demanding, because Creighton made them so, were the central councils of the Church. He took little part in the Convocation of Canterbury. Randall Davidson, shortly to become Archbishop of Canterbury, wrote after his death:

> Often I have envied his power as he sat steadily writing his letters during the whole course of a debate, and yet was ready at a moment's notice, if necessity arose, to make a substantial contribution as finished in outward form as it was solid in material. Again, in a long experience of committees, I have never known any chairman with a power comparable to his of reducing the outcome of tedious and troublesome discussion into a few clear and cogent paragraphs in the form of a report.

He became ill in the summer of 1900 and at first it was hoped that rest and dieting would effect a cure, but in December two operations became necessary and early in January 1901 he died with the word 'God' on his lips. Five years earlier he had written, 'Relations founded on a sense of lasting affection are the sole realities of life,' and his wife described her biography of him as 'The story of the life of one to whom love was the supreme revealer and life but an opportunity for loving.'

Kenneth Kirk

Kenneth Escott Kirk brought to the Bishopric of Oxford (1937–54) a combination of academic and pastoral gifts that enabled him to minister, as few modern bishops have been able to do, to the university, and also to make a considerable impact on the parishes of a large and mainly rural diocese in which he was greatly loved. Having begun life as a Methodist, he moved on to become the unchallenged leader of the Anglo-Catholic wing of the Church of England, but his learning, integrity and spirituality caused him to be held in the highest regard by the whole Church.

He was also a good administrator and the experience of running much of Oxford diocese's central organization without lay help during the 1939–45 war years led him to reflect, in the March 1946 number of the *Diocesan Magazine*, on the ministry of a bishop. His long article was occasioned by the centenary of the enthronement of one of his predecessors, Samuel Wilberforce, and the suggestion made in a newspaper that, as a consequence of his vigorous episcopate, bishops were now required primarily to have high administrative competence. Kirk recognized that bishops now carried a heavy burden of administration, but to choose them primarily for their administrative efficiency would, he believed, be to give a secondary requirement a quite fatal predominance in the life of the Church of England – 'In all ranks of the clergy we ask not for good organization (though a little organizing ability may go a long way) but for inspired teachers, pastors and evangelists; this is as true for the episcopate as it is for the parochial clergy.' Kirk returned to this subject in 1952 when he declared the Church of England to be in the almost impossible predicament of trying to combine two systems of government – the patriarchal and the democratic. The growth of councils and committees at every level of the Church's life had not been accompanied – and this for the best of reasons – by any lessening of the expectation that the bishop should be involved in the decision-making processes. Furthermore, because of their patriarchal role, the bishop was bound to serve as a court of appeal for anyone who disagreed with the results of these processes, and the more active the Church became in the diocese the more the pastoral presence of the bishop was required in the parishes. Kirk could see no way of resolving the conflict between the two systems of government and believed that, short of an impossibly expensive increase in the bishop's staff, nothing could be done except make the best of them. He was highly critical however of the increase of Westminster-based church activity and legislation which added to the episcopal burden. And he objected to the selection of ordination candidates being removed from the hands of the bishops who would ordain them. Yet, in spite of his serious reservations about the bishop's administrative role, he was able to present this in a positive light in a remarkable sermon on 'Beauty and Bands' preached at the consecration of his friend Glyn Simon as Bishop of Swansea and Brecon in 1954.

Kirk was born in Sheffield in 1886, his father being the not very well remunerated director of a steel works. His paternal grandfather was a well-known Wesleyan minister in the area and young Kenneth was baptized as a Methodist. When he was about thirteen he was however confirmed in the Church of England and, having won many prizes at Sheffield Royal Grammar School, considered the possibility of a career on the stage. Instead, and on the advice of an actor, he went to St John's College, Oxford, where he took a double first in classics, then began to study Theology. It was during his time at Oxford that he became a High Churchman and was also much influenced by the Student Christian Movement and the Inter-Collegiate Christian Union. He left Oxford in 1909 in order to undertake mission work among foreign students in London and in the following years joined the staff of University College London as warden of one of its halls of residence and assistant to the Professor of Philosophy. Remaining involved in the work of SCM, he travelled widely on its behalf until 1912 when he suffered a breakdown through overwork and was obliged to rest for four months. On his recovery he spent a term at Cuddesdon Theological College and was then ordained to a curacy in the large coal-mining village of Denaby Main in South Yorkshire. He was there for two happy years before appointment as a tutor at Keble College, Oxford, but the outbreak of war in 1914 removed most of his students and he also volunteered to serve as an army chaplain in France and Flanders. There he ministered to the heavy casualties in the first Battle of Loos and later in the Battle of the Somme.

Following demobilization in 1919 he returned to Oxford, first as Acting Principal of St Stephen's House – the Anglo-Catholic theological college – then as a Prize Fellow of Magdalen College. By this time he had written his first book *A Study of Silent Minds* (1918), which was about education through friendship, and in 1920 he published *Some Principals of Moral Theology*, in which he examined the ethical teaching of St Thomas Aquinas and of the seventeenth-century Church of England Bishops Sanderson and Jeremy Taylor. This was followed by *Ignorance, Faith and Conformity* (1925) and *Conscience and its Problems* (1927) and these three volumes did much to revive interest in Christian ethics after a long period of neglect. He had become Fellow and Chaplain of Trinity College, Oxford, in 1922 and, as a result of his books, was now widely known and in demand as a lecturer and preacher. In 1927 he was appointed Reader in Moral Theology and an invitation to give the

Bampton Lectures provided an opportunity for him to express his wide-ranging learning. The resulting book *The Vision of God* (1928) became a classic with its central thesis that the highest Christian action is worship, and worship holds the key to the solution of ethical problems. An invitation to become Principal of Cuddesdon was rightly refused in 1928 and five years later he became Regius Professor of Moral and Pastoral Theology and a Canon of Christ Church, Oxford. But then tragedy struck. In 1934 his wife died of pneumonia leaving him with five young children. His own life was to extend over another twenty years, but he never fully recovered from this blow and thereafter was always a lonely man. He published a commentary on the Epistle to the Romans in 1937 and in the same year was made Bishop of Oxford. At the time there was strong pressure for the appointment of a solely pastoral bishop but this was resisted and it was fortunate that Kirk had academic, pastoral and administrative gifts in equal measure. Faced with responsibility for 870 parishes spread over the counties of Oxfordshire, Buckinghamshire and Berkshire, he decided that each should have its own suffragan bishop who would also be the archdeacon. The diocesan administration was transferred from Cuddesdon to Oxford and the episcopal palace at Cuddesdon was abandoned in favour of a house in Oxford. Attention was also given to diocesan finances.

But there was no neglect of pastoral work by Kirk, who was soon out and about in the parishes where he quickly became a revered figure. He was a very good preacher, with the ability to present profound truths in simple language, and his remarkable memory enabled him to get to know his 650 clergy well. A particular concern to him was those of them who were in ill-health – sometimes through overstrain and too often through undernourishment because of low pay. During his holidays he usually served as a locum in a country parish outside the diocese. *The Diocesan Magazine* became an important part of his teaching ministry with high quality articles on theology, worship and parish life, and his university links enabled him to exercise an influential ministry in the colleges.

In February 1939 Kirk became seriously ill and was unable to return to duty until the outbreak of war in September. He strongly supported the war on moral grounds and shocked some by defending the use of atomic bombs on Japan in 1945 – 'While all is horrible and poignant to the last degree, it remains – so far as I can see – the more merciful course to have used the atomic bomb than to have refrained from using it.'

During the immediate post-war period he became dismayed by developments in the ecumenical fields particularly the scheme for a united church in South India. Like others who had migrated to Anglicanism from Free Church tradition he felt betrayed by the possibility of what had attracted him being abandoned, or at least seriously diluted. So he recruited a number of other Anglo-Catholic scholars to contribute to a symposium *The Apostolic Ministry* (1946), which sought to uphold the traditional Catholic view that bishops belonged to an unbroken succession which could be traced back to the first Apostles and thus guaranteed their authenticity and orthodoxy. The volume which might well have come out of the Vatican was immediately subjected to sharp criticism by other leading scholars, including many who recognized the importance of bishops but could find no evidence in either the New Testament or early church history to support the views of Kirk and his colleagues regarding their origin. They seemed to be defending the indefensible.

At the 1948 Lambeth Conference Kirk was the chief spokesman of those who opposed the South Indian Church's method of bringing together the ordained ministries of the participating bodies. They believed that any doubt about the validity of the new ministry cast doubt on the validity of the sacraments and must therefore be removed. But they lost this battle and afterwards Kirk appealed with success for mutual toleration and the avoidance of schism. In the longer term he also lost the battle to impose strict discipline on Christians who remarried after divorce. His speeches in the House of Bishops and the Church Assembly were always much less influential than might have been anticipated in one whose reputation was so high. His scholarly and somewhat oblique style was unsuited to powerful advocacy. During the final years of his episcopate Kirk was a sad figure who suffered much ill-health and some bouts of depression. He died suddenly in June 1954 and the crowds who lined the streets of Oxford at the time of his funeral in Christ Church testified to an admiration and affection greater than he had ever recognized.

Ian Ramsey

At a London Memorial Service for Ian Ramsey (Bishop of Durham 1966–72) Archbishop Michael Ramsey, then at Canterbury, said of his close friend, 'It will not be surprising if history comes to remember Brooke Foss Westcott and Ian Ramsey as the two bishops who made the biggest impact upon the Durham community.' Three decades later that prediction remains unchallenged. Ian Ramsey was a very remarkable man. Small of stature and with a Lancastrian accent, the initial impression was that of an affable north-country rural dean. He was kind, warm, approachable and interested in the lives of ordinary people. Yet he had the mind of a distinguished philosopher – good enough for an Oxford chair and able to engage the attention of the leading scientists, physicians, politicians and other philosophers of his day.

This combination of gifts made him an ideal choice for Durham when it fell vacant in 1966. Maurice Harland, who moved from Lincoln to Durham when Michael Ramsey became Archbishop of York in 1956, was a pastoral bishop. He lacked the intellectual gifts that had come to be expected of Durham's bishops and after fourteen years of good pastoral work, first as a suffragan, then as a diocesan, bishop he had become jaded. On hearing the name of his successor, Michael Ramsey exclaimed, 'Very good, very good, yes very good. But it must not happen again.' To be fair to Harland, he had no desire to move to Durham and during his early years there told gatherings of the clergy that he was no more than a 'hedge priest' who had accepted translation only because Archbishop Geoffrey Fisher would not countenance his refusal. It did not take Fisher long to recognize his mistake.

Ian Ramsey's appointment was greatly welcomed in Durham and seen, more widely, as a notable acquisition for the episcopal bench. And he did not disappoint. But six years later he was dead, aged 57, and at the end of his memorial service address Michael Ramsey raised a question that many others were asking:

> Is it possible for one man to lead the pastoral work of a diocese with its outreach to the community and at the same time to be taking part in national affairs and at the same time also to conserve the work of study, reading, thought and teaching?

The answer provided by Ian Ramsey was, 'Yes, but only for a short time,' and this answer was inseparable from his own personality for he was a man who found it impossible to say No to any invitation, who found it equally difficult to delegate and who was always too busy to sit down and establish personal priorities. It was, quite literally, a fatal mixture for a modern bishop, but no-one who knew Ian Ramsey believed that he could have behaved otherwise or ever regretted that he had been called to be a bishop.

Auckland Castle, with its towers and turrets, was far removed from the humble surroundings of his birth in Bolton in 1915. Although never himself on the breadline, he retained throughout his life memories of his early years when the decline of the cotton industry brought massive unemployment and dire poverty to Lancashire's mill towns. A scholarship took him to the local grammar school and thence to Christ's College, Cambridge, to read mathematics. His studies were however interrupted by tuberculosis and during a long convalescence he began to feel drawn to ordination. Returning eventually to Cambridge, he took firsts in mathematics and philosophy, and came increasingly under the influence of Charles Raven – a notable liberal theologian who was both Master of Christ's College and Regius Professor of Divinity. He then took a first in theology and went for ordination training to Ripon Hall, Oxford.

From 1940 to 1943 Ramsey was a curate at Headington Quarry, near Oxford, before going back to Christ's College as Chaplain, then as Fellow and Director of Studies in Theology and Philosophy. He remained there until 1951 when, aged 36, he became Nolloth Professor of the Philosophy of the Christian Religion at Oxford. His first book *Religious Language* (1957), with which he made his name, was followed by several more in which he developed the idea that, while the visible world and human life must be open to rigorous scientific analysis, there are experiences – he called them 'disclosure situations' – which go beyond the visible and require both their own language and personal commit-ment. He failed to win over all his fellow philosophers, but nonetheless indicated to them that there was a Christian case that needed to be taken seriously, and to the Church that the twentieth century required more than the traditional scholastic argument for God's existence and activity.

Besides his academic work, Ramsey threw himself into the life of Oriel College, where he was a fellow, became chairman of a hospital management committee, director of the Lambeth Diploma in Theology and chairman of several church groups concerned with social questions such as suicide, abortion and sterilization. His boundless energy, fertile mind and inability to say No was becoming increasingly evident. It was characteristic of him that when, following his appointment as Bishop of Durham, he went to pay homage to the Queen, he arrived at Bucking-ham Palace in a cloth cap. On completing the ceremony, he went into a philosophical and theological discussion with the Queen on the problems created by a recent disaster at Aberfan, South Wales, in which many schoolchildren were killed by a moving coalmine spoil. Equally characteristic was his enthronement sermon at Durham in which, after emphasizing the rich historic inheritance upon which he was entering, he evaluated a recent report of the Northern Economic Planning Council.

Wherever he went in the diocese for confirmations and institutions of new vicars his lengthy sermons were replete with stimulating ideas and, if not all of these were immediately accessible to either the clergy or the laity who heard them, the obscurity was quickly forgiven when the preacher shook hands with everyone as they left the church and then spent time in the church hall talking over the refreshments with little old ladies about their families. Once away from the parishes however he had many other demanding responsibilities to fill the remainder of his waking hours – the chairmanships of the Church of England's Doctrine Commission, of a commission on the future of religious education, of the Institute of Religion and Medicine, of William Temple College, and of the Central Religious Advisory Committee on Religious Broadcasting. On most Wednesdays when Parliament was sitting he travelled to London to attend the House of Lords where he spoke frequently on issues affecting the North-East and on wider social and moral problems.

In his perceptive, candid and affectionate memoir, David L. Edwards recorded that during the last quarter of 1971 Ramsey prepared 57 original speeches, talks and sermons besides the normal quota of confirmation addresses. It had become absurd and could not be maintained. On Easter Eve of the following year he suffered a heart attack which put him out of action for several months. This led some to hope that his pace of life would be reduced and his years lengthened, but one of his first engagements after returning to duty was to address a large gathering of church leaders in Birmingham at which, although the time allocated to him was 45 minutes, he spoke at breakneck speed for 75 minutes. He seemed to be on an express train that was out of control, and it was not long before he had another, this time fatal, heart attack after chairing an all-day meeting at Broadcasting House in London. Michael Ramsey said that he had been living 'in a whirl of mental and physical movement. The whirl became the whirlwind which swept Ian, like Elijah of old, to Paradise!'

Ian Ramsay was followed by John Habgood, who in turn was followed by the controversial David Jenkins, thus continuing for another twenty years the Durham tradition of the scholar-bishop. But then the supply of scholars dried up, not only for Durham but for the rest of the Church of England and by the end of the century no scholar of distinction, apart from Eric Kemp of Chichester, who had by then passed the normal retiring age by fifteen years, occupied an English bishopric. Two developments had conspired to bring this about.

The setting up of the Crown Appointments Commission in 1977 left the nomination of bishops virtually in the hands of the Church. The eight permanent members of the commission have always given careful consideration to the needs of the vacant diocese as discerned by the diligent Secretary for Appointments at 10 Downing Street, and the presence at commission meetings of four representatives from the diocese ensures that none of these needs is overlooked. The proceedings of these meetings are highly secret but it is no surprise to learn from leaks that the dioceses always ask for a pastor and never for a scholar. The struggling parish clergy hope for an experienced and sympathetic Father in God who will hold their hand, and the laity hope for a kindly bishop who will bring warmth to the services, not preach overlong, and spend time at the party in the parish hall afterwards. The idea of a scholar arouses fear of a distracted intellectual, lacking in parochial experience, impatient with the synodical bureaucracy, and likely to preach sermons which, if understood, may well disturb the faith of the theologically illiterate – both clergy and laity. Asked if scholar Christopher Wordsworth (Bishop of Lincoln 1869–85) was popular in his cathedral city, an inhabitant replied, 'He is as popular as a man can be, three-quarters of whom is in the third century and the other quarter in heaven.'

A surprising feature of the Crown Appointments Commission's activities is what appears to be a complete lack of strategy relating to the composition of the bench of bishops as a whole, and the need for it to contain a variety of gifts, including intellectual ability. Archbishop Robert Runcie, when asked about this, seemed shocked and replied that he believed such a strategy would be a serious mistake, since each appointment had to be considered in the light of local needs. So much for the concept of the bishop as an agent of the whole Church.

It is not to be supposed however that the universities house a large number of dons who are bitterly disappointed that a Prime Ministerial offer has never dropped through their letterbox. For a scholar with a vocation to think, teach and write, fewer posts on this earth could be less attractive than that of a bishopric. The incessant demands of pastoral administration and other duties, local and national, guarantee that serious, sustained study must end. This is by no means a recent development, as many of the lives in this volume demonstrate, but the problem is more serious than ever before and any serious scholar who might be approached about a bishopric would have good reason to beg to be excused. The early death in office of Ian Ramsey is a salutary reminder of the perils of being a scholar-bishop in the present age. It is also the case that theological scholarship has in recent years become divorced from the life of the Church. A distinctive feature of Anglican theology was for many years its broad pastoral aspect, but today's scholars – many of whom are lay and members of other churches – tend to be theological technicians concerned with narrow and esoteric fields of research which are of not much use to the Church and are unlikely to enchance an episcopal ministry.

The need for the bench of bishops to include some distinguished scholars is however wider than their particular theological expertise. While this is important when doctrinal matters – particularly the reinterpretation of the Christian faith in the light of contemporary culture – are under consideration, there are many other problems and opportunities facing the Church where strong intellectual gifts are necessary for the making of right decisions. Second-class minds tend to make second-class decisions, as the recent history of the Church of England all too clearly demonstrates. This serious problem will not be solved however until the Church has rediscovered the true role of the bishop in the modern world and reordered its life to make the exercising of that role possible.

4

The statesmen

Every so often the Church of England has enjoyed the leadership of a bishop who has not only exercised powerful influence in the Church but also made an important contribution to the life of the English nation as a whole. Sometimes particular circumstances, for example war, have called for such leadership and in some ways made it easier to offer. But in no circumstances can it be given unless some bishops are endowed with unusual gifts of vision, insight and courage, and – no less important – the ability to witness to their faith on the frontiers of church and society in such a way that even those who do not share this faith feel bound to take them seriously.

Archibald Campbell Tait

During the 60 years between 1868 and 1928 three of the five Archbishops of Canterbury were born in Scotland and brought up as Presbyterians before moving south and embracing the faith and polity of the Church of England. The first of these was Archibald Campbell Tait, who occupied the primacy from 1868 to 1882, having spent the previous twelve years as Bishop of London. A tall man, open-minded and tolerant, he was always concerned that the Church should express the religious aspirations of the whole nation, and no archbishop since the Reformation came to carry so much weight in Parliament or in the country generally. And it was during his primacy that Canterbury came to be recognized as the focus of the worldwide Anglican Communion.

Yet the beginning of his career was distinctly unpromising and he owed his appointments to London and Canterbury entirely to the insistence of Queen Victoria who was initially moved greatly by a tragedy that struck his family and then, having seen him in action in high office, much admired his qualities. Succeeding Thomas Arnold as headmaster of Rugby School in 1842 was never going to be an easy task, but he was not equipped for a headmastership and, although he tried hard and ran a strict regime, the most charitable verdict when illness forced him to resign in 1848 was no higher than 'worthy but dull'. On his recovery in 1850 he was appointed Dean of Carlisle where he found the cathedral poorly attended, various abuses in the affairs of the chapter, and the school in need of reorganization. 'At times I feel greatly depressed here by the uncongenial spirits amongst whom I am thrown,' he lamented.

He had however the consolations of a happy family life, with seven children. But between 6 March and 8 April of 1856 five of these children died of scarlet fever. This became national news and none was more affected by the fate of the children and the plight of their parents than the Queen. Within six months, and in the face of strong opposition from both High Churchmen and evangelicals, Tait had been appointed Bishop of London – the only priest for 200 years to go directly to the third place in the Church of England's hierarchy. When twelve years later his translation to Canterbury was suggested, the Prime Minister, Disraeli, declared himself against it on the grounds that, 'though apparently of a spirit somewhat austere, there is in his idiosyncrasy a strange fund of enthusiasm, a quality which ought never to be possessed by an Archbishop of Canterbury or a Prime Minister of England'. But the Queen got her way, and she was right.

Tait, born in 1811, was the youngest of nine children and his mother died when he was only three years old. His Scottish ancestors had been Episcopalians but became Presbyterians in the eighteenth century and it was not until he reached Glasgow University that young Archibald felt drawn to the Anglican Church and subsequently to Holy Orders. A scholarship to Balliol College, Oxford, led to a first in classics and election to a fellowship. Benjamin Jowett, Frederick Temple and Matthew Arnold were among his pupils. Following his ordination in 1836 he also took charge of the parish of Baldon, near Oxford, and in 1838 declined the offer of the Professorship of Greek at Glasgow University because he could not subscribe to the Calvinism of the Westminster Confession which was a requirement of those who held this post. His position was that of a liberal Churchman and he opposed the Tractarians, partly because he believed they would restrict the Church of England's openness and partly because he was anxious that non-episcopalians should not be unchurched.

His acceptance of the headmastership of Rugby School required courage, but clearly it was a mistake and, had not an appalling tragedy struck his family, he might well have spent many more years in the deanery at Carlisle to which he was rescued after his Rugby illness. Appointment to a commission responsible for recommending reforms at Oxford University indicated that some in authority were aware of his gifts, but his consecration as Bishop of London in 1856 caused great astonishment as well as opposition. On his arrival in the capital he announced that evangelism would be his chief priority and immediately set an example by engaging in open-air preaching. Westminster Abbey and St Paul's Cathedral were persuaded to hold Sunday evening services to which ordinary people might be attracted. A diocesan Home Mission was founded to facilitate missionary work among London's unchurched poor and, although handicapped by a club-foot, Tait was here, there and everywhere in the diocese – enthusiastic, generous and hard-working. He was essentially a man of action and, in spite of his early academic credentials, Gladstone doubted if he had ever read a theological book.

After two years in the diocese he delivered his primary charge in St Paul's Cathedral. This occupied five hours and consisted of a masterly survey of the Church's life in London and concluded with a call for greater efficiency and stronger emphasis on evangelism. In the great controversy then raging over the Church's rites and ceremonies, he took the line that, while the law relating to worship expressed in the Book of Common Prayer must be obeyed, the clergy could otherwise do whatever they considered necessary to advance Christianity in their parishes. When in 1859 there was rioting at St George's-in-the-East because of High Church practices he went down to the East End to restore peace and order, and later received a letter of thanks signed by 2,000 people.

On theological matters, about which he was nothing like as ignorant as Gladstone believed him to be, he was markedly more liberal than most other members of the bench. Back in 1847, when still at Rugby, he had supported R. D. Hampden's controversial appointment to the Bishopric of Hereford and later was the only bishop among the majority of Privy Councillors who upheld the right of the clergy to examine the Bible with the tools of modern criticism and to believe that the whole of human-kind would finally be saved. This brought widespread criticism from more conservative quarters. Undeterred, he next advocated the relaxa-tion of the legal requirement that the clergy should subscribe ex animo to the Thirty-Nine Articles of Religion and, although most of the clergy opposed this and the Convocation of Canterbury rejected Tait's pro-posal, he requested the government to enforce the change. When Colenso was charged with heresy and deposed from the Bishopric of Natal, Tait said that the case should be heard in an English court and that mean-while Colenso should remain in office. He was also among the bishops who supported a Divorce Bill which gave divorced people the right to be remarried in church, while leaving the clergy free to decide whether or not to officiate at such a ceremony. His speech in the House of Lords was influential in securing the Bill's passage.

August 1866 saw the outbreak of cholera in East London and Tait, well aware of what this involved for families, had some of the children whose parents had died in the epidemic brought to Fulham Palace – the bishop's home – to be cared for. He strongly supported the parish clergy who were ministering to victims and the crisis revealed once again the weakness of the Church's organization in the East End. The large parishes were thereupon divided, more clergy were drafted into the area, and Tait launched a Bishop of London's Fund to sustain the new work. In the first year over £100,000 was subscribed and the fund became – and remains – an important element in the financing of London diocese.

In 1862 he had declined an invitation to become Archbishop of York but six years later acceded to the Queen's request that he should go to Canterbury. The first major issue facing him was Gladstone's proposal that the Church of Ireland should be disestablished, and initially he was against this. But when a general election showed the country to be behind Gladstone he changed his mind and played an important part in the examination of the Bill's implications for the clergy. In the end its passage owed a great deal to Tait and his reputation was enhanced in consequence. Twelve months after his appointment as Primate, however, he suffered a heart attack, probably caused by stress and overwork, and during his convalescence, which extended to the spring of 1871, a Suffragan Bishop of Dover was appointed to share the pastoral work in Canterbury diocese.

As Primate he was required to devote more time than he found agreeable to ritual problems, but he continued to put his weight behind moves designed to safeguard the Church of England's inclusive character. In a House of Lords debate on a new Burial Act in 1880 he supported the right of Nonconformists to be buried in parish churchyards, and although the Anglican parish clergy were against this it was through his influence that Parliament approved the necessary legislation. He was less successful, however, in persuading the Convocation to make the use of the Athanasian Creed optional in worship, though it was agreed that its condemnatory clauses should be understood only in a general sense. Two royal commissions were set up at Tait's suggestion. The first was concerned to awaken the cathedrals to their responsibilities in the Church's overall mission, and the second to simplify the procedures of the ecclesiastical courts. Both reflected the reforming zeal and statesmanship which characterized his episcopal ministry right up to his death in 1882.

When he died the Queen asked for a lock of his hair. The inscription on his monument in Canterbury Cathedral reads:

A GREAT ARCHBISHOP,
JUST, DISCERNING, DIGNIFIED, STATESMANLIKE
WISE TO KNOW THE TIME AND RESOLUTE TO REDEEM IT,
HE HAD ONE AIM:
TO MAKE THE CHURCH OF ENGLAND MORE AND MORE
THE CHURCH OF THE PEOPLE: DRAWING TOWARDS IT
BOTH BY WORD AND GOOD EXAMPLE
ALL WHO LOVE THINGS TRUE AND PURE,
BEAUTIFUL AND OF GOOD REPORT.

Randall Davidson

Randall Davidson was Archbishop of Canterbury from 1903 to 1928 and before that Bishop of Winchester (1895–1903) and Bishop of Rochester (1891–1895). He was the first ever Primate to retire from office and was described by William Temple as 'The essence of kindness and sanity – without a glimmer of inspiration.' Yet he exercised enormous influence not only over the life of the Church, but also over that of the nation. He was for many years a central figure of the Establishment. This was due partly to the fact that his primacy extended over a quarter of a century, but chiefly to the fact that as the pace of social change accelerated in the new twentieth century he presented a reassuring image of wisdom and stability. And he was a consummate politician who knew how to operate in the corridors of power and, because he did not support causes or campaigns, won the trust of leaders of all the parties.

Although his early years were spent in Scotland and he was baptized in the Church of Scotland, the Anglicanism which he acquired while a schoolboy at Harrow was cast in the classical mould as expressed by the great sixteenth-century divine Richard Hooker. Church and state were seen as complementary elements in a single Christian society, each interacting with the other for the common good. If the Church had comments to make about political matters these would best be made, said Davidson, by reasoned, behind-the-scenes, discussion, rather than by any public shouting of the odds. In return, the Church might reasonably expect to have the government's support in the making of sound senior appointments, the promotion of ecclesiastical legislation and the offering of public witness.

Davidson's influence began when he was in his early thirties. After a three-year curacy at Dartford in Kent he was, on the recommendation of Crauford Tait, whom he had known at Oxford, appointed resident chaplain to his friend's father, Archbishop Tait. He soon married Tait's daughter and became so close to the archbishop that a good deal of the important Lambeth correspondence was delegated to him. He also became one of Queen Victoria's chaplains. On the death of Tait in 1882 he sent an account of the deathbed scene to the Queen who was 'greatly touched' and asked to see him. After the interview she wrote in her journal, 'I was seldom more struck than I have been by his personality . . . I feel that Mr Davidson is a man who may be of great use to me, for which I am truly thankful.' She immediately began to seek his advice on various senior church appointments and in the following year, when he was still only 35, she persuaded the Prime Minister, W. E. Gladstone, to nominate him for the Deanery of Windsor. He now became the Queen's confidante and adviser and his pastoral ministry to her at the time of the death of her youngest son, Leopold Duke of Albany, in 1884 created a close bond which continued until the end of her life. Davidson's influence at Court was enormous and he was confident enough to advise the Queen, in the most tactful way, against the publication of a second volume of her journal. This upset her and she demanded an apology and the withdrawal of his advice, which courageously he refused to do and offered his resignation instead. This was greeted with silence and normal relations were quickly resumed. During the next forty years he was never far from the centre of power.

Davidson was born in 1848 in Edinburgh where his father was a timber merchant. There were a number of Church of Scotland ministers among his ancestors, one of whom was a chaplain to Queen Anne. At Harrow he was greatly influenced by the headmaster, H. M. Butler, and by his housemaster, Brook Foss Westcott, the future Bishop of Durham. During the summer of 1866, however, immediately before his final year at Harrow, he was accidentally shot in the back while rabbit-shooting in Scotland and returned to school more or less a cripple. The effects on his health proved to be life-long and an immediate consequence was failure to secure a hoped-for scholarship at Corpus Christi College, Oxford. So he went instead to Trinity College, Oxford, as a commoner where a combination of poor health and inadequate tuition resulted in disappointing thirds in law and modern history. By this time he had felt drawn to Holy Orders and the next three years were spent trying to recover his health and preparing for ordination under the guidance of C. J. Vaughan, the Master of the Temple, who used time spared from this undemanding office to train young men, 'Vaughan's doves', for the ministry. Davidson's curacy at Dartford was happy but unremarkable and, unsurprisingly, provided few opportunities for displaying the gifts that were to be required of him in high office. Humanly speaking, it was mere chance that Crauford Tait recommended him to his father for the vacant chaplaincy at Lambeth, but his subsequent meteoric rise in the Church was without parallel in modern times.

Besides his work for the Queen at Windsor he wrote, with the help of William Benham, a two-volume Life of Archbishop Tait and most days he received a packet of letters from Tait's successor, Edward White Benson, with a request for comment and advice. In 1891 Davidson was appointed Bishop of Rochester, which had recently shed the counties of Hertford and Essex but acquired in their place the whole of South London. The Queen had wanted him to go to Winchester, which was also vacant, but the Prime Minister, Lord Salisbury, was unwilling to let so young a clergyman go to so senior a bishopric. Rochester turned out, however, to have been a mistake. Davidson chose to live in Kennington Park, not far from the Elephant and Castle, which was quite a change from Windsor Castle; he did not like urban work, and had three serious illnesses in the space of four years. Relief came in 1895 when the see of Winchester again became vacant and this time Lord Salisbury was ready to nominate Davidson. The expectation that his health would recover in the rural surroundings of Farnham Castle was soon realized, and the fact that Osborne House on the Isle of Wight was at that time in Winchester diocese enabled him to maintain close contact with the Queen. He had been at Winchester for less than a year however when Archbishop Benson died and the Queen pressed for him to be translated to Canterbury. Once again Lord Salisbury refused on the grounds of his age and appointed instead, with Davidson's approval, the now decrepit Frederick Temple. The suggestion that Davidson should succeed Temple at London was firmly rejected by the Queen because of the likely threat to his health. So he continued at Winchester for another five years, exercising a strong pastoral ministry and reviving a diocese which had since the death of Wilberforce suffered the lassitude of very ancient bishops. He was, naturally, present at the Queen's deathbed, saying the commendatory prayers, and, because of the archbishop's failing powers, played a large part in the planning of King Edward VII's coronation.

Soon afterwards he succeeded to the primacy and during the next 25 years found himself grappling with many new problems as the Church sought to respond to the demands of the twentieth century. In 1904 he became the first Archbishop of Canterbury to visit the USA and Canada. In the following year he denounced the actions of mobs against the Jews in Russia. The Lambeth Conference and a Pan-Anglican Congress, both held in 1908, enhanced his patriarchal status in the Anglican Communion and increasingly overseas bishops turned to him for advice. He crowned King George V in 1911 and served as one of the three Counsellors of State during the King's visit to India. During the 1914–18 war he was not among those who saw the conflict as a religious cause and he denounced the use of poison gas, attacks on civilians and propaganda designed to encourage hatred of Germans. Before the war he had sought to foster Anglo-German friendship. In 1916 he launched a National Mission of Repentance and Hope which attracted a lot of attention but it did not catch the mood of the times and turned out to be a flop.

After the war Davidson supported the Life and Liberty Movement's appeal for greater democracy in the life of the Church and displayed considerable cunning in persuading the House of Lords to pass the legislation required for the setting up of a Church Assembly on the grounds that it was no more than an administrative move designed to save parliamentary time. His support of Prayer Book revision in 1927–28 was however much less successful. In 1903 he had inherited many unresolved problems relating to the Church's worship and soon after becoming archbishop got the government to set up a Royal Commission on Ecclesiastical Discipline, but it soon became apparent that nothing less than a complete revision of the 1662 Prayer Book would meet the need. At this point Davidson's leadership was weak, chiefly because he was not himself convinced of the necessity of a great upheaval in the Church's worship. When the House of Commons finally rejected the proposed revision in 1928 he shed no tears and strongly opposed those in the Church who were calling for disestablishment. That such a call was being made by traditionally minded bishops such as Henson of Durham led him to recognize that the Church had now entered a new age, so wearily he retired, explaining that this would enable Archbishop Lang, whom he had treated like a son, to preside over the 1930 Lambeth Conference.

One of Davidson's critics said, 'He sat on the fence with both ears to the ground,' but this was not altogether fair, for besides his courageous wartime pronouncement he strongly supported President Woodrow Wilson's proposal for a League of Nations in 1919 and he was very much behind the 1920 Lambeth Conference historic Appeal to All Christian People for church unity. During the General Strike in 1926 his appeal for reconciliation included the suggestion that the government should subsidize the depressed coal industry and that the mine owners should cancel their proposed reduction of wages. This was controversial enough to cause him to be banned from making a broadcast appeal on the BBC.

He was an archbishop of sound judgement who enjoyed the exercising of influence and power, but he was humble enough to seek advice whenever he felt uncertain about any matter. In the end it was evident that he was essentially a Victorian figure who had lived long into a very different era and was unable to cope with its demands. When in 1920 Canon Peter Green, a renowned slum parish priest, declined the Bishopric of Lincoln on the grounds that episcopal palaces and stipends were a stumbling-block to the preaching of the gospel, Davidson confessed that he had never thought of this before. He died in 1930 and George Bell's *Life* is one of the great biographies of the twentieth century.

William Temple

William Temple, who was Archbishop of Canterbury from 1942 to 1944, having previously been Archbishop of York (1929–42) and before that Bishop of Manchester (1921–29), was one of the greatest English archbishops and the most remarkable of the twentieth century. His tenure of Canterbury was however one of the shortest ever, though he was there during a critical period in the nation's history, and his influence was no less great during his thirteen years at York.

The secret was a combination of an astonishing intellectual capacity which enabled him to apply his mind to many of the central issues of human life, a deep religious faith, and a warm, open personality. Thus equipped, he could hardly have failed, and his early death was lamented both nationally and internationally, and by many who were not associated with any church. He was described in the Press as 'The Churchill of the Church' and as 'The People's Archbishop'. A Yorkshire farmer, who knew little of his great gifts and wide influence, said that he was 'a jolly man'. His rotund figure was easily captured by cartoonists – he was rarely out of the Press – and he once confessed that climbing Great Gable, in the Lake District, destroyed once and for all his belief in the resurrection of the flesh.

Although Temple was in his day recognized as a considerable philosopher and, as an ecclesiastical statesman, made a considerable contribution to the reform of his own church and the development of the ecumenical movement, which in his Canterbury enthronement sermon he described as 'the great new fact of our era', his greatest and most lasting impact was as a social reformer. The roots of this were located partly in the idealist philosophy he imbibed during his time at Balliol College, Oxford, and partly in a Victorian understanding of the obligation of the rich to help the poor. He was also much influenced by the work of R. H. Tawney – an economic historian who had been a close friend since their schooldays at Rugby. But most important of all was his understanding – prompted by the teaching of F. D. Maurice, Westcott, Scott Holland and Gore – of the Incarnation which led him to believe that no part of human life was outside God's concern and that society as well as individuals needed to be challenged by and infiltrated by Christian values.

Temple was chairman of a ground-breaking conference on Politics, Economics and Citizenship attended by 1,500 people in Birmingham in 1924 and another on The Church and Social Issues held in Malvern in the darkest wartime days of 1941. Far more influential than either of these, however, was his paperback *Christianity and Social Order* which was published in 1942 and sold 150,000 copies in a matter of months. This was no more than a brief and hurriedly written essay which stated the basis of Christian social concern, outlined the principal issues, suggested a way in which the two might be linked, and in an appendix offered a personal view of what action in the interests of social justice and the building of a fairer society would be needed when the war ended. The timing of the book's appearance contributed greatly to its publishing success and influence, for, although the 1939–45 war was still at a critical stage and the victory of the Allied forces by no means certain, the British people needed something to lift their minds beyond the immediate danger and to fuel their growing belief that the heavy sacrifices of war must be rewarded with a better, more just society. Temple reflected a widely felt national feeling and contributed to a radical change in public opinion which brought a Labour government, with a landslide victory, to power in 1945. Professor Denys Munby, an Oxford economist, described *Christianity and Social Order* as 'one of the foundation piers of the Welfare State'.

Politically, Temple stood some way left of centre, though he always asserted that in Britain no political party could lay exclusive claim to Christian allegiance. There was nonetheless no possibility of the Conservative Party embracing many of the suggestions in his personal manifesto and some were even beyond the reach of the Labour Party, to which he had belonged in the 1920s. Among these were the nationalization of the banks and the public ownership of all urban land, but others, such as family allowances, the five-day week, and education until the age of sixteen, became all-party policies. His suggestion of a European Economic Community was a very long way ahead of its time. More than half a century after its publication *Christianity and Social Order* is open to some valid criticisms, and the absence of any reference to the role of women in society and to Third World problems is striking, but it remains one of the most significant contributions to social thought in the twentieth century.

William Temple, born in 1881, was the younger of the two sons of Frederick Temple, who was Bishop of Exeter at the time of his birth and subsequently became Bishop of London, then Archbishop of Canterbury. Young William went to Rugby School where he carried all before him, except at games, and at Balliol College, Oxford, secured a double first in classics, served as President of the Union and became a socialist. As a fellow of Queen's College and a lecturer in philosophy, he sought ordination in 1906 at the hands of the Bishop of Oxford, but was turned down because of his hesitations about the historicity of the Virgin Birth and the bodily Resurrection of Jesus. Two years later, with these hesitations more or less resolved, he was ordained by the Archbishop of Canterbury, Randall Davidson, and thereafter had apparently no doctrinal problems. His understanding of the New Testament and of traditional doctrine was on the whole quite conservative. During his time at Oxford he became much involved in the Workers Educational Association (of which eventually he became the president) and the Student Christian Movement – both recently formed and attractive to those seeking change in church and society.

In 1910, when only 29, he was appointed headmaster of Repton School. That was almost certainly a mistake, for, as he was himself ready to admit, he was not a born headmaster, he was no disciplinarian, and there were increasing demands on his time outside the school. Rescue came in 1914 but not in the way planned by those in authority. Two years earlier it was announced that he had been appointed to a Canonry of Westminster, to which was annexed the Rectory of St Margaret's, Westminster, but then it was discovered that he had not completed the six years in priest's orders required of those appointed to canonries. So he resumed the headmastership until the important parish of St James's, Piccadilly, in London's West End, fell vacant and on the eve of the 1914–18 war he moved there. During the war years large congregations assembled to hear his expositions of St John's Gospel and its message for those troubled times. The church became a key place of Christian witness. He was also editor of *Challenge* – a weekly newspaper which provided an outlet for his own views, and in 1916 was deeply involved in a National Mission of Repentance and Hope. The following year saw the publication of *Mens Creatrix* – a philosophical study which pointed to the Incarnation as the keystone of a rational world view.

At the same time his attention was increasingly being given to a new Life and Liberty Movement which aimed to press for the reform of the Church of England when the war ended. The best of the clergy serving on the Western Front and the more perceptive of the clergy who were manning the parishes at home were aware of the huge gulf that existed between the Church and the working classes. They were equally aware that, because of the close link between church and state, any significant proposals for change in the Church would require parliamentary approval. This, even if forthcoming, would be a cumbrous process requiring much parliamentary time, with inevitable long delays. The answer to this problem seemed to lie in the bringing together of the Convocations of Canterbury and York, along with the laity of the Representative Church Council, to which Parliament would delegate certain powers. The parishes would have their own church councils to assist the priest. Temple resigned from his parish in order to provide the movement with full-time leadership and he stumped the country speaking on its behalf. The result was an Enabling Act (1919) which gave the Church of England the freedom it sought but not the inspiration necessary for its effective use.

Temple had by now completed the required apprenticeship in Holy Orders and was once again offered a Canonry of Westminster. His time at the Abbey was however brief, for in 1921 he became Bishop of Manchester. He was only 40 and hesitated before accepting, not so much because it was a very large, heavily populated diocese beset by massive problems, but because he was reluctant to accept the constraints imposed by episcopal office. In the end the archbishops pressed him into service and during the next eight years he offered Manchester dynamic and prophetic leadership. His intellectual gifts and interests never got in the way of his enjoying a warm relationship with ordinary Lancashire people among whom he became a popular figure. This was to be a characteristic of his entire episcopate. During his years as Archbishop of Canterbury, when a multitude of problems occupied his mind, he was remarkably relaxed and accessible; his chaplains never found him rattled; and he was happy to travel about wartime London by bus – 'strap-hanging' when no seats were vacant. And no archbishop ever had so loud, and so frequently exercised, a laugh.

The new Diocese of Blackburn was hived off in 1927, but still left Manchester with 400 parishes and a population of 2 million. Temple also had many other irons in the fire. Besides the 1924 COPEC Conference, he was chairman of an Archbishops' Commission on Christian Doctrine and deputy chairman of a section of an international Faith and Order Conference held at Lausanne in 1927. Time was also found for the writing of several books, of which *Christus Veritus* – a sequel to *Mens Creatrix* – was the most important.

Temple's translation to York in 1929 surprised no-one and for the next thirteen years he was at the height of his powers. He was in constant demand for sermons and lectures in all parts of the world and his mission to Oxford in 1931 greatly influenced many future church leaders. Deep involvement in the ecumenical movement led to the chairmanship of a Lambeth Conference Church Unity Committee and an Edinburgh Faith and Order Conference. When the World Council of Churches was formed in 1939 he became its provisional chairman and by this time he was one of the outstanding leaders of the quest for church unity. That so heavily engaged a church leader could also find time to prepare the Gifford Lectures, published in 1934 as *Nature, Man and God*, was considered extraordinary at the time and in retrospect seems unbelievable. His *Readings in St John's Gospel* (two volumes, 1939–40) became a classic and his literary output totalled 35 books and innumerable articles. A senior episcopal colleague said that what took him two or three mornings to prepare was accomplished by Temple in twenty minutes and was better.

When Cosmo Gordon Lang eventually retired from the Archbishopric of Canterbury at the end of 1941 there could be no doubt about the name of his successor and Winston Churchill, who disliked Temple's views on social questions, described him famously as 'the only sixpenny item in a penny bazaar' and reluctantly appointed him. During the war years his broadcast talks, started when he was still at York, had large audiences and were models of how Christian insight can illuminate a dark human crisis. He travelled tirelessly the length and breadth of the country addressing crowded meetings, and a series of addresses given in a number of large cities in 1942–43 under the title 'The Church Looks Forward' attracted wide attention. From 1943 onwards he expressed deep concern at the Nazi persecution of the Jews and pleaded for government support for any who might escape to Britain. But the response to his proposals was by no means universally favourable and there were frequent complaints about his alleged 'interference' in social, economic and political matters. A lecture to the Bank Officers' Guild on 'A Christian View of the Right Relationship between Finance, Production and Consumption' (what archbishop before or since could have tackled such a subject?) drew a particularly hostile reaction from the City of London. He lived just long enough to provide the support essential to the passing of R. A. Butler's 1944 Education Act. In the end the strain was too much and he died quite suddenly on 26 October 1944. President Franklin D. Roosevelt of the United States sent the King a telegram of condolence.

George Bell

Was George Bell, Bishop of Chichester 1929–57, the best Archbishop of Canterbury the Church of England never had? The question was asked at the beginning of 1945 when, to the dismay of many, it was announced that Geoffrey Fisher, then Bishop of London, would succeed William Temple at Lambeth. More than half a century later it continues to be asked whenever Bell's name is mentioned, and the course of the Church's history during that time has served only to reinforce the widely held conviction that the passing over of Bell was a disastrous mistake.

Temple's death could hardly have come at a more inopportune moment. He had been at Canterbury for only two years and the outstanding leadership he had displayed in both church and state during the critical years of war would be needed no less urgently in the approaching era of peace. Vision and courage would be essential in an archbishop responsible for inspiring the Church's necessary renewal and reform. Bell, an outstanding Bishop of Chichester, was a recognized leader in the world Church. He had a fine mind, a wide vision of the Church united, and a deep commitment to the service of the poor and oppressed. He had engaged in pioneering work in the relationship between the Church and the arts and written a great biography of Archbishop Randall Davidson, whose chaplain he had been. And there could be no doubting his courage, for in February 1944 he had spoken in the House of Lords against the obliteration bombing of German towns and cities which had become Allied policy. In the circumstances of that time this required courage of almost foolhardy proportion, though many military historians now question the policy's strategic wisdom.

When the Archbishopric of Canterbury fell unexpectedly vacant the Prime Minister, Winston Churchill, was not the only person in authority who felt incensed by Bell's intervention. The occupants of Buckingham Palace were equally annoyed and Bell was well aware that there was not the slightest possibility of his being appointed to the primacy. To be fair to Churchill, however, it has to be remembered that for the past five years he had been leading the nation in a life or death struggle against the most evil forces ever to have appeared on the human scene. At the time of Bell's speech preparations were being made for an invasion of continental Europe that might well involve a horrendous number of casualties as the price of success. The maximum pressure must be applied to Germany and bombing by the RAF was one of the few available weapons. In such a situation it was hardly to be expected that a Prime Minister who had little interest in church affairs would wish to promote a bishop who had challenged the morality of a key element in war policy. It may also have been pointed out to him that, although Bell had remarkable gifts, he lacked a charismatic personality and was actually a dull speaker. He was essentially a shy man who did not command the wholehearted support of his fellow bishops. Moreover Temple himself evidently had some doubts about Bell's suitability for Canterbury when he confided to his wife, 'I must retire early enough to give Geoffrey (Fisher) a go', though Temple, in common with some other great men, was notoriously a poor judge of ability and character.

Bell was born in 1883 within sight of Chichester Cathedral, his father being Vicar of nearby Hayling Island. He was the eldest of nine children and two of his brothers were killed in the 1914–18 war. Early academic promise was confirmed by the award of a scholarship to Westminster School, and at Christ Church, Oxford, he obtained a first in Mods and a second in Greats, as well as winning the Newdigate Poetry Prize. As an undergraduate he was the general editor of the *Golden Anthologies* of verse. At Wells Theological College he joined the recently founded Student Christian Movement and began a lifelong commitment to church unity and the Church's involvement in social and political affairs. He became a curate of Leeds Parish Church in 1907 and his social concern deepened during a three-year ministry among the poor in the city's back streets.

Bell taught at Christ Church, Oxford, from 1910 to 1914 and soon after the outbreak of war became one of Archbishop Randall Davidson's chaplains. Over the course of the next fourteen years a close and highly effective partnership developed between the two men. Davidson became confident enough of Bell's ability to feel able to delegate a considerable amount of work to him and to use him for the preparing of briefs and the drafting of speeches. It was a remarkable role for a priest still in his early thirties, though it had a recent precedent in Davidson's own experience as chaplain to Archbishop Tait. In both instances the chaplains learned the importance and method of episcopal involvement in public affairs. Bell was entrusted with the convening of an ecumenical conference of church leaders to consider the issues raised by the 1914–18 war and at the 1920 Lambeth Conference, of which he was assistant secretary, he was largely responsible for the private discussions which led to the unity Appeal to all Christian People.

In 1924 the Prime Minister, Ramsay MacDonald, prompted by Davidson, appointed the 41-year-old Bell Dean of Canterbury. 'It is not a very exacting post,' Davidson told his chaplain, 'just what you make it, and there are still many things you could keep in touch with at Lambeth.' In the event, Bell made a very great deal of it and in the space of five years brought about a revolution in the cathedral's life. The building was opened more to the public, admission fees were abolished, pilgrimages encouraged, a Friends' organization started, Free Church preachers invited to the pulpit, and services regularly broadcast. The cathedral also provided scope for Bell's love of the arts, and the performance of the specially commissioned play *The Coming of Christ* by John Masefield, with music by Gustav Holst, was the first use of drama in an English cathedral since the Middle Ages. Other dramatic productions followed and it was at Bell's suggestion that T. S. Eliot's *Murder in the Cathedral* was commissioned for the Canterbury Festival in 1935. Beyond the cathedral he was involved in matters related to education, housing and unemployment, and in the development of the East Kent coalfield. In 1925 he attended the landmark Stockholm Conference on Life and Work, where he came under the lasting influence of Archbishop Söderblom of Uppsala, took a very active part in its deliberations and edited the English edition of the proceedings. He was now well on the way to becoming a key figure in this aspect of the ecumenical movement.

It was evident also that he was destined for high office in the Church of England and when he became Bishop of Chichester in 1929 he brought to that diocese the reforming zeal which had characterized his time at Canterbury. A Liturgical Missioner was appointed to help raise the standard of worship in the parishes and to relate worship to a revival of mission. A Director of Religious Drama, a Bishop's Chaplain for Schools and a Canon Teacher were also appointed and this pointed the way to specialist appointments in other dioceses. Bell himself worked long hours, and spent much time visiting parishes where a retentive memory greatly assisted his pastoral work. He had a particular concern for education.

At the same time he retained his international links and, having chanced to attend an ecumenical meeting in Berlin at the time Hitler came to power, was one of the first to discern that the Nazi threat would become the central issue in Europe. His knowledge of developments in Germany was aided by a deep friendship with a young theologian Dietrich Bonhoeffer, and this was to have dramatic consequences when war came. During the 1930s Bell wrote many letters to *The Times* on the German problem and, following a meeting of the Life and Work executive committee chaired by him at Novi Sad in Yugoslavia in 1933, he wrote on behalf of the committee to the leaders of the German Lutheran Church expressing concern about the treatment of Jews and the restrictions placed upon freedom of speech. Two years later Life and Work put its weight behind the German Confessing Church, which had been formed to uphold more strongly the Christian witness and in 1935 Bell met Rudolf Hess, Hitler's deputy, and urged on him the need for the German Churches to have an independent place in the life of their nation.

As war became increasingly likely, Bell favoured negotiations, pointing out that, although the Nazi regime was undoubtedly evil, there was another, quite different, side of Germany that needed to be taken seriously. Soon after the outbreak of war in 1939 he wrote in the *Fortnightly Review* about the Church's role in wartime, emphasizing the need for the Church to be at all costs the Church, exercising an authority independent of the state. It must guard moral principles by speaking out against the bombing of civilians, the propaganda of lies and hatred, and policies of extermination or enslavement. In August 1940 he spoke in the House of Lords against the automatic internment of enemy aliens, and in April of the following year wrote to *The Times* appealing for an end to the night bombing of German towns, provided the German government would do the same. None of which made a scrap of difference to the prosecution of the war, but Bell was still sufficiently well regarded as to be sent on a three-week visit to neutral Sweden in May 1942, along with T. S. Eliot and Kenneth Clark, the art historian. The purpose of the visit was to maintain contact with influential Swedish people and secure whatever support they could for Britain's war effort. During the course of their stay, however, Dietrich Bonhoeffer arrived from Germany with news of the growth of an underground movement and a request that the British government should encourage its further development by declaring that when the war ended special consideration would be given to those who had opposed and helped to undermine Hitler.

Bell conveyed this request in great secrecy to the Foreign Secretary, Anthony Eden, but the government at this critical stage of the war felt unable to take such action. In any event, the agreement of the other Allies would have been needed and Russia was unlikely to be enthusiastic. Bell always believed the policy of unconditional surrender to have been morally and strategically wrong. His speech against obliteration bombing in 1944 was heard with respect in the House of Lords, but the Dean of Chichester asked him to withdraw from preaching in the cathedral on the anniversary of the Battle of Britain and he was much abused by certain sections of the Press. When the war ended he pleaded for the generous rehabilitation of the German people and for the cessation of the war crimes trials.

There were to be several more clashes with the government during the post-war era. He opposed the setting up of a Central African Federation on the grounds that the proposed terms were unfair to Africans. The Suez Crisis in 1956 provoked him to severe criticism of government policy, as did the Cyprus crisis in which he was one of the few public figures in Britain to support Archbishop Makarios in his campaign to rid the island of British rule and Turkish influence. He believed that Communism could not be overcome by economic and military measures but only by the propagation of a better religion and truer philosophy. In home affairs he strongly supported the campaign for the abolition of capital punishment. His concern for church unity was unceasing. He had enthusiastically backed the proposals for the creation of a united Church of South India, which came into being in 1947, and at the inauguration of the World Council of Churches in the following year he was elected chairman of its Central Committee. When the Anglican–Methodist unity conversations began in 1956 he was joint-chairman and he worked hard for local unity schemes in Sussex.

Following his retirement early in 1958 his health deteriorated rapidly and he preached his last sermon later that year at a service in Denmark to mark the tenth anniversary of the foundation of the World Council of Churches, of which he was now an Honorary President. At a service in Chichester Cathedral held on 10 October 1958, when his ashes were interred near the altar of St Richard, the Archbishop of Canterbury, Geoffrey Fisher, said:

He will go down in history as one of the special glories of the Church of England: in days to come when the Catholic Church recovers again its lost unities, men will still remember the debt for that recovery owed to George Bell . . . All his life he has had to be an elder statesman and has carried his share of responsibility for us. But he has never been old at heart: as all young people do, he was looking forward, seeing visions, dreaming dreams, contriving, devising.

It is hardly to be expected that every generation of bishops will produce men of the calibre of Tait, Davidson, Temple and Bell, and in a period when the most able people are not involved in the full-time service of the Church the chances of such leaders emerging are obviously greatly reduced. But it would be unduly defeatist to suggest that the bench of bishops can no longer include some men (and hopefully women in the near future) who have a broad vision of how the affairs of church and nation might best be ordered and what particular steps are required in the ecclesiastical and political institutions to secure this end. Reading, consultation and reflection are needed for this, and over-busy bishops, who are preoccupied with the running of their dioceses and the central bureaucracy of the Church, are unlikely to fill the bill.

When the American and British armed forces launched their first attacks on the Taliban regime in Afghanistan in October 2001 a *Church Times* commentator congratulated the Archbishop of Canterbury on his statesmanlike silence. There are of course times when wisdom decrees silence, but the outbreak of war can hardly be one of them and a depressing feature of the period following the catastrophic terrorist actions against the World Trade Center in New York and the Pentagon in Washington was the lack of any serious attempt by English church leaders to apply Christian ethics to the deep crisis in which the world had suddenly found itself. The Roman Catholic bishops, followed by the Archbishop of York, turned to the classical doctrine of the just war, first formulated by St Augustine of Hippo in the fourth and fifth centuries and now impossible to apply to modern terrorist action. The Archbishop of Canterbury and some other church leaders issued a necessary call to prayer, and a few bishops declared themselves to be against any armed intervention, chiefly it seemed on pacifist grounds. It was left to the Chief Rabbi to provide a thoughtful analysis of the moral issues at stake and an indication of what might be the greater and lesser evils in a situation where politicians and the military were required to make decisions of the utmost gravity. It is impossible to believe that Tait, Davidson, Temple and Bell and many other bishops of their eras would have ducked the problem. A month after the outbreak of hostilities the Archbishop of Canterbury said, while on a visit to the Middle East, that he believed the war to be 'a necessary conflict'.

In spite of their apparent lack of skill in handling, with Christian insight, a matter as important as the response to global terrorism, the bishops are nonetheless fighting to retain the 26 seats presently allocated to them in the House of Lords. This number was settled when there were no more than 26 dioceses and every bishop was a spiritual peer of the realm, but now, in the long overdue proposals for House of Lords reform, it is recommended that their number should be reduced to sixteen. This is part of a much-needed general reduction in the size of this House, and also intended to make room for representatives of other churches and religious faiths.

The bishops are resisting this, though the number of them who attend regularly and speak in the debates is small. On some important occasions their absence verges on the scandalous. Obviously it is far from easy for busy bishops whose dioceses are a long way from London to spend long hours in Westminster, and pastorally minded bishops are natually reluctant to break parish engagements in order to attend unexpected debates in the House of Lords. Part of the reason for their reluctance to have their number reduced is that this would require them to attend more frequently for the conducting of prayers and for speaking in debates of particular concern to the Church. Here it is necessary to acknowledge that the professional politicians in the House do not look kindly on bishops who speak on matters other than those deemed to be the Church's business, such as education and personal morality. This inhibits some, though not all, and many of the episcopal speeches are of a high quality, especially those based on expert briefs from the General Synod Board for Social Responsibility.

There is now much to be said for Archbishop Geoffrey Fisher's surprising proposal, made to Prime Minister Clement Attlee as long ago as 1949, that the number of bishops with seats in the House of Lords should be reduced to ten, including the two archbishops, and be confined to those with particular expertise who would be able to play a full and useful part in the work of the House. This would need to be taken into account when episcopal appointments were made, and it would have to be understood that involvement in the House of Lords was a major piece of responsibility, exempting the participants from involvement in most other aspects of extra-diocesan work. It would also be understood that the representatives of other churches could be left responsible for stating the Christian position on political questions. Such a reform would not of itself produce statesmen but it might well bring a few to birth and encourage them to develop.

5

The prophets

Although all Christians are called to continue the prophetic ministry of Jesus Christ by challenging those aspects of human life – personal and social – which are contrary to the revealed will of God, the number of those whose witness has earned them the title prophet has always been very small. And this is true of the bishops, as indeed it is of all church leaders, for institutions do not normally appoint to positions of influence those who are likely to rock the boat. Thus ways have usually been found to exclude from the episcopate anyone who might seriously threaten the stability of the political and ecclesiastic orders. It is also the case that some prophetic characters have excluded themselves inasmuch as they have been unwilling to accept the compromises inevitably involved in the leadership of an essentially conservative institution. Yet prophets have sometimes appeared among the Church of England's bishops and emerged from a variety of backgrounds. And, like all prophets, they were courageous.

John Percival

John Percival (Bishop of Hereford from 1895 to 1917) was described by his biographer, William Temple, as 'A true prophet, refusing and forbidding to compromise the moral law. He was a man who lived by faith in God.' Charles Gore knew him as President of Trinity College, Oxford, and never forgot his sermons in the college chapel – 'We felt that a great, strong righteous will was expressing itself amongst us with profound astonishment at our being content to be such fools as we were; and this was to one very bracing.' At Hereford he was far from popular and Prebendary Wynne Willson, who was Percival's chaplain during the early part of his episcopate, then became Rector of St Nicholas, Hereford, wrote – 'His hindrances were heavy. He was a radical among bigoted conservatives, a liberal churchman and reformer amid a population whose soft relaxing climate caused them to dislike effort and whose remoteness made them suspicious of new thought.' On the first day of the twentieth century Percival prayed fervently that the Church would 'shake herself free from that spirit of political subservience and timidity which paralyses her prophetic powers'.

He was born in Westmorland in 1834 and never lost his Cumbrian accent. His father, a farmer and prize wrestler, required young John to work on the farm as well as attend Appleby Grammar School, from where he won a scholarship to Queen's College, Oxford. After taking firsts in classics and mathematics, he was elected to a fellowship, but then his health broke down due to a combination of hard work and spartan living. By 1860 he was sufficiently recovered for him to be ordained and take a teaching post at Rugby School. He found teaching fourteen-year-olds tedious and after two years applied speculatively for the headmastership of the newly founded Clifton School. To his own great surprise and that of his colleagues, he was appointed. He shared the ideas and methods pioneered by Dr Arnold at Rugby, built up a brilliant staff, imposed strong discipline and introduced natural sciences, so that within ten years Clifton was regarded as one of the leading public schools in the country.

In 1879 he left to become President of Trinity College, Oxford, and this again occasioned surprise, since it was unprecedented for an Oxford college to elect someone not already connected with its own life. His liberal reputation also caused some misgivings and he soon crossed swords with the fellows, most of whom saw no need for reform. His austerity also rankled, for he objected to smoking in public and one fellow complained that he felt obliged to go round to the Oxford wine merchants and apologize for the small consumption of wine accomplished by Trinity undergraduates under Percival's rule. It was not a happy time for Percival either, though college numbers increased and new buildings were erected. A further outlet for his reforming zeal appeared in Bristol where, as an honorary canon of the cathedral, he undertook regular preaching and social work in the city and strongly supported the infant trades union and co-operative movements. He edited the journal of the National Agricultural Labourers' Union. Back in Oxford he was one of the chief movers in the foundation of Somerville College for women and as its first chairman worked hard for the admission of poor students.

In 1887 however he leapt at the opportunity to become headmaster of Rugby School, the life of which was now at a low ebb. Public confidence needed to be restored and a new era of reform was signalled at the beginning of the Lent term in 1888 when five boys were expelled on the spot, their names being publicly struck off the school list, and many more were dismissed at the end of term. Percival, a formidable figure, of considerable height and stern countenance, flogged delinquent boys and made scathing remarks between the strokes – 'It'll hurt ye, but it's for your good. I mean ye to remember it every day of your life.' One of his victims recalled, 'The rod in his left hand was no toy' and when young William Temple was observed sucking a sweet during a chapel service a powerful voice boomed out – 'How dare you come gorging and guzzling into the presence of your Maker?' Nonetheless Percival was greatly respected and put the school back on its feet. One of the masters later reported, 'Under Percival we were always moving towards noble ends along a sure road; but he sometimes forced the pace to such an extent that we almost dropped from fatigue.' In 1894 there was however a considerable outcry when he wrote to *The Times* supporting the disestablishment of the Church in Wales and it was his views on this explosive subject that led the Prime Minister, Lord Rosebery, to offer him the Bishopric of Hereford, disregarding the strong opposition of Queen Victoria who rightly discerned that sending such a man to a diocese which had thirteen of its parishes in Wales would be specially provocative.

Rosebery also had it in mind that Percival needed a less strenuous job, though he soon found plenty to do in his diocese and one of his chaplains, who as a journalist had been used to a fourteen-hour day, later complained that the bishop had worked him off his feet. He conducted confirmations impressively, preferring them to be held on Sundays when most people could attend, believed that the laity should have more power in the parishes, especially over forms of worship, and ordered there to be a church council in every parish. His Protestant sympathies were never in doubt and he opposed elaborate ritual in worship on the grounds that 'it ministered to the sensational and emotional cravings of a materialistic age and would strengthen the Church as the Church of the upper and wealthier or materialized classes'. Yet he was always kindly disposed to Catholic Anglicans and his notably generous hospitality was offered to all.

In the cathedral he got the chapter to agree to the cessation of the use of the Athanasian Creed – 'How terrible it sounded,' he declared, 'those innocent choir boys repeating the awful words "without doubt he shall perish everlastingly"' – but a minor canon said that the law required it to be used, so it was settled that it would be said on Sundays at 8 am Mattins, but at no other service. Appointments to parishes in what had previously been known as 'The Dead See' soon engaged his attention and he was criticized for favouring liberal clergymen for senior appointments. He justified this on the grounds that they were frozen out elsewhere. Percival's third charge to the diocese in 1904 declared that clergy and laity must be involved in the social and political affairs of the country, with a particular concern for the poor, the weak and the suffering, because –

concern for the poor burns and shines, as a light from heaven above us, on almost every page of the Gospel story, making this story the Magna Charter of all true popular and democratic progress. Such, as I apprehend it, is the Christianity of Christ, and none other.

This was the last thing that Hereford wished to hear and widespread complaint followed. His own political involvement was considerable and he often spoke powerfully in the House of Lords. During the 1895–1906 debates on education he opposed the archbishops and bishops who were seeking more government money for church schools. He argued that the Church should not encourage a separatist policy, and that Nonconformist teachers should be employed in church schools. His special interest in education led him to publish a pamphlet advocating the foundation of university colleges in all the major English cities and he played an important part in the establishing of University College, Bristol, which was open to both men and women and later became Bristol University. His proposal that Oxford and Cambridge should grant degrees to women was defeated in 1897.

A considerable fuss followed Percival's decision to mark the coronation of King George V in 1911 with a service of Holy Communion in Hereford Cathedral to which Nonconformists would be invited. The Bishop of Winchester, E. S. Talbot, protested against this in the House of Bishops, claiming that the proposed service was 'a contradiction of sacred principles with which we have no right to interfere'. To which Percival tartly retorted, 'I am not conscious of contravening Christian principle by our kneeling together at the Table with those who believe in the same God and accept the same Creed.' Hereford protesters received an even sharper response in a letter to the Archdeacon of Hereford who had signed the protest:

> I have looked at your protest and it certainly does little credit either to its composer, whoever he was, or to the men who signed and presented it. Its tone is contemptuous, in an insolent way, to Nonconformist bodies, and offensive to the Bishop . . . I am truly sorry that you all have so far allowed your minds and feelings to be warped by prejudices and party spirit.

There is no doubt that he would have been happier in an urban diocese and for a time he entertained the hope that when the aged and ailing Archbishop Maclagan either retired or died he would succeed him at York. The Prime Minister, Campbell Bannerman, had more or less promised him this but inconveniently died shortly before Maclagan resigned and his successor, H. H. Asquith decided, not unreasonably, that at the age of 74 Percival was too old for so senior a post.

So he soldiered on at Hereford until 1917 when ill-health drove him to resignation. His final years in the bishopric were dogged by controversy and he became increasingly unpopular and lonely. His prophetic witness had also isolated him from most of the other bishops who regarded him simply as a loner. But his innate goodness was widely recognized and he marked his 80th birthday by gifts to the poorer clergy of his diocese.

Edward Lee Hicks

When the saintly Bishop Edward King of Lincoln died in 1910 the choice of his successor was never going to be easy and the Archbishop of Canterbury, Randall Davidson, disagreed with the Prime Minister, H. H. Asquith, who insisted on nominating Edward Lee Hicks, Canon of Manchester Cathedral and Rector of the largely slum parish of St Philip's, Salford. He occupied the bishopric until 1919. In his letter to Hicks, Asquith was frank in telling him that his first choice had been Edward Stuart Talbot of Southwark, who had declined, and he went on to point out that Lincoln diocese contained a large Nonconformist population which presented difficult problems. He would therefore rely on Hicks's 'large and broad-minded conception of the true function of a chief pastor of the Church under democratic conditions worthily and adequately to face these problems'. Hicks, now in his 67th year, was astonished to be asked but replied by return of post, expressing his own sadness that Talbot felt unable to leave Southwark (he went to Winchester in the following year) and indicating that in these circumstances he was willing to undertake the task and try to do his best. This best turned out to be very good indeed, for he not only continued and expanded his predecessor's pioneering pastoral work but also made his own distinctive mark as a prophet and radical social reformer.

In his farewell sermon in Manchester Cathedral Hicks said, 'If any class of men may seem more than any other to have kinship with the spirit of Christ and his Gospel, it is those who have at heart the interest of Labour, who champion the claims of the unenfranchised, the unrepresented, the unemployed and the unprivileged.' This was not quite what conservative Lincolnshire was used to hearing, for, although Edward King loved the poor and they loved him, his politics were Tory. Soon after Hicks's arrival in the diocese fellow travellers on a rail journey were surprised to hear their bishop complain in a loud voice to his neighbour that the Church was dominated by the Tory Party and the Party by the brewers. Silence reigned for the remainder of the journey. More was to follow, and in his primary visitation charge to the diocese in 1912 Hicks asked a series of questions:

How are we as Christians, as Churchmen, to feel and act in respect of the enfranchisement of women, the restriction and suppression of the liquor traffic, the prevention of the state regulation of vice, the peace movement, and other forms of social and moral agitation? In particular, seeing that liberty is no longer seriously menaced by the claims of the aristocracy of birth, how are we to prevent the domination of the plutocrat and the corrupting influence of the millionaire?

He went on to forecast that traditional Christianity would be open to serious criticism and experience tremendous shocks if it could not find a practical answer to those questions. His episcopate was devoted to seeking the answers.

Hicks first came to public notice as a scholar. Born in Oxford in 1843, he took a double first in classics at Brasenose College, was elected to a fellowship at Corpus Christi College, and before long had become a leading authority on ancient Greek inscriptions. He retained this interest and authority to the end of his life. But at Brasenose he became a friend of John Ruskin, who enthused him with a love of the arts and also a concern for social reform to improve the lot of the poor. It was Ruskin's influence that inspired his prophetic zeal and two years after his ordination in 1870 he left Oxford to become Rector of Fenny Compton in Warwickshire. He remained there for fourteen years, during which time the parish was enlivened by a combination of diligent pastoral work and various new-style church organizations. An agricultural depression, described in terms remarkably close to those used for the rural problems of the early twenty-first century, caused him great concern and from his own glebe land he allocated a number of half-acre spade allotments to unemployed village labourers. These proved to be very successful, so he tried – but in vain – to persuade wealthy Christ Church, Oxford, to do the same with some of their landholdings in the parish. The arrival of the co-operative movement in the area was greeted with his warm approval.

In 1886 he became Principal of Hulme Hall in Manchester. This was a new venture that provided a hall of residence for Church of England students attending Owen College – the beginning of what was to become Manchester University. There he undertook pastoral work and some teaching, but the academic standard was far below his teaching capacity and his gifts were still not fully exploited when he became Lecturer in Classical Archaeology in the embryonic university. It was during this time however that Ruskin's earlier influence began to be much more powerfully felt by Hicks and his appointment in 1892 to a Residentiary Canonry of Manchester Cathedral, to which was annexed the Rectory of St Philip's, Salford, provided fertile ground for its expression.

The combination of the two posts, which occupied him for the next eighteen years, taxed his physical and spiritual strength to the utmost. It was an absurd set-up designed to remedy an earlier situation in which the Canons of Manchester were scandalously underemployed. St Philip's parish, which included some of the city's worst slums, had a population of 10,000. The Church's ministry had long been neglected and the church building, which had large galleries and seated 2,000, had become an impediment to mission. Hicks, who had the assistance of curates, met this challenge with a threefold policy which he pursued with great vigour. First, evangelism, including open-air preaching, of which he did a great deal himself; second, the care and training of the young, which was focused on a hugely attended Children's Service and Catechism held every Sunday at 9.30 am; third, social work designed to improve the welfare of the many parishioners who lived in dire poverty. Seeing in the slums the devastating effects of alcohol abuse, Hicks came to believe that there would be no social progress until this evil had been overcome. Thus temperance became one of the major concerns (some said obsessions) of his ministry both as a parish priest and as a bishop.

His preaching in Manchester Cathedral was acknowledged to be of a very high standard, though his political comments did not please everyone and his strong opposition to the Boer War aroused a hostile reaction. Nonetheless, he was offered the deanery in 1906 and only declined because of certain conditions attached by the Prime Minister, Campbell Bannerman, who had been got at by evangelical extremists. There was also the point that he had just accepted an invitation to join J. H. Moulton in the preparation of a New Testament Lexicon of Classical Greek. Besides which he was teaching in the diocesan Clergy Training School, serving as rural dean, contributing regular articles to the *Manchester Guardian* and presiding over the excavation of Roman Manchester.

As a bishop, he played little part in the House of Lords and Canterbury Convocation, but the 580 parishes of Lincoln diocese were quite enough to keep him fully occupied. The train service covered only part of the territory and getting about was still difficult, but he covered a lot of ground, as his diary for June and July 1916 clearly indicates:

June 1	Preach at Welby: visit Wilsford and Heydour
4	Preach at Broughton and Cadney
5	Visit Denton and Harlaxton
6	Grant institution and licences
	Address Loveden Rural Deanery Chapter
7	Attend SPG Women's Jubilee
8	Attend meeting at Lincolnshire Home for Girls
9	Visit Sempringham

11	Preach at Grainthorpe
13	Attend charity meeting at Huntingdon
14	Dedicate memorial at Bardney
15	Attend garden party at Swineshead
16	Attend executive committee of Diocesan Conference
17	Address candidates for ordination
18	Ordain priests and deacons
19	Send forth pilgrims of prayer
20–22	Conferences of Archdeacons, Rural Deans and Inspectors
24	Confirmation at Old Palace
25	Preach at Navenby and in Cathedral
26–27	Preach at Bilsby (reopening) and Farlesthorpe
28	Attend model Sunday School at Old Palace
29	Preach at Cleethorpes (Jubilee)
July 1	Bless new vicarage at Gosberton Clough
2	Preach at Spalding (National Mission)
4–7	Attend Convocation
7	Consecrate churchyard at Gonerby
8–10	Visit West Walshcroft Rural Deanery
12	Diocesan Missionary Festival
14	Visit Sleaford (National Mission)
15	Confirmation at Diocesan Home, Boston
	Consecrate churchyard at Skirbeck
16	Preach at Fleet and Gedney (National Mission)
18–19	Visit Alford and Spilsby (National Mission)
20	Visit Willingham-by-Stow
22–24	Visit Horncastle (National Mission)
25	Address Mothers' Union
27–28	Visit Isle of Axholme (National Mission)
29	Grant institution and licences
30	Preach at Rowston and in cathedral

Besides these engagements and the necessary preparation for them, there were many interviews to be given and letters to be written, as well as books to be read, for he remained an international authority on Greek inscriptions and was a regular contributor to the *Journal of Hellenic Studies*. What seems rather surprising is that in the year of the Battle of the Somme there is no indication of his involvement in anything directly connected with the war, though the National Mission of Repentance and Hope, launched by the archbishops in response to the wartime crisis, obviously claimed quite a lot of his time. As President of the Church of England Peace League he was initially against the 1914–18 war, declaring that war served the interests only of financiers and armaments manufacturers, but he came to see this particular war as a necessity and concentrated instead on supporting conscientious objectors, whom he likened to the early Christians.

Another of his special concerns was the women's movement and, as President of the Church League for Women's Suffrage, he gave it bold support. Maude Royden said that Hicks was the only bishop who would have accepted the presidency, but he would not follow her when she moved on to promote the ordination of women to the priesthood. Within the diocese he dealt with what the Prime Minister had described as 'the difficult problem' of a large Nonconformist population by getting on with the Methodists and others extremely well. They liked his concern for temperance and other social issues so much that wherever he preached the chapels were closed and their congregations migrated to the parish church, where they were treated to strong doses of Anglican doctrine for he was essentially a High Churchman. On the other hand, he had a scarcely concealed horror of the Roman Catholics.

Unlike Percival, his contemporary, Hicks did not suffer the unpopularity that normally accompanies a prophetic ministry. Part of the explanation of this was that his pastoral touch was more gentle. The people of Lincolnshire were prepared to tolerate his views because he so obviously loved them and cared for them. He also seemed very human, in spite of his extraordinary gifts, and a layman said, 'He was the only Bishop I knew who made you forget, while he was talking to you, that he was a Bishop.' One of his clergy added, 'There was nothing about him that was not great.' He died, on the eve of his retirement, in 1919 and large crowds gathered in Lincoln for the funeral. His body was cremated, he being one of the early advocates of this method of disposal.

John A. T. Robinson

John Robinson, who held the suffragan Bishopric of Woolwich from 1959 to 1969 achieved a fame and influence that would have been utterly impossible had he remained a Cambridge don. Like many another prophet, however, his prophetic ministry ended in frustration and disappointment. A paperback of no more than 150 pages, condensing in an accessible form the work of three important twentieth-century academic theologians and written by the Dean of Clare College, Cambridge, would have passed largely unnoticed. But, with the name of a bishop attached to it, it was explosive. The original print order was 6,000 copies for the United Kingdom and another 2,000 for America, but these all went on the day of publication and in the end over one million copies were sold in seventeen different languages. The controversy and consequent publicity was immense and, although Robinson wrote bigger and better books, his name will always be inseparable from *Honest to God*.

The late 1950s saw a mini-boom in church attendance and at the same time a questioning concern among the laity and the younger clergy about the veracity of the Church's orthodox teaching. Scholars were aware that theologians such as Bultmann, Bonhoeffer and Tillich had challenged orthodoxy at its deepest levels but the results of their work had not reached the ordinary churchgoer or indeed many of the clergy. By the early 1960s the bottle of belief was ready to burst and a bishop was needed to remove the cork. Robinson was ideally suited to this purpose for he had an uncanny ability to discern the issues of his time that were exciting interest and to interpret these in the light of his very considerable knowledge of the Bible and the rest of the Christian tradition.

Thus the headline – 'Our Image of God must Go' – on an article by him in *The Observer* on the Sunday before the publication of *Honest to God* spoke to millions and aroused the greatest interest in what was to follow. And this was enhanced by the knowledge that the author had been involved controversially in the defence of D. H. Lawrence's novel *Lady Chatterley's Lover* in a widely reported trial at which an attempt was made to have the book condemned as obscene. *Honest to God* was written when Robinson was off duty with a severe back problem and he saw it as no more than a personal confession of faith and an attempt to be honest about the big truth questions involved in faith. He recognized that what he had written would seem to be radical, and to many heretical, but added, 'The one thing of which I am fairly sure is that, in retrospect, it will be seen to have erred in not being radical enough.' That was a prophetic utterance, too.

He received over 4,000 letters about the book, most of them expressing gratitude or asking questions, but the Archbishop of Canterbury, Michael Ramsey, who as a professional theologian ought to have known better, criticized it on television! 'It is utterly wrong and misleading to denounce the imagery of God held by Christian men, women and children: imagery that they have got from Jesus himself, the image of God the Father in Heaven, and to say that we can't have any new thought until it is all swept away.' Some other bishops joined in the condemnation without taking the trouble to read the book. Among many of the younger clergy and the thoughtful laity, in all the churches, however, Robinson was a beacon of hope, for he lent episcopal authority to the asking of questions about fundamental Christian beliefs and indicated that such questioning did not require abandonment of the Church. Yet the bishop who created a sensation and made the greatest episcopal impact during the second half of the twentieth century was a very shy man and by no means easy to get to know. After his resignation from the Bishopric of Woolwich he was quite unable to cope happily with the demands of community life at Trinity College, Cambridge, where he became Dean of Chapel, and this offered further evidence of the difficulties that prophets normally have with traditional institutions.

Robinson was born in 1919 and brought up at the heart of the ecclesiastical Establishment. His father was a Canon Residentiary of Canterbury Cathedral and a member of a clerical dynasty that included the notable scholar dean, Armitage Robinson, and a revered scholar-saint, Forbes Robinson. He went from Marlborough College to Trinity College, Cambridge, where he obtained a first in theology and a good second in classics. He was also President of the Cambridge Student Christian Movement and at one of its conferences in the summer of 1939 was deeply impressed by Reinhold Niebuhr – the American 'realist' theologian. He prepared for ordination at Westcott House, Cambridge, and, having attended a retreat conducted by Mervyn Stockwood, became one of his curates at St Matthew's, Moorfields, in Bristol. From 1945 to 1948 he was involved in the life of a lively inner-city parish and also found time to complete a Ph.D. thesis on the thought of the Jewish philosopher Martin Buber and its relationship to Christian theology. At the same time he forged a close friendship with Stockwood which proved later to be of the greatest significance.

He then became chaplain of Wells Theological College and while there wrote his first book *In the End God* (1950) – a short essay on eschatology. This was well received, but his wider questioning of Christian tradition and ministry proved to be disturbing in a rather conservative college. His appearances on Labour Party platforms during the 1950 general election were equally disturbing to many of Somerset's churchgoing electors. On the recommendation of Michael Ramsey, at that time Regius Professor of Divinity, he moved to Cambridge in 1951 as Fellow and Dean of Clare College and University Lecturer in Divinity.

The movement for liturgical renewal spearheaded by Parish and People was now gathering pace and Robinson used its insights in a revision of the worship in his college chapel. This attracted a lot of interest and led to a book *Liturgy Coming to Life* (1960) in which he described the changes and the reasons for them. His contribution to a controversial, and in the end influential, collection of essays, *The Historic Episcopate* (1954) included a statement which he often repeated and others quoted during the turbulent 1960s:

Just as the New Testament bids us have as high a doctrine of the ministry as we like, as long as our doctrine of the Church is higher, so it commands us have as high a doctrine of the Church as we may, provided our doctrine of the Kingdom is higher.

He also became one of the translators of the New English Bible.

Mervyn Stockwood moved from Bristol to become Vicar of Great St Mary's, Cambridge, the university church, in 1955 and when he was appointed Bishop of Southwark in 1959 he invited Robinson to join him as Bishop of Woolwich. But Geoffrey Fisher, the then Archbishop of Canterbury, was strongly against this proposal, partly because he believed that Robinson would be better employed for some more years as a Cambridge academic, partly because he considered him too young at 39 for such a post in the Church, and partly because he did not like the idea of a diocesan and suffragan bishop sharing the same convictions about the development of church life. In the end, however, Fisher decided not to oppose Stockwood's strongly expressed wishes, and when the appointment was announced the widow of George Bell of Chichester offered him some of his serviceable episcopal robes. These he wore with great pride.

Consecrated on Michaelmas Day 1959, he proved to be a high-calibre bishop in South London, overcoming much of his shyness and offering strong support and encouragement to the hard-pressed parish clergy. His preaching and teaching gifts were put to good use and his confirmations and institutions of new vicars were memorable occasions of devotion, stimulation and hope. The forging of links between the Church and the secular community was one of his special concerns and Stockwood entrusted him with responsibility for establishing the Southward Ordination Course. This pioneering venture was designed to train for the priesthood men who, for one reason or another, could not undertake a residential college course and needed to remain in their secular occupations. It was the expectation and hope of the two bishops that those so trained would stay in these occupations as worker-priests, and during the early years of the scheme many did so, but they were nearly all professional men from offices and schools and most of them eventually moved into full-time parish ministry. The prophetic vision was unrealized, chiefly because its practical implications had not been fully worked out.

Robinson had been a bishop for only thirteen months when the *Lady Chatterley's Lover* trial put him on national and international headlines and confirmed Archbishop Fisher's worst fears. The fact that a bishop had come to the defence of the book made all the difference and in the course of his evidence Robinson went so far as to claim that Lawrence had tried to portray the adulterous relationship between Lady Chatterley and her gamekeeper as 'an act of holy communion'. The court found the novel not to be obscene, but the archbishop told the Canterbury

Diocesan Conference: 'In my judgement the Bishop was mistaken to think that he could take part in this trial without becoming a stumbling block and a cause of offence to many ordinary Christians and I think I ought to say so here where I am above all a pastor among you and by my office your chief pastor.' Five leading Cambridge theologians wrote briefly to *The Times* :

> We regret that on one of the infrequent occasions when a bishop has caught the ear of the nation in a manner befitting a spokesman of the National Church he should have been publicly rebuked by the Archbishop of Canterbury.

Throughout the 1960s Robinson was deeply involved in the movements for church reform and very active in the Church Assembly where his speeches were always heard with respect. His book *New Reformation* (1965), based on lectures given in America, presented reform as a theological imperative and became another best-seller. A further collection of 1960s lectures and essays, *Christian Freedom in a Permissive Society* (1970) also aroused much interest.

After ten years in South London where the tension between his diocesan responsibilities and the demands of a national and international prophetic ministry was tearing him apart, it became evident that a change of sphere was essential, and the opportunity to move to Trinity College, Cambridge, seemed God-sent. He was now 49 and it was not in his own mind or that of anyone else who recognized his special gifts that he would remain there for the rest of his life. Rather would this fairly undemanding job provide the opportunity for personal renewal, writing and teaching – and preparation for the next phase of his episcopal ministry. In bodies such as the Church Assembly he was now highly respected and it was not unreasonable to suppose that before long he would be appointed to a major diocesan bishopric. In all-round ability he stood head and shoulders above his contemporaries.

But this is not how things turned out and he was simply left at Trinity where he was never happy, but where he wrote several more good books, of which the best was *The Human Face of God* (1973) – one of the most important contributions to the study of Christology made by an English scholar during the twentieth century. His final book *The Priority of John* (1984) argued ingeniously, but not to the satisfaction of other New Testament scholars, that John used sources earlier than those employed by the writers of the first three Gospels. But academic as well as ecclesiastical preferment eluded him and he did no university teaching. When his application for the Lady Margaret Chair of Divinity at Cambridge was unsuccessful, his friend Professor Charlie Moule explained:

I don't think that John would rank as a 'learned' scholar. To the end, I doubt if he knew much Hebrew, let alone any other Semitic language. I don't think he was really intimate with the Hellenistic Judaism of Philo and Josephus. Nor, I think, did he read much patristic literature.

A distinguished American theologian, Professor John Knox, valued him differently – 'He was one of the most brilliant and productive scholars of our time.'

Just why he was never invited to become a diocesan bishop when many other, far less able, men were being elevated to the bench remains unclear, even when it is recognized that the chances of a prophet being appointed to a position of leadership in a declining church are remote. A formidable obstacle was presented by R. A. Butler, a former Conservative Deputy Prime Minister, who was now Master of Trinity College, and with whom Robinson had more than once crossed swords. Butler let it be known at Downing Street that he considered Robinson unsuitable for a diocesan bishopric. Faced with this influential judgement, the evangelical Donald Coggan, who had succeeded Ramsey at Canterbury and was busy with an unheeded 'Call to the Nation', was apparently unwilling to press his case. Some of Robinson's friends also wondered if he would really have been happy under the constraints imposed on late twentieth-century bishops, but all agreed that he should have been given the opportunity to try. The clergy of South London were still on hand to testify to Robinson's great pastoral gifts which, as demonstrated by Edward Lee Hicks's occupancy of the Bishopric of Lincoln half a century earlier, allow the prophet as much freedom as he can reasonably expect. The fact that four-tenths of Eric James's fine biography of Robinson is occupied with his final fourteen years at Trinity College, Cambridge, is the measure of the Church of England's loss. He died in December 1983 after a six months' battle against cancer that turned his college critics into admirers.

Ted Wickham

E. R. (Ted) Wickham, Suffragan Bishop of Middleton 1959–82, was not born to be a bishop, neither did he make a good one. Although a bishop for 23 years, his most important work came earlier when he was, from 1944 to 1959, the pioneer leader of the Sheffield Industrial Mission. In this he was a true prophet. His attempt to engage the Church with the largely alienated industrial working class was based on deep sociological, as well as theological, insight and under his dynamic leadership the mission attracted world-wide attention and some emulation. But in its radical form it did not long survive his departure from Sheffield and the Church of England failed to learn its lessons. In this there is a close parallel with the worker-priest movement in France, which was active during the same period as the Sheffield Industrial Mission and suffered much the same fate. Wickham was in close touch with the French experiment, though his approach was significantly different inasmuch as he did not believe that the British situation required priests to be working on the shop floor. Neither did he believe it desirable for the official representatives of the Church in the industrial sphere to ally themselves with a particular political party.

Wickham was born in London in 1911 and never lost his assertive Cockney style. Fairly small of stature, decidedly scruffy, with tousled hair and a no-nonsense manner, people were often surprised to discover that he was a priest, and later that he was a bishop. Yet his commitment to the Bible and to worship and prayer was not less than his passionate belief that the Church needed to be deeply involved in the life of the secular world. During his own industrial experience in East London in the 1930s, which enabled him to claim that he was the only bishop ever to have stood in a dole queue, he felt drawn to Holy Orders and, having taught himself Latin, Greek and Hebrew, obtained a London University BD. He then went to St Stephen's House, Oxford, for a few terms and in 1938 became a curate in a poor Tyneside parish. This heightened his awareness of the gulf between the Church and the working class – a concern he shared with the Archdeacon of Northumberland, Leslie Hunter, with whom he would later have a fruitful partnership in Sheffield.

A single night's bombing in 1941 more or less flattened Wickham's parish and he moved to become chaplain of a Royal Ordnance factory in Staffordshire. This vital component in Britain's war effort employed 25,000 people and Wickham began experimenting with chaplaincy methods that went beyond pastoral care and into discussions with the workers of current social and ethical issues. It was on the strength of this, and admiration of his ability, that Leslie Hunter, who had become Bishop of Sheffield, invited him in 1944 to

> find out by trial in the next two years whether there might be a full-time job for a man with his experience on the shop floors of the big steel works if managers and men invited him.

Initially, Wickham was, for financial reasons, obliged to combine his work with the half-time chaplaincy of an almshouse, which was hardly appropriate to his gifts and interests, but through the good offices of the managing director of a major steel works, who became a strong supporter of industrial mission, he gained access to a sphere in which he established a pattern of work that remained for the next twelve years. This always involved obtaining the agreement of the trade unions as well as management before any work commenced.

The basic element in the mission's work involved the chaplain wandering around the shop floor, talking to the steelworkers as opportunity arose, getting to know them and learning about the issues that concerned them. He was to remember always that he was a guest, with neither status nor rights. Before long Wickham found himself involved in a great deal of pastoral work which would never have found its way to the local vicarage. Next came the arranging of informal gatherings in snap-breaks. The steel-making processes at that time allowed breaks during which the workers could have sandwiches or simply pause for a smoke. Wickham used these to initiate discussions on a variety of subjects – some suggested by himself, others by the men; some with a direct religious dimension, many raising ethical, social and political issues. Anything from 20 to 100 would gather and quick-witted Wickham was adept at stimulating discussion and encouraging involvement. And, since many subjects were too big to cope with in 15–20 minutes, further meetings were arranged out of working hours and away from the factory – in a home or a pub or a hall. The aim of all these activities was to build a modest bridge between the Church and the industrial community – managers as well as workers – to encourage the discussion of important human and social problems, and to encourage the small number of active Christians in the steel works to see their responsibilities not so much in the service of their parish churches but rather within their working environment where they might serve as shop stewards and trade union officials or simply demonstrate with sensitivity their love of their neighbour. Wickham saw this as the Church coming alive within industry.

News of the development spread quickly and he was soon invited to visit several other companies. Long before the two-year experimental period was completed it became clear that there was scope for this kind of mission and the work continued to develop. In 1949 a meeting of 142 industrialists convened by the Master Cutler agreed on the need for urgent expansion of the mission and for its financial support, and this was endorsed on the following day by a meeting of trade union officials. In 1950 the Sheffield Industrial Mission was formally inaugurated. Wickham moved from the almshouse chaplaincy to a residentiary canonry at the cathedral, which left him more or less free to devote all his time to the mission. An advisory committee, drawn from both sides of industry, was formed, a staff of chaplains, including a woman, recruited, and the work steadily expanded to take in the steel works at Rotherham and the Sheffield railway depot. Theological students came in large numbers for pre-ordination courses, which included work experience on the shop floor, and during the late 1950s chaplains moved from Sheffield to Teesside and Manchester to establish missions there. Others were started in Nigeria and Detroit.

Wickham took time off in 1955 to reflect on the significance of the Sheffield experience and this resulted in a seminal book *Church and People in an Industrial City* (1957) which revealed him as a considerable theologian as well as a mission pioneer. In some parts of the book however the parochial system and the parish church were sharply criticized, and the fact that Wickham, who never suffered fools gladly, sometimes gave voice to his criticisms in public seriously compromised relations between the Industrial Mission and the Church in the diocese. Bishop Hunter spent much time trying to keep the peace. Conflict also arose, though it was not of Wickham's making, over a proposal that a national secretariat for industrial mission should be established. A report *The Task of the Church in Relation to Industry* (1959) containing this proposal was accepted by the Church Assembly (the forerunner of the General Synod), but there was never any possibility of the bishops relinquishing control over their own industrial missions to an independent body with Wickham at its head.

This left him high and dry, for he was needing a larger sphere of influence than that provided by Sheffield, important and influential though its industrial mission continued to be. He was bitterly disappointed, for he had a vision of the Church becoming permanently present in large sections of British industry exercising a mission parallel with that of the residential parishes and with himself as its episcopal leader. It would become a new manifestation of Christian witness in a twentieth-century missionary situation. It was not to be and in the end, and for the want of anything better, he accepted appointment as Suffragan Bishop of Middleton in Manchester diocese.

This was not a sensible appointment. Neither by temperament nor inclination was Wickham suited to the traditional, pastoral role of a bishop, and his low opinion of many of the parish clergy had become known about far beyond the boundaries of Sheffield. So his early years in Manchester were not easy, but in time he learned how to minister effectively to clergy and people in inner-city parishes and he found ways of carrying out his long-held belief that bishops should serve local secular institutions as well as the structures of the Church. Thus he played a large part in the development of a new Salford University, serving as chairman of its council, then as Pro-Chancellor. And he wrote three more stimulating books – *Encounter with Modern Society* (1964), *Growth and Inflation* (1975) and *Growth, Justice and Work* (1985). Meanwhile his successor in the leadership of the industrial mission and a new Bishop of Sheffield sought to turn back the clock by linking the work more closely to the Church's established institutions and traditional pastoral methods. Most of the chaplains who had been appointed by Wickham left or were dismissed and his radical creation was dismantled virtually overnight, and without a word of protest, or even regret, from anyone on the bench of bishops. He died in 1994.

These are not the only prophets to have held episcopal office during the last two centuries. Others are to be found elsewhere in this volume, and had space permitted it would have been good to have included Neville Talbot, who returned from the Bishopric of Pretoria in 1933 and, having failed to be appointed to an English diocese, ministered for ten years like a caged lion as Vicar of Nottingham; Joseph Fison burned himself out as Bishop of Salisbury in the 1960s; Trevor Huddleston was one of the truly prophetic figures of the twentieth century.

At the beginning of the twenty-first century there are few signs of prophecy in the Church of England's institutional life apart from the important witness of those who are still fighting to secure an acknowledgement of the rightful place of women in the ordained ministry. The battle for their ordination to the priesthood was won in 1993, but there are now clear signs of discrimination against them over appointments and much remains to be done if women are to play their full part in the Church's life. Evangelicals are now the most active group in the Church and are well represented in the episcopate but they have a greater affinity with old-style revivalism than with the prophetic challenge that comes through insight into the way that God is at work in the secular world as well as in the Church.

Looking to the future, it must be acknowledged that the present method of appointing Church of England bishops is unlikely to produce episcopal prophets. The three priests and three lay people who, together with the two archbishops, form the permanent element in the Crown Appointments Commission are elected by the General Synod and for the most part represent party interests. Inevitably, compromise rules and in such circumstances prophecy cannot flourish. Ironically, but understandably, there was a better chance of prophetic bishops emerging when the choice was made by Prime Ministers who had no ecclesiastical axe to grind and, from a semi-detached position, could discern more clearly the true needs of the Church and the place of bishops in the life of the nation.

There can be no going back to that system and it may be that painful experience will eventually lead to a different method of appointment that will provide more dynamic and visionary leaders. In the meantime it seems hardly unreasonable to hope that all those who are appointed to bishoprics – men and women – will display some prophetic gifts. The outstanding prophet who is inspired by God to exercise a special ministry is a rarity, but all who are called to leadership in the Church should be capable of discerning the signs of the times through their daily encounter with the Word of God revealed in the Bible, the Christian tradition, and the life of the world.

This should make them ready to encourage and support any signs of prophetic activity relating to the Church or to social reform that may emerge within their dioceses. The prophet expects opposition, not least from those in authority, but it is in the best interests of the Church that he or she should be heard and that the response should always be 'Why not?', rather than 'Why?' This may well involve the taking of risks and departure from tradition, but the greater danger is always that of failing to hear what God is saying to the Church.

6

The pastors

The traditional symbol of the bishop's office is a pastoral staff, which may be simple or elaborate but is always based on the shape of a shepherd's crook. It serves as a reminder of the caring ministry that Jesus, the Good Shepherd, entrusted to all his followers and which finds a special focus in the work of a bishop. The Book of Common Prayer order for the ordaining and consecrating of an archbishop or a bishop makes the implications of this abundantly clear:

> Be to the flock of Christ a shepherd, not a wolf; feed them, devour them not. Hold up the weak, heal the sick, bind up the broken, bring again the outcasts, seek the lost. Be so merciful, that you be not too remiss; so minister discipline, that you forget not mercy: that when the chief Shepherd shall appear you may receive the never-fading crown of glory.

It is hardly surprising therefore that the most serious criticism that can be levelled against any bishop is that he is not a good pastor. Considerable courage is needed if this word is to be omitted from an episcopal memorial stone. The strong emphasis on the pastoral role of a bishop and indeed of the clergy as a whole also owes much to the fact that from the Middle Ages until the mid-nineteenth century the Church had a secure place in a relatively stable society. The main task of the clergy in this situation was to exercise a pastoral ministry among those who worshipped in the parish church on Sunday and lived and worked nearby during the week. George Herbert, the saintly rector of the Wiltshire parish of Bemerton in the seventeenth century, was the exemplar of this kind of ministry. Little prophetic or pioneering work seemed to be called for and the task of the bishop was to pastor the parish pastors.

But not every bishop was diligent and even when he was the combination of huge unwieldy dioceses and transport limited to horseback and carriage meant that parishes often went for several years without so much as seeing their bishop. Periodic visitations provided a degree of contact between the bishop and his clergy, but these official events could be demanding or even threatening, particularly to the negligent, and they were never popular. Nonetheless, the pastoral ideal remained and the nineteenth century witnessed the emergence of some outstanding episcopal pastors.

Edward King

Chief among these was Edward King who was Bishop of Lincoln from 1885 until his death in 1910. In his sermon at King's consecration Henry Parry Liddon forecast that the new bishop would one day 'rank with those which in point of moral beauty stand highest on the roll of the later English Church – with Andrewes, with Ken, with Wilson, with Hamilton'. Another Canon of St Paul's, Henry Scott Holland, on hearing of King's appointment declared, 'It shall be a bishopric of love.' Rarely have clerical prophecies been so amply fulfilled. They were not, however, very difficult prophecies to make, for King had already displayed unusual marks of holiness and pastoral sensitivity during his time as Regius Professor of Pastoral Theology at Oxford. The learned Bishop Stubbs congratulated the Prime Minister, W. E. Gladstone, on having made 'the best appointment since St Anselm'.

Born in 1829, King was the third of the ten children of an Archdeacon of Rochester and his grandfather was Bishop of Rochester. Childhood ill-health required him to be educated at home and although he secured a place at Oriel College, Oxford, it was deemed wise for him to aim only for a pass degree, rather than attempt the more strenuous honours. Nonetheless he became fluent in French, German and Italian, studied in Germany, and always applied an acute mind to the theological issues of the day. More importantly, Oriel brought him under the influence of the Tractarian Movement, particularly through his friendship with Dr Pusey and Charles Marriott.

Following a visit to the Holy Land, King was ordained by Bishop Samuel Wilberforce in 1854 and spent the next four years as a curate at Wheatley. In this rough parish about five miles from Oxford he demonstrated his love of the poor and ability to influence young men. He then became chaplain of the theological college recently founded by Wilberforce at nearby Cuddesdon and in 1863 succeeded to the principalship and to the vicarage of the parish. Over the next ten years his influence on the Cuddesdon ordinands and on the pattern of ordination training in the Church of England was enormous. Towards the end of his life he wrote to one of his former students – 'Paradise will be like Cuddesdon again.'

Among these students was one of Gladstone's sons whose reports to his father, allied to strong pressure from several bishops, led to King's appointment to the Oxford Chair of Pastoral Theology. But not everyone favoured this move. Some Oxford dons complained about his 'lack of university distinction', while Archbishop Tait of Canterbury twice tried to dissuade Gladstone on the grounds that the appointment of so dangerous a High Churchman would 'shake public confidence in the theological school at Oxford'. In the event King held the post, and the Canonry of Christ Church to which it was attached, for twelve remarkably successful years. Although attendance at his lectures was not compulsory, they were always crowded – sometimes by as many as 300 students. On Friday evenings he also gave devotional addresses in a chapel created from a disused outhouse in his garden and, as death removed the early fathers of the Tractarian Movement, King became the most influential religious force in Oxford.

Although widely welcomed, his appointment as Bishop of Lincoln provoked some protests from the Church's extreme evangelical wing and these were to take a more serious turn later. But the day of his enthronement at Lincoln was one of unbridled rejoicing. Soon he embarked on the first of the tours of parishes which were to occupy the greater part of his ministry over the next 25 years. In this he was greatly assisted by the rapid development of the new railway network, though this did not extend to the remoter parts of Lincolnshire. At the end of every rail journey he paused on the platform to thank the driver and the guard.

Confirmations were always a special joy to him. He was not a great orator, but he spoke simply and directly and with what Archbishop Benson described as 'heavenly mindedness'. Few forgot his beautiful, penetrating eyes. He had in fact only four or five different sermons – he once said that he had one lantern in which he inserted fresh slides – but each was refreshed with homely illustrations from rural life – 'If I were cutting a hedge . . . or shepherding a lamb.' After one confirmation a candidate was heard to say, 'The bishop's a wonderful man. He must have been a stable-boy himself; he knows all about us.' And he was thrilled when another village boy sent him a letter which began, 'I could never write to you as if you was a gentleman.' If a baby cried while he was preaching or confirming he would pause to speak to the mother – 'I don't mind, if you don't. You needn't take it out, you needn't take it out. I don't mind, if you don't.'

Sometimes he walked, in shabby clothes and worn boots, between the villages he was visiting and often stopped to speak to those who were working in the fields. A labourer, who had evidently heard about the controversy over church ceremonial, asked him to explain the reason for placing candles on an altar and, having received an illuminating response, said, 'I see, sir, that yours is a yon side religion.' It certainly was, for King radiated an intense and compelling spirituality.

It was therefore exceedingly stupid of the ultra-Protestant Church Association to lodge a formal complaint to the Archbishop of Canterbury against Edward King for allowing lighted candles on the altar, mixing wine and water in the chalice at the Eucharist and ceremonially washing the vessels afterwards, permitting the Agnus Dei to be sung after the Consecration, and absolving and blessing with the sign of the Cross. They could not have chosen a more difficult target, for by 1888 King was the most revered member of the episcopal bench, and having heard the case the archbishop found largely in his favour, thus overthrowing earlier judgements by the secular courts and the Judicial Committee of the Privy Council. There could be no denying that King was a High Churchman, but he never sought to impose his likes and dislikes on the parishes. He became the first English bishop since the Reformation to wear a mitre – some friends presented him with one at the time of his consecration – but he only wore it, and Eucharistic vestments, if the parish he was visiting was happy for him to do so.

He was nonetheless hurt by the trial and thereafter went to London much less frequently, confining his visits mainly to the Convocation and Bishops' Meetings. There was more than enough to occupy his time in Lincoln, for he made a special point of being accessible to the clergy and indeed to anyone else who wished to consult him. This was the chief reason for his decision to abandon Riseholme – a large country house some three miles from Lincoln – and recreate a house within the old palace near the cathedral. The poor clergy could not, he said, be expected to pay 2s 6d for a cab to see their bishop.

They came to him in large numbers and, as was the custom at the time, were instituted to benefices or licensed to curacies in his chapel. If they came in the morning they were invariably invited to stay for lunch, and a wide variety of people from all walks of life attended his dinner parties. He regarded these gatherings as only a little less important than general councils of the Church. By common consent he was no great organizer and his study was usually a chaos of unsorted papers which drove some of his chaplains to despair. His archdeacons were apt to be annoyed when he dealt gently with erring clergymen, and his examining chaplains were sometimes vexed when he accepted for ordination candidates who, in their view, were not up to scratch. 'Better to be overcharitable than overstrict,' he counselled them. This was the hallmark of the countless letters he wrote to those who sought his advice on spiritual matters, and a collection of these, published after his death, became a classic.

In 1887 King began a particular pastoral ministry to criminals in Lincoln prison who were under sentence of death. Much time was spent with them in their cells and in some instances he confirmed and gave Holy Communion to a prisoner before accompanying him to the scaffold. In a final message to the diocese a few days before his own death in 1910 he wrote: 'My great wish has been to lead you to be Christlike Christians,' and after his funeral a member of the vast congregation said, 'We have buried our saint.' They had and Edward King now has a place in the Church of England's calendar of saints.

William Walsham How

Very different in character from King, but not less gifted as a pastor, was William Walsham How who became the first bishop of the newly created Diocese of Wakefield in 1888. A small man who needed a platform in the pulpit to make himself visible to the congregation, he was neither a scholar nor a great preacher, but he cared deeply for people of every sort, especially children, and he was an enthusiastic organizer who got things done. He also wrote some fine hymns, including 'For all the saints', 'It is a thing most wonderful' and 'Soldiers of the Cross arise', and his little books of devotion were widely read by lay people. A communicant manual, published in 1868, remained in print until the Second World War and sold over a million copies, while a Commentary on the Four Gospels sold nearly 300,000.

Educated at Shrewsbury School and Wadham College, Oxford, where he took a third in classics, he then read theology at Durham and after a couple of curacies became Vicar of Whittington in Shropshire in 1851. He remained there for 28 years, exercising a remarkable rural ministry while at the same time keeping in touch with events in the wider world. In a delightful book *Lighter Moments*, published after his death, he recounted how, at the height of the Colenso controversy about the historical accuracy of the early books of the Bible, a timber merchant in the parish calculated the alleged size and weight of Noah's Ark and found them unbelievable.

In 1867 Walsham How made a great impression with a speech on the Anglican position at a church congress in Wolverhampton and from then onwards was regarded as one of the leaders of the moderate High Church party. Attempts were now made to woo him away from his country parish with offers of the livings of Brighton and All Saints, Margaret Street, in London's West End, but these he declined as also the Bishoprics of Natal, New Zealand, Montreal, Cape Town and Jamaica. In 1879, however, he accepted an invitation from the Bishop of London, John Jackson, to become a suffragan bishop (the office had only recently been revived) in the East End of his diocese. In spite of the earlier church building efforts of Bishop Blomfield and the evangelistic concerns of Bishop Tait, this still rapidly growing area of slum housing remained largely unchurched and Jackson perceived that a bishop on the spot was needed to provide effective leadership.

His choice of Walsham How was inspired and demonstrated the Victorian preference for ability, rather than experience, since the new bishop had exercised only a rural ministry. And it worked, even though he had, absurdly, to be known as the Bishop of Bedford, this being the only legal title available, and in order to secure an income was also a Canon of St Paul's and rector of a City parish. He set about the task with extraordinary vigour and was soon said, with perhaps pardonable exaggeration, to be worth 100 curates. Another massive church-building programme was financed by his visits to wealthy parishes in places such as Brighton and Tunbridge Wells, but his main contribution was to be out and about in the East End. This earned him the sobriquet 'The Omnibus Bishop', though he was equally well known as 'The Children's Bishop', for he was dearly loved by them. The clergy were welcomed to his home in Clapton and every weekend was spent with one or other of them in their parishes. If in the long run Walsham How was unable to save the day for the Church of England in London's East End, he nonetheless established the basis for much notable pastoral and social work and while he was there made an important contribution to the work of a Royal Commission on the Housing of the Working Classes.

In 1885 he declined the offer of the Bishopric of Manchester, believing it to be his duty to remain at his post in the East End, but in the same year Frederick Temple was translated from Exeter to London and immediately decided to reduce the autonomy of his suffragan and required him to minister also in other parts of the diocese. This was unsatisfactory to Walsham How and provided an early warning of the vulnerable position in which suffragan bishops would find themselves whenever there was a change in the diocesan leadership. The solution in this instance was to translate the suffragan to a diocese of his own where his gifts and experience would be equally valuable. Wakefield, in the southern part of Yorkshire's West Riding, had more than its fair share of slum property and poverty.

Once again he tackled the task with energy and flair. New parishes were formed, Wakefield Parish Church was established as a cathedral and, after the custom of the time, a large bishop's residence was erected. But most of his time was devoted to pastoral work in the parishes and in 1893 he shared in the conducting of funerals for 92 of the 137 men who were killed in the Thornhill colliery disaster. After a mere three years of vital pioneering work in a difficult territory he was, with the lack of strategic sense that has generally characterized episcopal appointments, offered the Bishopric of Durham. This he very properly declined. In the same year Queen Victoria, who thought a great deal of him, mentioned his name as a possibility for the Archbishopric of York, but this was not acceptable to the Prime Minister, Lord Salisbury, so he stayed at Wakefield until his death in 1897. Earlier that year the Queen had commanded him to write, at very short notice, a hymn for her Diamond Jubilee thanksgiving service. The first attempt, made by the Poet Laureate, had been rejected as unworthy of the music composed by Sir Arthur Sullivan, but although Walsham How's effort proved to be acceptable it offered incontrovertible evidence that the good bishop posed no permanent threat to the holder of the Laureateship:

> Thou hast been mindful of Thine own,
> And lo! we come confessing –
> 'Tis Thou has dower'd our queenly throne
> With sixty years of blessing.

Yet it showed that his heart was in the right place and that he was not lacking in the common touch. This, combined with a disciplined devotional life, was the secret of his pastoral power.

Edward Woods

There was nothing at all folksy about Edward Woods who was Bishop of Lichfield from 1937 until his death in 1953. It seemed perfectly natural that he should live in a palace large enough to house most of the present Lichfield Cathedral School. A friend of the King and Queen, he was accustomed to entertaining 25–30 people for lunch and enjoyed his days off shooting on country estates. None of which occasioned any surprise, not even among those in the Black Country part of the diocese who had endured the worst effect of the 1930s economic depression. This was the place in society where bishops belonged.

Woods was in fact every bit as popular a bishop as Walsham How had been. A tall man with a fine presence, he exhibited an engaging simplicity and humility, and what many recognized as sheer goodness. He came of Quaker stock and married into one of England's leading Quaker families – the Barclay bankers – and was possessed by an evangelistic zeal which, in its concentration on Christian essentials, resulted in a markedly liberal outlook. His style of preaching – direct, uncomplicated, well stocked with anecdotes and addressed to individuals – attracted large congregations and translated easily into radio talks which made him a household name.

Woods was born in 1877 in Hereford where his father was the vicar of one of the city parishes. His mother was a grand-daughter of Elizabeth

Fry and his elder brother, Theodore, became Bishop of Peterborough, then of Winchester. Young Edward went from Marlborough College to Trinity College, Cambridge, where he took a second in theology. He prepared for ordination at Ridley Hall, Cambridge, and from 1901 to 1904 combined three part-time posts in Cambridge – curate of Holy Trinity Church, chaplain of the Pastorate, which involved pastoral and evangelistic work among undergraduates, and chaplain of Ridley Hall. He was also active in the World Student Christian Federation, sharing its optimistic belief in 'the evangelization of the world in this generation'.

He then became the full-time Vice-Principal of Ridley Hall, while continuing much of his evangelistic work in the university, but he was struck down by tuberculosis in 1907 and was not fully recovered until 1912. Even then he was deemed strong enough only for the light duties of the English chaplaincy in Lausanne, Switzerland. On the outbreak of war in 1914 he returned to England and enlisted as an army chaplain, expressing a keen desire to serve at the front in France. But because he was said to be 'good with young men' he was sent to Sandhurst to minister to the officer cadets and remained there for the rest of the war. A book *Knights in Armour* was written for the cadets, most of whom were destined to be killed within weeks of leaving Sandhurst, and emphasized the virtues of courage, chivalry, purity and loyalty. Visits to Sandhurst by the King and Queen led to his admission to royal circles.

Following demobilization in 1918 he returned to Cambridge as Vicar of Holy Trinity Church and, although this was a major pastoral responsibility – pioneered by one of the most famous of all pastors, Charles Simeon, during the years 1783–1836 – he so organized the work that he had the freedom to pursue other, mainly national, interests. When William Temple became Bishop of Manchester in 1921 Woods took over the chairmanship of the Life and Liberty Movement and, believing that the movement now needed 'spiritual power', he started large annual conferences for parochial church councillors. These were largely inspirational in content and continued to be held for several decades. He was also in demand for preaching on big occasions and for conducting missions.

In 1927 he became Vicar of Croydon – a very large parish, the life of which had been built up by the hugely gifted Pat McCormick, who left to succeed Dick Sheppard as Vicar of St Martin-in-the-Fields. Woods's name had also been mentioned for this post. On his arrival in Croydon he recruited three curates, embarked on intensive pastoral and evangelistic work, and before long was preaching to crowded congregations. After three years his responsibilities were increased by the additional appointments of Bishop and Archdeacon of Croydon, and he continued to attend committees, lead missions elsewhere, and conduct a monthly broadcast service. It was a hectic life, inimical to sustained pastoral ministry, and he came to hope for appointment to a diocesan bishopric, believing that the conflicting claims on his time and energy would thereby be reduced.

In this he was correct. When the call to Lichfield came in 1937 he found himself responsible for a diocese covering Staffordshire and Shropshire, with 463 parishes and over 600 clergy, but he delegated much of the administration and concentrated on pastoral work and preaching. Every year, apart from wartime when petrol was rationed, he travelled 20,000 miles by car and, following the example of his brother at Winchester, undertook some pastoral visits on foot. These involved an 8–9 mile walk, clad in purple cassock and carrying his pastoral staff, and included conversations with others on the road and labourers in the fields, as well as services in village churches. In all, he carried out 23 of these expeditions. The regular invitations to preach at Windsor and Sandringham continued and he supplied members of the Royal Family with books and pamphlets on spiritual subjects.

Ironically, the central government of the Church, the democratic enlargement of which he had fought for through the Life and Liberty Movement, tended to bore him. But he had a deep involvement in the burgeoning movement for church unity and took part in many of the national and international conferences that sought to promote what he saw as essential to wider evangelism.

Sophisticated critics were apt to say that Woods's charm was ingenuous and that he lacked intellectual originality. Others complained that his irrepressible optimism owed most to his unwillingness to face facts, and it is certainly the case that he saw the Christian faith almost exclusively in personal terms. But he was his own severest critic and in his journal in January 1944 he wrote, 'I know that I cannot be a "great" bishop but I think that I might – long to – sort of outdo my clergy in being just a *Christian* in the very fullest sense of the word.' That was a high and laudable ambition for any bishop to hold, and his biographer, Oliver Tomkins, who knew him well and was not easily deceived, said 'he made things loveable'. His death attracted national attention.

Launcelot Fleming

Of the 534 Royal Navy chaplains who served in the 1939–45 war, 25 subsequently became bishops. None of these was more admired than the first – Launcelot Fleming, Bishop of Portsmouth, 1949–59, then of Norwich, 1959–71. He joined the Navy in 1940 from Cambridge where for the previous seven years he had been Fellow and Dean of Trinity

Hall and also a member of an important expedition to the Antarctic. His induction as a naval chaplain lasted no more than a week before his appointment first to an officers' training establishment, then in November 1940 to the battleship HMS *Queen Elizabeth*, which after service in the North Atlantic became the flagship of Admiral Cunningham, the Commander-in-Chief of the Mediterranean Fleet. Operations in the Eastern Mediterranean, including the closing stages of the Battle of Crete, brought the ship under frequent attack. During an engagement Fleming, who never wore uniform – preferring a flannel suit and a battered soft hat – would often ascend the bridge and use the intercom to give a running commentary for the benefit of the majority of the crew who were working below and could see nothing of the action.

On 25 November 1941 he used the intercom for a unique spiritual purpose. Twenty-four hours earlier, the *Queen Elizabeth*, in company with two other battleships – *Barham* and *Valiant* – sailed from Alexandria but, in spite of an escort of eight destroyers, *Barham*, which was close to the *Queen Elizabeth*, was struck by three enemy torpedoes. The ship turned on its side, blew up, and within minutes was sunk, leaving 450 survivors in the water and more than 850 others, including the captain, dead. All this was witnessed from the *Queen Elizabeth* and amid the chaos Fleming obtained permission to say prayers for the dead and dying, and for the Fleet, over the intercom system. Shortly before *Barham* left Alexandria its chaplain, Gerald Ellison, who was destined to become Bishop of Chester, then of London, left the ship following a disagreement with its captain. His successor was among those who were killed. Just over three weeks after the *Barham* disaster, the *Queen Elizabeth* was herself hit by a torpedo while in the harbour at Alexandria and so badly damaged that repairs and refitting occupied more than eighteen months. This led to Fleming's appointment in 1943 as senior chaplain of HMS *Ganges* – a large training establishment at Shotley, near Ipswich – and inevitably a sense of anti-climax after what had gone before.

Born in Edinburgh in 1907, and the son of a distinguished physician, he went from Rugby School to Trinity Hall, Cambridge, where he took a first in natural sciences. He then studied geology at Yale University in the United States. Trinity Hall was anxious to reclaim him but could not afford to pay a fellow to teach geology, so at the suggestion of another fellow, and after much careful thought, he decided to seek Holy Orders and thus qualify for the position of Fellow and Dean, for which money was available.

His training at Westcott House was interrupted by involvement in an expedition to Iceland in 1932, and in the following year, a week after his ordination and election to a fellowship he was off again as chief scientist of an expedition exploring the ice-cap north of Spitsbergen. Not surprisingly, he hesitated before accepting an invitation in 1934 to join a three-year expedition to British Graham Land in the Antarctic, but the Master of Trinity Hall urged him to go. This, the first major British expedition since Scott's ill-fated journey in 1911, involved long sledge journeys with 45 dogs, six of which had at one point to be destroyed because of insufficient food. Fleming served as a geologist and also as chaplain to the expedition, conducting services on its sailing ship *Penola* or in a hut at the base camp. On their return in 1937 all were decorated with the Polar Medal by King George VI.

A shy and humble man, Fleming had a gift for friendship and the personal influence he exercised on the polar expeditions was soon felt in Trinity Hall when, finally, he took up the office of Dean. Although always an indifferent preacher, his personality shone through his sermons and there was a constant stream of people seeking counsel in his rooms. He was also an enthusiastic rowing coach and it was with difficulty that he found time to supervise undergraduates who were reading geology. Before returning to Trinity Hall after the war he spent two years in Westminster as Director of Service Ordination Candidates, having been released early from the Navy in order to take up this key job.

Back in Cambridge in 1946, he resumed his college duties and was also appointed Director of the Scott Polar Institute at a time when its activities were expanding considerably. To this he added membership of the council of the Royal Geographical Society. But it soon became clear that the Church would want to make use of him and, having declined the Principalship of Westcott House, Cambridge, and the Bishopric of Edinburgh, he finally decided – largely because of its naval associations – to go to Portsmouth. In the event, this small diocese of only 135 parishes suited him rather well. At first some eyebrows were raised because of his total lack of parochial experience, but he delegated most of the committee work to his archdeacons and concentrated on pastoral work in a way that soon won the admiration and affection of the clergy. The laity, many of whom had served in the Royal Navy, or were still serving, enjoyed having a bishop with his background.

He had no interest in the Bishops' Meetings or the Church Assembly, but his ability to get on with young people led to appointment as chairman of the Church of England Youth Council and to involvement in the founding of the Duke of Edinburgh's Award and Voluntary Service Overseas. In 1953 he spent eleven days with a British North Greenland expedition and his maiden speech in the House of Lords was – surely uniquely for a bishop – concerned with cruelty to whales.

In 1959 came translation from the second smallest to the second largest diocese in the Church of England. The retiring Bishop of Norwich – Percy Mark Herbert – was a saintly man but he came from an aristocratic family and was somewhat remote. The diocese was facing an acute problem created by the existence of 700 church buildings, many of them architecturally magnificent, in a rural area of declining population, and also by a growing shortage of clergy. Fleming announced that his first task would be to visit all the clergy and their families in their homes. This was accomplished in sixteen months and, as in Portsmouth, he won their hearts if not always their ready acquiescence to his plans. These, when they emerged, involved the formation of group ministries, consisting of sometimes as many as a dozen parishes served by teams of clergy, and insistence that all the clergy of the diocese should attend monthly chapter meetings in order to further collaboration and overcome loneliness. Refresher courses and summer schools were also introduced and a campaign to raise clergy stipends was successfully concluded. By the time he left, 18 per cent of the clergy were working in teams. A commission on the future of the many churches in the city of Norwich reported towards the end of his episcopate and led to conversions and alternative use and some closures. The foundation of the University of East Anglia was another of his special concerns and absorbed a good deal of time.

Fleming drove himself hard and, to the alarm of other Norfolk road-users, his car even harder. He still played hockey, tennis and squash and, following the death of his mother who had lived with him for many years, found time to marry Jane Agutter – a widow who provided him with strong support for the remainder of his days. In April 1965 a friend met him outside Westminster Abbey and, after talking about this and that for a while, the friend offered him a lift in a taxi. Fleming graciously declined: 'No, thank you. You see, I am just going inside to be married.'

By 1970 however his health was causing concern and, although he had no thought of early retirement, an invitation to become Dean of Windsor was attractive inasmuch as it offered the possibility of his being able to continue in full-time work until he was 70. In the event, the experience at this Royal Peculiar was less than happy. He enjoyed the role of Domestic Chaplain to the Queen, who much valued his wisdom and pastoral concern for the Royal Household. He was responsible for the funeral service of the Duke of Windsor in 1972 and in the same year that of the young Prince William of Gloucester, whom he knew well and who was killed in an air crash. The work of St George's House, established by his predecessor, also greatly interested him, for he was a man of liberal mind who found discussion with lay people on the issues of the day stimulating.

The problem lay with the canons. Endless bickering destroyed any semblance of collegial spirit and Fleming found himself presiding over a small but divided community. A crisis point was reached when Fleming called in management consultants to report on the chapel's creaking administrative and financial arrangements. They proposed among other things that a competent layman should be appointed to handle finance but, to Fleming's great dismay, this was rejected on the grounds that it would infringe the ancient rights of the canons. Some years later, after Fleming's retirement in 1976 and when the canons had also gone, the reform was implemented. But the Windsor experience was a disappointing end to a distinguished ministry. He died in 1990.

Virtually all of today's bishops see their ministry primarily in pastoral terms and it is the intention of the Church that they should. The tension between the demands of pastoral care and administration has however become acute in most dioceses and unbearable in some. In an outspoken statement explaining her resignation from the post of Adviser in Pastoral Care in Counselling in Southwark diocese in February 2001, Dr Susan Walroud-Skinner, one of the leading practitioners in this field, said:

> I dissent from the current culture of the Church, which is not confined to the diocese of Southwark but which is manifested in a particularly uncompromising way here: a culture of management that all but denigrates the culture of pastoral care, and makes it increasingly difficult for pastoral care to flourish. The dominant culture is pervasive, and dissent is hard to articulate. Yet, I believe that, if we are to be true to the Gospel, dissent is now vital. Christians, and those who may be drawn into belonging to Christ, do not want primarily to be managed, they want to be pastored. Where a bishop disclaims that role by his words and actions, the task of the diocesan adviser in pastoral care is to call attention to this situation. The non-negotiable part of a Bishop's role is that of pastor.

The Bishop of Southwark, Dr Tom Butler, was reported as having told some Southwark Cathedral deanery chapters soon after his appointment in 1998, 'I am not a pastor, I am a manager.' The Diocese of Southwark, founded in 1905, embraces the whole of Greater London south of the Thames, except for two boroughs which are in Rochester diocese and a few parishes which are in Guildford. Its population is about 2.4 million who are served, theoretically anyway, by 357 stipendiary clergy, and have the opportunity to worship in 381 churches. Besides the diocesan bishop, there are three area bishops – one responsible for South-East London, the other for South-West London, and the third for Croydon – and six archdeacons. The diocese – in which the alienation of the urban masses from the life of the Church is most marked – makes it a particularly difficult episcopal assignment, and the task of the bishop is not eased by the existence of strong evangelical parishes in the stockbroker-belt of Surrey which exert undue financial power.

The Diocese of London, which embraces most of London north of the Thames and has a population of nearly 3.5 million in 410 parishes, shares most of Southwark's problems. Besides the diocesan bishop, it has four area bishops and a suffragan bishop, together with six archdeacons. But, unlike the Bishop of Southwark, the Bishop of London has for some years retained pastoral responsibility for a small part of his diocese – the Cities of London and Westminster – and successive bishops have taken this seriously, becoming well-known figures in the parishes and active in national, civic and commercial life. Thus, although he carries great administrative responsibilities within the diocese as a whole, his pastoral skill has continued to be exercised – and noticed. The tension between the pastoral and the administrative is not, it should be noted, a new one:

> In these days when the disciples were increasing in number, the Hellenists murmured against the Hebrews because their widows were being neglected in the daily distribution. And the twelve summoned the body of the disciples and said, 'It is not right that we should give up preaching the word of God to serve tables. Therefore, brethren, pick out from among you seven men of good repute, full of the Spirit and of wisdom, whom we may appoint to this duty. But we will devote ourselves to prayer and the ministry of the word.'   *Acts 6.1–4*

Gregory the Great in the sixth century and Bernard of Clairvaux in the twelfth reminded the bishops of their time of the priority of prayer over business, and in the nineteenth century the zealous reforming Bishop Samuel Wilberforce of Oxford and Winchester was sometimes accused of destroying the tranquillity of his episcopal colleagues and their successors.

Before loosing the bonds of episcopal administration today however the strong pastoral element in much of a bishop's desk-work should not be overlooked. A good deal of his time is spent facilitating the Church's ministry in the parishes where, hopefully, the priest spends most of his time on pastoral work. Letters and interviews relating to the appointment of clergy have an obvious pastoral significance and, since the introduction of wide consultation and the power of parishes to veto nominations, this consumes more time than ever before. Time devoted to training schemes, ecumenical relations, contacts with non-parochial ministries and much else also has important pastoral implications. Increasingly the financing of pastoral work demands episcopal leadership in the raising and spending of money. Administration is not to be despised, especially when carried out by a bishop with a pastoral heart and a sensitivity to pastoral need.

Yet the bishops need to be freed from an excessive burden of administration, though not, as is commonly supposed and as they may wish, in order to spend more time in the parishes holding the hands of the clergy and preaching at special events. Most of this can and should be left to the suffragan or area bishops, for if the Church of England is to continue in its historic role of accepting pastoral responsibility for everyone who lives within its parishes a new strategy for the deployment of its clergy and the use of its money can be delayed no longer. Such a strategy will need strong and imaginative leadership by the diocesan bishop, and such leadership requires time for consultation and reflection. If, as in London, the bishop retains direct responsibility for some small part of the diocese, this will enable him to keep in touch with pastoral need, but his main task is to lead the Church in mission, of which pastoral care is an important, but not the only, part.

7

The controversialists

Most, perhaps all, bishops have at some time or another been involved in controversy, if only of the minor sort. This is inevitable given the nature of their office. As leaders of an essentially conservative Church, any proposals for change in its life they may make are likely to provoke opposition – some of it fierce, since deep religious emotions may be involved. Since also they are the chief spokesmen of a religious faith which frequently challenges the current ideology and actions of the society in which the Church exercises its mission, it is only to be expected that bishops – if they are doing their job properly – will find themselves publicly opposed. During the sixteenth and seventeenth centuries several English bishops were executed or imprisoned for their controversial views and actions. This remains a constant risk in some parts of the world, but not in England where the chief danger springs from the fact that nearly all the bishops are uncontroversial figures who offer little significant challenge either to conventional belief or to the values of secular society. A notable exception to this at the end of the twentieth century was David Jenkins, who was Bishop of Durham from 1984 to 1994 and because, happily, he is still alive does not qualify for inclusion in this book.

Nonetheless he offers a useful example of the fact that in this country a statement made by a Church of England bishop is still more likely to be noticed and regarded – at least by the media – as controversial than is a similar statement made by a theologian. During his thirty years as an academic at Oxford and Leeds, and as a member of the staff of the World Council of Churches, Jenkins held moderately liberal theological opinions and a left-of-centre political position. But he was virtually unknown to the general public. When however his appointment as Bishop of Durham was announced and, in the course of a television interview, he expressed doubts concerning the historical veracity of the Virgin Birth and the physical Resurrection of Jesus, a storm of protest arose and he was accused of denying the Christian faith. And when, three days after his consecration as a bishop in York Minster, the building was struck by lightning and a large section of its roof destroyed by fire there were even some who saw this as a sign of divine disapproval of his appointment. Thereafter his views on almost any subject attracted media attention and often caused a stir. The learned professor had gone unnoticed, the controversial bishop was rarely out of the spotlight.

The reason for this is not difficult to discern inasmuch as a bishop is the holder of high office in the Church and is seen therefore as a spokesman for the Church, whereas the professor speaks for no-one but himself and, by tradition, may well have eccentric opinions. This is undoubtedly an inhibiting factor for many bishops who believe it to be their chief duty to uphold the mainline teaching of the Church and not step out of line by expressing publicly their own insights and questions. In a period of insecurity in the Church, such as is now being experienced, there is pressure for its leaders to 'sing from the same hymn sheet' lest controversy further weaken its life and witness. But lack of controversy indicates lack of life, since there is no single, infallible understanding of the Christian faith or of how society might be ordered if it were to express Christian values more accurately. And it is in the frank exchange of opinions, and the controversy which sometimes ensues, that truth is more clearly perceived.

Herbert Hensley Henson

Herbert Hensley Henson (Bishop of Hereford, 1918–20, then of Durham, 1920–39) was one of a handful of nineteenth- and twentieth-century bishops whose appointments were surrounded by controversy. At one point the Archbishop of Canterbury, Randall Davidson, contemplated resignation rather than preside over his consecration. Unlike the others, however, he was a controversialist by design, rather than by accident, and the greater part of his episcopate was spent tilting at ecclesiastical and political windmills. He combined a complex personality and dislike of innovation with a mind like quicksilver and the ability to express himself in what his friend Cyril Alington called 'the stainless steel of perfect English prose'. This made him one of the strangest-ever bishops and his combative temperament made him many enemies, yet both church and state were greatly enriched by his ministry. He would have made a formidable lawyer and might conceivably have been a happier man if he had chosen that profession.

The controversy over his appointment as Bishop of Hereford concerned an issue far removed from the life or death choices facing those occupying the Flanders trenches at that time. It had to do with Henson's declared agnosticism over the historicity of the Virgin Birth and the physical Resurrection of Jesus, and his apparent support of some who had been ordained in spite of their denials of these beliefs. In the end Henson, at the request of the archbishop, signed a statement professing his adherence to the Nicene Creed, but only seven other diocesan bishops shared in his consecration and questions were raised about Crown appointments to bishoprics. But Henson was no liberal; indeed, he was markedly conservative in other doctrinal matters, particularly the Incarnation, and later was highly critical of the modernist movement in the Church of England – Bishop Barnes of Birmingham attracting his most vehement condemnation. One of his favourite texts was, 'Jesus Christ is the same, yesterday, and today, yea for ever' and the depth of his faith was expressed remarkably and movingly in a poem he wrote in a café in Munich when only a young man and feeling depressed:

> Oh Christ, Thou knowest hearts – my heart – can'st tell
> Why thoughts of heaven jostle thoughts of hell,
> Why the sweet ardours of my love for Thee
> Are elbowed ever by foul blasphemy.
> I know not how it is, yet this I know
> That I do love Thee best of all below,
> And yet – is it some madness of the thought?
> Some devil rioting in a mind distraught?
> I know not: yet I would that I could know
> Whence come the tyrants which torment me so.
> Then might my heart its waxing terror lose,
> Then could I know I love the thing I choose.
> Then could I face the infamy within,
> And in the hour of sinning loathe the sin.
> Then, O my Saviour, might the loyal will,
> Amid the daily treasons, love Thee still,
> Yet now I think I love Thee – only think,
> And in th'abyss, O Christ, I deeper sink,
> I know not, and I cannot know – but Thou,
> Thou knowest that I love Thee, here and now.

As a young man, Henson felt powerfully drawn to the service of the poor and was on the verge of embracing a Franciscan-like vocation, but he was at Durham during some of the twentieth century's worst industrial strife and when the coal miners came into conflict with the government in 1926 he sided with the government. This destroyed his reputation in the mining communities of the diocese and was long remembered there after his death. It was by no means unusual for him to change his mind. From the time of his ordination in 1887 until the end of his ministry as Vicar of Barking in 1900 he was a High Churchman of the non-ritualist sort, but when he was made a Canon of Westminster he became, and remained for the rest of his life, one of the fiercest champions of Protestantism. Linked to this was a high doctrine of the state which led him for many years to uphold the place of the Church of England as a national church, yet after the 1927–28 defeat of the Revised Prayer Book in the House of Commons he demanded disestablishment. Earlier he had strongly opposed the Life and Liberty movement and the setting up of the Church Assembly to give the Church a measure of freedom from the state and a semblance of democracy in its own life.

Whatever his opinions and whatever the subject, Henson could however never be ignored. He was one of the finest orators in the country and his utterances compelled attention because he quickly got to the heart of a matter and expressed himself in a pugnacious style. Some of his speeches in the House of Lords were said to be among the best ever heard in that chamber, and for most of his life the Press were in attendance wherever he was preaching or speaking. Rarely did he disappoint. In his relentless quest for the truth he could nonetheless be exceedingly cruel in his judgement of people. Half his clergy were, he said, 'made' by their wives, the other half ruined by them. The appointment of Theodore Woods to the Bishopric of Peterborough would 'add physical, rather than intellectual, weight to the bench'. The country clergy 'loiter through life in discomfort and discontent, steadily degenerating as age strengthens their prejudices, diminishes their natural powers, and destroys the effects of such efforts as they make'.

Born in Broadstairs in 1863, Henson had a deeply unhappy childhood. He was the sixth child of his father's second marriage, and his father, who had made enough money to retire early, was an ex-Anglican turned Plymouth Brother and exhibited a militant evangelicalism that caused the future bishop to distrust all forms of fanaticism – religious or political. The death of his mother when he was only six brought family crisis and for a time he was brought up in the home of the local Congregational minister, another evangelical, and did not attend school until he was fourteen. His entry into Broadstairs Collegiate School owed everything to his father's third wife, a German Lutheran, who insisted that her stepchildren should be properly educated and backed young Herbert's future development. This soon started to be stormy, for after two years in the school he fell out with the headmaster and ran away to Brigg in Lincolnshire where he was taken on as a pupil-teacher at the local grammar school. Meanwhile, as a result of attending a mission in Ramsgate, he had been baptized and confirmed.

The headmaster at Brigg soon recognized in Henson unusual talent and encouraged him to go to Oxford. His father, with whom he always had a most difficult relationship, opposed this and, having by now lost most of his money, could not subsidize his entry to a college. But his step-mother again supported him and he became a non-collegiate student at Oxford, living frugally in lodgings and literally reading for a degree, with very little in the way of tuition. Nonetheless, he took a first in modern history and, when not quite 21, won one of Oxford's most coveted prizes – a fellowship of All Souls' College. It was an astonishing feat. Never before had anyone of such a social and educational background climbed so high, but he quickly settled into the life of the elite college and did not hesitate before expressing his strongly held opinions to the more distinguished members of the fellowship. Still short of money, he was driven to move to Birkenhead for six months to coach the son of an MP and while there became specially aware of the plight of the underprivileged. Ordination seemed to him to be the best way to their service, so on his return to Oxford he again became an undergraduate and read theology.

He was ordained by the Bishop of Oxford in July 1887 and a month later was appointed Head of Oxford House – a recently established centre of social work in London's East End. He tackled this responsibility with great enthusiasm, but it was not really his job and after less than a year, and when still a week short of his 25th birthday, All Souls used its patronage to appoint him Vicar of Barking. This large and rapidly expanding East End parish needed enlivening and Henson, with a team of curates, soon had things humming. They saw their work as primarily among the poor, but soon 1,000 and more people of all sorts and conditions were crowding the church to hear the vicar's striking sermons. He quarrelled with many parishioners, too, but raised enough money to restore the church and later came to regard his six years at Barking as the best in his ministry.

But the strain of the heavy workload proved to be too great and in 1895 Lord Salisbury came to the rescue by making him chaplain of Ilford Hospital – an almshouse for a few old people. All Souls re-elected him to a fellowship and he was in Oxford from Monday to Friday studying and writing. In 1900 Lord Salisbury offered him a Canonry of Westminster to which was attached the Rectory of St Margaret's, Westminster, believing that this would make better use of his preaching gifts. It did. Crowds came to the Abbey whenever he was in the pulpit and at St Margaret's he quickly provoked the resignation of its distinguished organist in order that the emphasis in worship should change from music to preaching. His carefully prepared sermons offered an intelligent exposition of basic Christianity spiced with controversy. By this time his affair with Anglo-Catholicism was over and there was a period when, with Charles Gore, the leader of the High Church wing, also a member of the Westminster Chapter, the Abbey congregation had the stimulating experience of hearing these two brilliant canons preaching against each other on alternate Sunday afternoons.

In 1908 Henson declined the offer of the Professorship of Ecclesiastical History and a Canonry of Christ Church, Oxford, hoping that one day he might succeed Armitage Robinson as Dean of Westminster. But in this he was destined to be disappointed and went instead to be Dean of Durham in 1912. He saw this as a national rather than a local appointment. Cathedral deans and canons were, he believed, required to study and make the fruits of their learning available to the wider Church. Neither need they confine themselves to theological matters. Henson opposed votes for women on the grounds that they would introduce into politics an undesirable element of emotion. On the outbreak of war in 1914 he appealed to men to join the forces and later advocated the conscription of the clergy. A wartime appeal for abstinence from alcohol was strongly supported by the Bishop of Durham but equally strenuously opposed by the Dean of Durham. Henson was in fact a very moderate drinker who sometimes took a glass of wine with his dinner, but the Temperance movement labelled him the 'Brewers' Friend' and later the 'Liquor Bishop'.

One Sunday in March 1917, and against the wishes of the Bishop of London, Winnington-Ingram, of whom he had a particularly low opinion, he preached twice in London's City Temple – the leading Congregational Church – and was immediately accused by Anglo-Catholics of 'heresy and schism'. In December of that year the Prime Minister, Lloyd George, appointed him Bishop of Hereford, thus unleashing a fierce controversy that Henson was never to forget, nor to forgive. He once described the day of his consecration in Westminster Abbey as 'the unhappiest in my life'. In the event he proved to be a popular bishop in Herefordshire, being the first bishop of the diocese to make use of a car and thus become widely known in the parishes. But he never really settled because of a broad, and improper, hint from Lloyd George that if he did well there he would be translated to something more significant. Only two years were to pass before the Prime Minister, as good as his word and strongly opposed by the Archbishop of York, Cosmo Gordon Lang, moved him to Durham.

Thus began an eighteen-year-long episcopate that can only be described as unique. Durham soon knew that it had a bishop and the rest of the country was not long in recognizing that Durham had a bishop. During the 1930s even Hitler and Mussolini knew that Durham had a bishop, for Henson denounced them both – as Winston Churchill was quick to note. He was however uncertain as to his role in the diocese and shortly before the enthronement wrote in his journal:

What shall be the line of my special contribution to the tradition of Durham? I cannot be a 'saint' like my predecessor, or a prophet like

Westcott, or a scholar like Lightfoot, or a princely magnate like Van Mildert. The role of statesman, which I think I might have played under the conditions that once obtained, is hardly possible now. I may possibly impress the diocese as an orator, though *that* is a reputation which I do not greatly value; and I might (if God should give me time and strength) put forth two or three charges which might rise above the level of most such utterances. There remains the humbler but perhaps not inferior part of a just and vigilant governor. This I must attempt, but I doubt my competence. *Justice* I can bring to my episcopal administration, for I do hate oppression of any kind; but *vigilance* implies that continuing purpose and steady habit which accord ill with my shifting and paradoxical temperament. This review of possibilities is certainly depressing. For the deeper requirements of great spiritual office – a disciplined character, personal piety, and habits of religion – I can say nothing that is promising. God Himself must make me sufficient as a minister of a new covenant, not of the letter but of the 'spirit'. Of myself I can be, and do, nothing here.

In spite of his supremely self-confident manner in public, Henson was often given to feelings of self-doubt such as this, but they never got in the way of his firm governance of Durham diocese. Discussion, consultation and the sharing of insight formed no part of his method, for he was an autocrat, and, since he refused to have a telephone in Auckland Castle, his primary means of communication was by letter. Recipients treasured these, even when their contents were unwelcome, and the two collections of them published after his death are classics of the epistolary art. Four must now suffice:

Auckland Castle
May 5th 1929

My dear Rector,

I note with considerable surprise that only two girls were presented for Confirmation from your parish, and I think that there must be some . circumstance unknown to me which can do something to explain so disconcerting a fact.

When I was myself a parish priest, it was commonly accepted that 20 persons reached the age of 14 every year in a thousand people, and this was held to be an indication of what we had to undertake.

The population of . . . is stated to be 2,304, *which would suggest that not less than 45 persons arrived at the age for Confirmation during the year.* Making large allowance for Roman Catholics and

Nonconformists, it seems difficult to believe that there were no more than two girls to be brought to the Bishop for Confirmation.

I should like to hear from you what explanation occurs to you as adequate.

With all good wishes,
I am,
Sincerely your Bishop,

Herbert Dunelm

Unfortunately the response of the Rector, who was probably already disappointed and depressed by his apparent failure, has not been preserved. He might well have resented the fact that his Father in God treated him as if he were a negligent sales representative whose figures were below target. Others might wonder if legitimate episcopal concern could not have been expressed in gentler, more sympathetic language, and thereby achieved more.

The colonel who may have witnessed army chaplains dedicating military band instruments would have been unwise to invite any bishop to perform a similar task, but only Henson would have replied in these terms:

January 16th 1929
To Lieut-Colonel F. W. Cluff
Barclays Bank Ltd, Durham

My dear Colonel,

I hardly think *a religious dedication of the silver Bugles would be suitable*. A line has to be drawn somewhere in these things in order to prevent 'our good being evil spoken of'. A few years ago I was asked by a triumphant Football Team to dedicate the shield which was the prize of victory, and I felt bound to decline. The Bugles have a stronger claim, but not strong enough.

With kind regards,
Yours sincerely,

Herbert Dunelm

The Vicar of St Peter's, Bishop Wearmouth, who sought his bishop's permission to hold a parish mission and employ a missioner from another diocese could hardly have been encouraged by this response:

May 26th 1926

My dear Mr Silva White,

I will sanction your Mission and grant leave to the Rev Hinton Knowles of St Paul's Church, Middlesbrough to act as Missioner.

I notice with some concern the multiplication of Missions of one sort or another in the Diocese. When I was a parish clergyman, it was generally said, and I think with substantial truth, that missions were 'superfluous in a well-worked parish, and mischievous in an ill-sorted one'. I wish in the Diocese generally that there was a greater confidence in steady parochial work, visiting from house to house and teaching, and less resort to this modern fashion, in which Nonconformists so freely indulge, of keeping the people in a state of constant surprise by repeated 'stunts'.

Yours sincerely,

Herbert Dunelm

Henson's fellow bishops, with most of whom he quarrelled at some time or another, became used to this kind of missive and Winnington-Ingram of London cannot have been surprised by the content of the following letter and its affectionate ending.

January 30th 1931

My dear Bishop,

Thank you for letting me see the enclosed. It is of course quite impossible for me to allow Mr . . . to work in my diocese. It would be 'asking for trouble'. I return to you the documents you were good enough to send.

I hope you have noticed the letters in the *Spectator*, calling attention to the neglect of the Westminster clergy to visit the people. They do certainly coincide with my own observations. Instead of this incessant prating about a 'Way of Renewal', and a multiplying of 'Quiet Days', and the Lord only knows what other Latter-day Quackeries which may distract us from our obvious duties, what we want is nothing more than an honest pedestrian fidelity to pledged and acknowledged obligations. As it is, we are living more and more in the ever-closer atmosphere of our ecclesiastical Common-Room, and going on our knees for Litanies when we ought to be about our parishes in and out of the houses.

But there: I am, and I must consent to be, that most abhorred of figures – A BACK NUMBER.

Affectly yours

Herbert Dunelm

Small of stature and with unusual eyebrows – pointing diagonally out-wards–Henson was a daunting figure on parish visits and never hesitated before making his wishes known. Clergy assembled in copes were ordered to remove them; a member of the congregation who coughed during his sermon was asked to desist or to leave the church. The sermons were always carefully written and brilliantly delivered, though their subjects – which tended to be determined by what he was interested in at that moment – were not always pastorally helpful or even fully understood in the mining communities. Yet no-one could ever doubt that they were in touch with a brilliant mind. A visitor to Auckland Castle observed a tank of goldfish in the entrance hall and asked: 'Bishop, why are these small black fish (they were the immature ones) called goldfish?' 'Because we are what we aspire to become', came the instant reply. In spite of his formidable mind and style, however, those who knew him best and were closest to him spoke of his affectionate nature. This was displayed par-ticularly to his chaplains and to about half-a-dozen young men whom, in the absence of children of his own, he came to regard as substitute sons. And he was deeply loved by his wife's companion, Fearne Booker, who thought of him as a father and was at his bedside when he died.

Cosmo Gordon Lang moved from York to Canterbury in 1928 and there was then much talk of Henson succeeding to the Northern Arch-bishopric, but this was never a realistic expectation for so dedicated an individualist. The post went to William Temple and Henson's only regret was that he had been denied the opportunity to decline it. Retirement in 1939 gave him the chance to prepare for publication the journal which he had kept since 1885 and which appeared, together with some other autobiographical material, in three volumes as *Retrospect of an Unimp-ortant Life*. The candid character of its contents caused some eye-brows to be raised and there were those who regretted that it failed to convey the gentler side of its author's nature. On his leaving Durham tribute was paid not only to 'a great episcopate', but also to 'a generous episcopate'.

During the dark days of 1940 Winston Churchill got Henson to return to Westminster Abbey as a canon in the hope that his preaching would lift the spirits of a nation at war. But this proved to be a fiasco, for on his first appearance in the Abbey in April 1941 he discovered that his eyesight was now too poor for the reading of the Lessons. He resigned immediately and retired to Suffolk where in his 81st year he conducted the services in his local village church during an eleven-month interreg-num. In Durham he was now well on the way to becoming a cult-figure. Clergy were proud to have been ordained by him and recollections of his sayings and stories of his doings were retailed with relish. His like would never be seen again and he died gently on 28 September 1947.

Ernest William Barnes

In his journal entry for 28 July 1930 Henson painted a vivid picture of
Ernest William Barnes (Bishop of Birmingham 1924–53) in action at the
1930 Lambeth Conference:

> He is a striking figure, the very model of a 'heresiarch'. He might
> have been Huss in front of the fathers of Constance, or Luther at the
> Diet of Worms. Tall, pallid with much study, with stooping shoulders,
> and a voice at once challenging and melancholy, he commands atten-
> tion as well by his manner and aspect as by his opinions, which are
> almost insolently oppugnant to the general mind. He is a good man,
> but clearly a fanatic, and in a more disciplined age, could not possibly
> have avoided the stake.

In his presidential address to the Convocation of Canterbury in 1945
Archbishop Geoffrey Fisher also paid tribute to Barnes's character and
sincerity, but then attacked his recently published *The Rise of Christianity* and concluded, 'If his views were mine I should not feel that I could
continue to hold episcopal office in the Church of England.' Archbishop
Cyril Garbett took a similar line at York Convocation but Barnes was
unmoved and, not surprisingly, his book enjoyed considerable literary
success. Some theologians believed that its contents were of a higher
quality than Fisher's condemnatory address, but few regarded it as a serious contribution to theological debate. This was the time when the Biblical Theology movement was still flourishing in Britain and it is possible
that it would have attracted less hostility had it been published a quarter
of a century later. Offering a broad-brush account of the development
of Christianity over the centuries, Barnes argued – or, rather, simply
stated – that the Gospels were of a late date and presented an unreliable
account of Christianity's origins. All that could be known about Jesus, he
asserted, was that he lived, taught, suffered and died. Much more could
be known about his teaching than about his life, and any miraculous element in his life had to be rejected as incompatible with modern scientific
knowledge.

Reverence for scientific knowledge lay at the heart of Barnes's quest
for truth and influenced his understanding of the Christian faith. For
him, the gospel was no more, and no less, than the teaching of Jesus as
recorded in the New Testament. He was a distinguished mathematician
who frowned on any kind of compromise and believed that early in its
development Christianity became infected with pagan superstition. Thus
Barnes questioned much traditional sacramental doctrine, in particular

the mode of Christ's presence in the Eucharist and he not only denied the Roman Catholic doctrine of transubstantiation but also seemed to question any kind of sacramental presence of Christ in the Eucharistic elements. The implications of this were serious, for Birmingham diocese contained many Anglo-Catholic parishes in which Reservation and other forms of Eucharistic devotion were central to their life. Conflict was inevitable and caused anxiety and anger far beyond Birmingham. His views on various social questions were no less controversial.

But like many, perhaps most, notable bishops, Barnes was a complex character and his apparently outrageous opinions were expressed through a warm, generous personality. A smile spread over his face whenever he greeted anyone and many intelligent people, who admired his courage, found his essentially simple faith allied to deep ethical and social demands close to their own understanding of Christianity. He was born in Altrincham, Cheshire in 1874 but his family moved to Birmingham when he was still young and he went from King Edward's School to Trinity College, Cambridge, as a scholar. There he carried all before him, being bracketed as Second Wrangler in mathematics and finding time to become President of the Union. By the time he was 35 he would be a Doctor of Science and a Fellow of the Royal Society. As a fellow of Trinity College he taught mathematics and some of his contemporaries said that, having gone to Cambridge as an atheist, he had some sort of conversion experience during his time there. In 1902, and without much preparation, he was ordained by the Bishop of London. At this time he was a shy and somewhat arrogant young man and the fact that the few sermons he preached in the college chapel tended to be about the need for greater social justice and reform did not endear him to the other fellows. Crisis came with the outbreak of war in 1914 when he began to advocate pacifism. This was too much for Trinity and he was driven to resign his fellowship and leave.

He was however immediately appointed Master of the Temple – one of the most coveted posts in the Church of England – and the next five years were the happiest of his life. The official duties in the London legal enclave were not onerous, and confined mainly to preaching on Sundays. In spite of the war, the lawyers, whom he described as 'wistful agnostics', were ready to tolerate his pacifism as the price of erudite and stimulating sermons on a wide range of subjects. His theology at this stage was relatively orthodox and he described himself as a liberal evangelical, but things began to change when in 1920 he moved to become a Canon of Westminster. The Abbey congregation were startled by the first of what became known as his 'gorilla sermons', in which he declared that the theory of evolution had overthrown the traditional Christian understanding of life's meaning and purpose, and that the doctrine of the Fall must be abandoned. In 1922, having taken part in the wedding of Princess Mary and Lord Lascelles, he wrote to the Press deploring the use of 'archaic language' in the service.

Barnes was now well established as a controversial churchman and it may well have been this, as well as high regard for his intellect, that led Ramsay MacDonald, Britain's first Labour Prime Minister, to appoint him to the Bishopric of Birmingham in 1924. The fears of those who criticized the appointment were by no means allayed by an enthronement sermon which first expressed the hope of Anglican/Free Church reunion then went on to deplore 'the spiritualism, stoical pantheism and pagan sacramentalism which has entered into Latin Catholicism and pretends it can create the Bread of Salvation by some magic of ritual and formula'. This was a theme to which Barnes would often return, and sometimes in language so colourful that it was bound to cause offence –

A wafer by itself has no more value than a penny placed in the hand of a dying man to pay his fare to the grim ferryman who shall take him safely across the Styx.

Again, in a Westminster Abbey sermon in September 1926 –

Magical sacramentalism, Second Adventism and spiritualism are variants of primitive belief whose day is past . . . The alternatives of religious evolution or religious decay lie before us. What is the path of religious evolution? I find it in the words – 'Follow me and leave the dead to bury their dead.'

This led to strong protests from Anglo-Catholics but even greater offence was caused by a lunchtime address given in Birmingham Parish Church in October 1927 in which he asserted, 'There are among ourselves today men and women whose sacramental beliefs are not far from those of the cultured Hindu idolater.' This was widely reported and drew protests from the Bishops of London and Southwark as well as a demonstration in St Paul's Cathedral when Barnes preached there a few days later.

Throughout his 29 years in Birmingham Barnes demonstrated his ability to make surprising and sometimes shocking statements on a great variety of subjects, and as he grew older this ability was in no way diminished. The occasions of these utterances could also be surprising. At confirmations his address was usually devoted to what was in the forefront of his mind at the moment, for example, The case for a fixed Easter, and The deceased wife's sister Bill. This was perplexing to many a congregation, yet the confirmation candidates often felt that they had been in contact with a saint. During the 1930s he embarked on an extensive

church-building programme to cater for Birmingham's still rapidly growing population and, unsurprisingly, he insisted that the new churches
should be simple, multipurpose buildings uncluttered by statues or
liturgical frills.

The outbreak of war in 1939 drew attention once again to Barnes's
uncompromising pacifism and created many problems. Throughout the
1930s he had been a fierce critic of Nazism in Germany and had attacked
Pope Pius XI for authorizing the singing of the Te Deum in Italian
churches following the occupation of Abyssinia in 1936. At the same
time he constantly advocated disarmament and when the war came
steadfastly refused to attend any service or event at which there was a
military presence. During the dark days of 1940 he accused the Cement
Makers' Federation of being a ring of monopolists who were holding
back supplies of concrete required for the building of air-raid shelters
in order to maximize their profits. This led to a High Court action for
slander which Barnes lost, but lay friends raised the £1,600 required
for the damages and legal costs. Later he repeated the accusation in the
privileged surroundings of the House of Lords. In 1943 he said that after
the war there should be a united Europe with a single currency and no
trade tariffs.

When peace came in 1945 Barnes spoke against the division of
Germany and in favour of co-operation with the Soviet Union. He also
favoured the rapid release of German prisoners of war and the ending of
conscription in Britain. Although critical of some aspects of Communism, he described Lenin as primarily a social reformer and Communism
as a politico-social movement for the welfare of the common man.
This brought a sharp criticism from Winston Churchill in the House of
Commons and the Lord Mayor of Birmingham described the speech as
'rubbish'. There was more to come. In 1950 Barnes declared Britain to
be over-populated and afflicted by too many bad stocks. Sterilization,
euthanasia and birth control were, he said, the only answer to these
problems. He forecast a time to come when 'the greatest geneticist will be
accepted as one of the leading agents of Christian progress'. In the meantime immigration should cease, though those already in Britain should be
treated compassionately and justly. When the learned Bishop of Derby,
A. E. J. Rawlinson, described Barnes as 'the stormy Petrel of the English
episcopate' few were inclined to disagree. He retired in May 1953 and
died a few months later. He would not easily be forgotten.

––––––––––––

These are not the only controversial figures to feature in the pages of this
volume and they chance to have exercised their episcopal ministries at

more or less the same time during the first half of the twentieth century. Among their colleagues were William Temple and George Bell, and the existence of four controversial bishops at that time serves to highlight the absence of this important element in the Church's life today. This suggests a lack of passionately held convictions, which may not be fair to all, or even any, of the bishops since the skill necessary for effective public debate is not given to everyone, and there may be widespread weariness arising from daily routine responsibilities. It is also the case that when, as today, the media attempts to turn every difference of opinion, however sincere, into a major controversy, it is difficult for bishops and other serious commentators to make their voices heard above the din. And let it be readily and gladly acknowledged that from time to time the utterances of some bishops cause minor controversy.

There is however nothing minor about most of the controversies in which Richard Holloway is embroiled and his example is instructive. As Bishop of Edinburgh from 1986 to 2000 and Primus of the Scottish Episcopal Church for the last eight of these years, he was the most controversial and for many the most stimulating churchman in Britain. His background is Anglo-Catholic – altar boy in a poor Glasgow parish, vocation to the religious life tested at the Society of the Sacred Mission, Kelham – but he came to see that a truly Catholic faith must be open to development and never allow itself to stagnate. His support for the ordination of women to the priesthood led some to accuse him of betraying the Catholic cause, while the latest of his 23 books *Doubts and Loves* (2001) caused some to suggest that he has abandoned the Christian faith itself. This is a common charge against the controversialist and such a judgement obviously depends on what the prosecution supposes the Christian faith to be.

What is not open to question however is that Holloway has never failed to declare the truth as he has discerned it with his acute theological mind, has never been afraid of sharp controversy (in Bangor Cathedral in 1996 he described the opponents of women priests as 'miserable buggers' and 'the meanest minded sods you can imagine') and, in consequence, has earned the gratitude of a multitude of people both inside and outside the Church's life. In 1991 there was some talk of his becoming Bishop of London but the chances of so imaginative an appointment being made were always slim and the freedom provided by his much lesser responsiblities in Scotland enabled his gifts to be employed more usefully. His election as a bishop, then as Primus, in Scotland owed everything to the fact that he was the most able of the candidates and it is to the credit of the electors that they recognized this and were ready to take the risks involved.

Like Holloway, Henson and Barnes had greater freedom to think and speak than any present-day English bishop and what they had to say was never less than thought-provoking and challenging. Their utterances in speech and writing were always concerned with that which is deep, rather than that which is trivial, and this is always the content of true Christian controversy. There is much in the life of the Church and the world today that urgently requires serious discussion and it is impossible to believe that this can be undertaken without the risk of lively controversy.

8

The headmasters

Not the least among the remarkable developments in English society during the Victorian era was the expansion of the old public schools and the foundation of many new ones based on the mediaeval and sixteenth-century models. It seemed perfectly natural to the new founders that their headmasters should be clergymen. The schoolmaster and the clergyman had similar roles in society – teaching, pastoral care and the upholding of Christian moral standards. Moreover, a high proportion of the most able scholars of the first half of the nineteenth century were, because of Oxford and Cambridge fellowship requirements, in Holy Orders. There was much to-ing and fro-ing between the colleges and the schools.

So the great Victorian headmasters were all ordained, and their influence on the life of the nation was enormous, for they educated its leaders in virtually every walk of life, including of course the Church. Neither was the movement in one direction. A number of headmasters became bishops and deans, and again this seemed not unnatural, since a man who was capable of running a large public school might well have the gifts of leadership, administrative skill and pastoral insight required in a bishop. What they nearly always lacked was any first-hand experience of the Church's administration but during a period when the Church of England had only a minimum of central organization this was not important and the presence on the bench of bishops of men with first-class minds more than compensated for their ignorance concerning the machinery of the Ecclesiastical Commissioners or the politics of the Convocations.

During the twentieth century, however, when the requirements of headmasters and bishops changed considerably, the movement between the two vocations gradually ceased, though two of the century's Archbishops of Canterbury, William Temple and Geoffrey Fisher, had been headmasters and as late as 1949 a former headmaster of Winchester, Spencer Leeson, became Bishop of Peterborough. Nearly all those who became bishops were men of some distinction who made a notable contribution to the life of the Church of England both in their dioceses and nationally. No-one has taken their places. The weakness of their contribution lay in the fact that they were essentially establishment figures who, with the significant exception of William Temple, saw the Church of England and the public schools as occupying the same ground in their unfailing support of a society based on privilege, wealth and class. Few of them recognized the radical changes taking place in the world in which they lived, or the demands that these changes were making of the Church. But in this they were hardly different from the great majority of the bishops who had not been headmasters.

Frederick Temple

Frederick Temple was not only an outstanding headmaster of Rugby School – comparable, it was said, to Thomas Arnold – but also a most notable Bishop of Exeter (1869–85) then of London (1885–97). If his impact as Archbishop of Canterbury (1897–1902) was less than that which he made in his previous appointments this was because he was 75 and almost blind when he moved to Canterbury, and had less than six years in office.

As a boy he was driven by poverty to work on his widowed mother's farm, and never lost the style and manner of a farmer. He was a rugged character, with a rough accent, and could be brusque to the point of downright rudeness. Yet beneath a formidable and seemingly wintry exterior there was real warmth and deep compassion, and an emotional element which was often expressed in tears. During his years as a headmaster it was said, as with Temple, that his whereabouts could usually be determined by the sound of laughter.

He was among the bishops whose appointment caused considerable controversy and for reasons which now seem incredible. Soon after he became headmaster of Rugby he gave an address in the school chapel on 'The Education of the World'. This was subsequently adapted to meet the requirements of a university sermon, and when invited to contribute to a series of *Essays and Reviews* in 1860 he economized on time by submitting this sermon. Apart from the fact that it espoused the cause of free enquiry in religious matters and made a few interesting suggestions about education, the sermon was quite unremarkable. Some of the other essays were however regarded as dangerously liberal and the volume was condemned by the Convocation of Canterbury in 1864. Temple had not even seen these essays before their publication, but the fact of his association with them was sufficient to drive Dr Pusey and the Earl of Shaftesbury to mount a campaign against his appointment as Bishop of Exeter. Several bishops joined in the protest and only three bishops assisted the Bishop of London, who was standing in for the ill Archbishop of Canterbury, at the consecration service in Westminster Abbey.

Temple's appointment was also strongly opposed in Exeter by Tractarian and evangelical churchmen who believed that a bishop of heretical beliefs had been imposed on them. He was in fact nothing of the kind. True, he believed the early chapters of Genesis were best treated as inspired stories, and that the findings of science needed to be taken seriously, but for the rest he was impeccably orthodox. During his undergraduate days at Oxford he was interested in, and to some extent influenced by, the Tractarian movement, but he never became identified with it and there was a strong evangelical element in his beliefs which often found moving expression in his preaching on the redemptive power of the Cross. When celebrating the Eucharist he always stood, after the Protestant custom, at the north end of the altar, and when a London vicar once ventured to say in the vestry before a service, 'My Lord, it is the custom in this church for the Celebrant to take the Eastward position,' there came the curt reply, 'It will not be the custom this morning.' On the other hand, he told Protestant trouble-makers that it was absurd to call a thing Roman or Popish because it was very like, or even identical with, something done in the Church of Rome.

The thirteenth of fifteen children, seven of whom died young, Frederick Temple was born in 1821 on Ionia Island where his father, an army officer, was the sub-inspector of militia. Returning to England, the family settled on a Devon farm, but this did not prosper and the father took up another overseas appointment – this time in Sierra Leone. Within two years, however, he was dead and the children were educated for two hours a day by their widowed mother; the rest of the day was spent working on the family farm. In 1834 enough money was found to send young Frederick to Blundell's School at Tiverton, from where he won a scholarship to Balliol College, Oxford. He lived there in poverty, wearing patched clothes and badly worn shoes, and was unable to pay for the private tuition normally required by those who aimed for high honours. Nonetheless, long hours of study earned him a double first in classics and mathematics, which led to a college fellowship and a lectureship in mathematics and logic. He was ordained by the Bishop of Oxford, Samuel Wilberforce, in 1846.

His own experience drew him to educational work among the less privileged and, after spending a year as an examiner in the Education Office in Whitehall, he was appointed Principal of Kneller Hall, Middlesex. This was a new training college for workhouse schoolmasters, but after five years the experiment failed and Temple was back in Whitehall as Inspector of Men's Training Colleges. In 1857 he was appointed headmaster of Rugby and during the next twelve years restored the school to its pre-eminent place among the English public schools. The dawning of a new era in its life was marked by his arrival from the station carrying his own bag. He was himself a stimulating teacher and introduced into the regular curriculum natural science, music and drawing. New buildings were erected and the chapel was enlarged. He worked long hours and, although an uncompromising taskmaster, was admired by the teaching staff and loved by the boys, one of whom wrote a letter to his parents, 'He is a beast, but a just beast.'

In 1869 he declined Gladstone's offer of the Deanery of Durham, but a few months later was invited to choose between the Bishoprics of Oxford, Exeter, Bath and Wells and Manchester – all of which had fallen vacant at about the same time. He arrived in Exeter unceremoniously on a farmer's cart, there having been a misunderstanding over the provision of a carriage, but crowds turned out to greet him and the diocese soon became aware that it had been sent another masterful bishop. Visiting the parishes was always his priority and there was an annual visit to every deanery to give a substantial lecture on a practical subject, such as worship, preaching, pastoral visiting, or on a theological issue, such as biblical inspiration or Christology. Meetings with the laity were also held, Sunday School examinations introduced, and a Diocesan Council of Religious Education established. Education was always a major concern and soon after his arrival in Exeter he said that the conditions of the working classes should be improved and that this would best be achieved by helping them to help themselves through better education. The ancient endowments of some privileged schools were therefore diverted to new secondary schools that were open to the poor, and exhibitions were provided to enable them to rise through the best county schools to the university. By the time Temple left Exeter, Devon schools were deemed to be the best in the country. He also saw temperance as necessary to self-help and social improvement and lost no opportunity to advocate total abstinence from alcohol. This remained one of his hobby horses and when, as Archbishop of Canterbury, he was invited to address the General Assembly of the Church of Scotland he surprised his audience by urging them to temperance, rather than to church unity.

Another of his special concerns was the patronage system, in particular the sale of advowsons which he described as 'a most serious scandal and one that does serious mischief'. He blamed the clergy for tolerating the system and begged them to accept the need for reform in order that parishes might have the most suitable priests. In spite of all his efforts, however, reform had to await the 1898 Benefices Act. His suggestion that the Dean and Chapter should become more active in the cathedral and diocese also met stiff resistance, and reformation there had to wait even longer. A few years earlier his fund-raising capacity was employed in the creation of the new Diocese of Truro. His predecessor had demonstrated that it was impossible for one bishop to exercise an effective ministry over both Devon and Cornwall, but a proposal to divide the diocese was postponed for want of money to finance the stipend of a second bishop and a basic diocesan administration. In 1875 Temple launched an appeal for the endowment of a Truro bishopric and, with his customary frankness, announced, 'I am decidedly against the creation of a new set of bishops at lower salaries; bishoprics so endowed will either be filled by men of less ability, or be made stepping stones.' The new diocese was inaugurated in 1877 with Edward White Benson, another former headmaster, as its first bishop.

In the following year he headed a movement for the relief of about 2,000 people who had been seriously impoverished by the failure of the West of England Bank, and later formed a society for the promotion of good manners which he called the Semper Fidelis Society. He was one of the first bishops to recommend the formation of parochial church councils and the first Bishop of Exeter to licence lay readers – some 238 of these being enrolled and trained during his episcopate. He next called for the ordination of permanent deacons, who would exercise a pastoral ministry and lead worship while remaining in their secular occupations, but there is no evidence that any of these were ever recruited. Few were surprised when he said, 'I do not have time to think.' He did find time, however, to get married in 1876 to Beatrice Lascelles – the granddaughter of an Earl. Their two sons, Frederick and William, were born at Exeter.

The announcement of Temple's translation to London in 1885 caused great distress in Exeter, where he was widely admired, and some wondered if he would successfully make the transition from a provincial to a metropolitan diocese. In fact he soon made his presence felt in the capital. 'Granite on fire' was how he was described when much younger and he never changed. His annual output of work was prodigious: 10,000 letters, 3–4,000 of them written in his own hand; 500 public or committee meetings; at least 150 priests or deacons ordained, each one personally interviewed; 70 confirmations; conferences for every deanery. Letters could be brief – 'Dear Mr ——, Are you disposed to accept the charge of the parish of ——? Yours faithfully, F. Londin.' Likewise interviews: a delinquent clergyman was informed by the Suffragan Bishop of Bedford that he must resign, and when he refused to do so his case was referred to the diocesan bishop. On his appearance before Temple and the suffragan he was greeted with the question, 'The Bishop of Bedford has informed you that you must resign your benefice, has he not?' 'Yes, my Lord' came the reply. 'Then you will resign at once; good morning.'

But as soon as he had gone Temple exclaimed in great sorrow, 'What can we do for that poor fellow?' Unlike Bishop Blomfield, whose church-building and parish-creating had transformed the London scene during the 1840s and 1850s, Temple was generally against the division of parishes, considering it to be more important to spend the money on additional clergy and to keep them in teams. He established an Order of Diocesan Readers in 1891.

Shortly before Temple's move to London, Edward White Benson had been translated from Truro to Canterbury, and Temple became the new archbishop's closest adviser. Hardly a day passed without letters and documents passing between Lambeth Palace and London House, and he was an assessor when Bishop Edward King was tried for alleged ritual offences. He was greatly upset by Benson's death in 1896 and, although the Prime Minister, Lord Salisbury, considered him to be the obvious successor in the primacy, this was challenged by Queen Victoria who said that he was too old. Her preference was for Randall Davidson, but in the end Canterbury was offered to Temple in the expectation, and hope, that he would decline. This proved to be a misjudgement, for he accepted with great enthusiasm – 'I do not feel that I have any right to refuse the call which Her Majesty has made upon me' – and at 75 he became the oldest man ever to be appointed Archbishop of Canterbury.

Inevitably, he could be no more than a caretaker, but he was by no means inactive. 'I think the day is past when the Archbishop of Canterbury should appear as a country gentlemen,' he declared soon after his enthronement, and then sold Addington Palace, near Croydon, in order to enlarge a house in the precincts of Canterbury Cathedral. There he stayed most weekends, ministering in the diocese and, as always, never declining an invitation unless it was absolutely impossible. Sometimes he would drop into a village church for Sunday Evensong and simply occupy a seat at the back. On one occasion, having endured a particularly lengthy and disjointed sermon, he enquired why the preacher had no script. The explanation was that he had once been congratulated on a scriptless sermon and vowed never again to take notes into the pulpit. Whereupon Temple declared, 'I, Frederick by divine providence Lord Archbishop of Canterbury, Primate of All England and Metropolitan, do hereby dispense you from your vow.'

In 1901 Temple officiated at the funeral of Queen Victoria and in the following year crowned King Edward VII. The coronation was postponed because of the King's illness and the service had to be shortened to avoid undue strain upon him. Fears that the archbishop would be too weak to carry out the ceremony proved to be unfounded, though failing sight caused him to place the crown on the monarch's head back to front and when he knelt in homage he was unable to rise. The King helped him to his feet and when he was upright Temple laid his hand on the crown and in a voice of deep emotion said 'God bless you, sir; God bless you; God be with you.' The King responded by kissing his hand and at the conclusion of the service sent him a bowl of soup which had been kept in the robing room in case the King needed sustenance.

Although Temple was now near his 81st birthday, he maintained a punishing schedule of engagements, travelling to various parts of England for sermons and speeches, delivering visitation charges at diocesan centres, consecrating a new Bishop of Melbourne, and attending innumerable meetings. When leaving a meeting to catch a train one evening it was raining heavily and someone asked, 'Shall I fetch a cab?' 'A cab! No! I'm not made of sugar,' came the response. But soon afterwards, while speaking in an education debate in the House of Lords, he had a seizure and, although he made a partial recovery, he died nineteen days later. Forty years on, his son William became Archbishop of Canterbury – the only instance of father and son occupying the throne of St Augustine.

George Ridding

Frederick Temple was well established and had made his mark at Rugby when George Ridding, Bishop of Southwell (1884–1904) began what amounted to a revolution at William of Wykeham's foundation in Winchester. He was born there, in 1828, when his father was the Second Master; was educated there; and, after a brilliant career at Oxford, returned as Second Master in 1863. Three years later he succeeded to the headmastership; his father-in-law, Dr George Moberly, had held this post for the previous 31 years.

The timing of Ridding's appointment was significant. Although Moberly had carried out some reforms, the school was still essentially corrupt. The warden and fellows, who constituted the governing body, claimed half of the endowment revenue for their personal use and were regarded by the headmaster as enemies. The amount of money remaining was totally inadequate for the payment of the teaching staff and the life of the school was, both educationally and morally, far removed from the high ideals of its fourteenth-century founder. The government, aware of the problems at Winchester and in the other old foundations, appointed a commission whose radical proposals were formulated in the 1868 Public Schools Act, and the warden and fellows of Winchester took pre-emptive action by appointing as headmaster a sound Wykehamist who would not, they believed, take reform too far.

They could not have been more mistaken. Ridding combined vision, high intelligence, energy, unusual administrative ability – and a private income. He encountered some opposition when he took over the head-mastership, but quickly won the support of the teachers, while the senile bursar, who held the purse strings, was powerless to object. Within five years the school had been transformed. A massive building programme, extended playing fields and other facilities (many of these paid for by Ridding), a totally restructured school system and a revised curriculum led to his becoming known as Winchester's 'Second Founder'.

In 1883 he was offered the Deanery of Exeter but, as his second wife, Lady Laura Ridding, remarked later in a biography of her husband, 'he felt no call to leave his work for the leisure of a Deanery'. Gladstone took the hint and in the following year appointed him as the first Bishop of Southwell. It was to be a formidable task. The new diocese, comprising Nottinghamshire and Derbyshire, had been hastily cobbled together in response to urgent requests from the Bishops of Lincoln and Lichfield who could not cope with the burgeoning industrial communities developing on the edges of their overlarge dioceses. No consideration had been given to the difficulty of uniting ecclesiastically two very different counties, to the necessary administrative structure and how the enterprise was to be financed. It had been decided, however, that the cathedral would be Southwell Minster – a delightful, historic building, but located in a large village near the eastern border of the diocese, some fifteen miles from Nottingham, the chief town, and virtually inaccessible from most parts of Derbyshire. To these and many other problems Ridding immediately applied the skill and energy which had wrought such a transformation at Winchester College, and what he lacked in church experience was more than compensated for by the possession of an acute theological mind, a deep spirituality and a compassionate concern for people. In many ways his outlook was that of a layman and at first he was treated warily by the clergy, but before long he was admired and respected, and at the end of the day greatly loved.

The parishes of the new diocese had, chiefly for geographical reasons, been neglected for many years by their former bishops. Many of the church buildings were decayed and the bishops had often yielded to the temptation to despatch their problem clergy to the far-flung corners of their empires. During the twenty years of his episcopate Ridding was tireless in visiting the parishes – usually by train – and sometimes he stayed for several days in the main centres of population. Besides administering confirmation he discussed with the clergy and churchwardens all aspects of parish life, taking careful notes for future reference. He was also a firm believer in town missions, in which he often took a prominent part, and in the course of a mission held in Derby in 1888 he gave 23 addresses in twelve days. This included visits to all the public houses in the town, and licences were subsequently refused to 113 public and beer houses where dancing and other attractions were deemed to make them places of special temptation to the young. Avoiding temptation – especially impurity – was a frequent theme of Ridding's sermons and this came as no surprise to the many Wykehamists who came to serve as priests in the diocese.

Yet he was no dyed-in-the-wool conservative. His theological outlook was distinctly liberal and the importance of the quest for truth, which had caused a stir in Oxford when he made it the subject of a University Sermon in 1864, remained with him to the end of his life. 'Life is better than custom,' he often said, and sometimes added, 'Archaeology is neither authority nor law.'

A major coal industry strike from July to November 1893 affected 100 parishes in the diocese and Ridding gave these special attention during what came to be known as the Coal War. He addressed 3,000 miners at an outdoor meeting, but his attempts at mediation between the miners and the colliery owners were unsuccessful. In better times the building of new churches in areas of increasing population continued apace and between 1896 and 1898 he consecrated 36 new churches. As at Winchester, much new work was financed from his own pocket and during his twenty years in Southwell he received £68,000 in official stipend and spent over £69,000 on diocesan work.

A reluctant visitor to London, Ridding played little part in the House of Lords, except during the time of the controversial 1902 Education Act, and he had little enthusiasm for Bishops' Meetings, though he was a trusted adviser of Archbishop Frederick Temple during his years at Canterbury. He believed strongly that his place was in his diocese and that his time was best spent in visiting the parishes and conducting Quiet Days for the clergy. A Litany of Remembrance which he used on these occasions was widely used as a prayerful form of self-examination by clergy of the Church of England for half a century after his death.

Inevitably, the punishing programme of work he adopted began to tell on his health as he grew older. A breakdown kept him off duty from May 1888 until Easter 1889, after which a Suffragan Bishop of Derby was appointed to ease the strain. He declined the offer of translation to Lichfield in 1891 and continued to provide Southwell with outstanding leadership until illness again intervened in January 1899. It was not until September of that year that he was well enough to resume work and the final years of his episcopate were marked by a good deal of acute pain. He died in 1904 shortly before the day of his announced retirement. A new Diocese of Derby, which he had recommended, was not created until 1927.

Neville Gorton

One of the last headmasters to become a bishop, and the most unusual of them all, was Neville Gorton, who went to Coventry in 1943, not long after its cathedral had been destroyed, famously, by wartime bombing, and was there until 1958, by which time a new building was rising phoenix-like from the ashes of the old. Before his consecration as a bishop he spent 28 years, first as a house tutor and form master at Sedburgh School, then as headmaster of Blundell's School. In both places he had many devotees who enjoyed his eccentricities, exasperating though these could sometimes be, and flourished under his loving pastoral care. Archbishop William Temple described him as 'That quaint saint', and someone else said, 'He was a man such as St Francis might have been had he been Balliol-trained.'

There was general agreement that preaching was not his *métier*. His mind was filled with so many visionary ideas and his heart with such burning passion that ordered language could not express coherently what he desired to share with others. Thus after a sermon in Eton College chapel, when his struggle with words ended in apparent failure, he stood in the chancel, as the organist was playing over the final hymn, and shouted out, 'What I really meant to say was – You damned well all need to be converted.' His impact did not depend however on his use of words. There was something about his presence that made people feel he was a man close to God, and when arrangements for his funeral were being made a group of workmen asked if they might have seats – 'He was our Bishop.'

Gorton was among those for whom the arts are their primary means of communication. He was a gifted painter and, besides enlisting the aid of notable artists for his educational work at Blundell's, encouraged some of them to make an outstanding contribution to the new cathedral. He was deeply involved in its planning and largely responsible for the replacement of Sir Giles Gilbert Scott by Basil Spence as its architect. In the end however he lost his battle to have the building designed around a central altar and was driven by Spence and the reconstruction committee to accept a neo-Gothic ground plan. It was a serious mistake. But he recruited Jacob Epstein to create a dramatic figure of St Michael – the cathedral's patron saint – and worked very closely with Graham Sutherland in his design of the great tapestry that went behind the main altar. Sadly, he did not live to see the completion of the building and it was left to his successor, Cuthbert Bardsley, to preside over its consecration.

Gorton was born in 1888 in Manchester where his father was a parish priest and an honorary canon of the cathedral. He went from Marlborough to Balliol College, Oxford, where he read classics and prepared for ordination at the theological college run by the Community of the Resurrection at Mirfield. During his twenty years on the teaching staff at Sedburgh he acquired the nickname 'Gorky' which continued to be used by his friends for the rest of his life. He was noted for the strange array of clothes he wore beneath his tattered gown and, as with Temple, the sound of laughter was always a clear indication of his whereabouts in the school. But he was valued above all as a gifted and inspiring teacher who gave much time to his less able pupils and knew how to stimulate the others, provided they could keep pace with his thoughts, darting from one subject to another without warning.

The chief feature of his headmastership of Blundell's was the tailoring of subjects to fit the interests of pupils. This was, he believed, the best way of creating a foundation on which a broad liberal education could then be built. Such an education required involvement in the arts and crafts and, having reorganized the school's workshops, he engaged Eric Gill and other sculptors, painters and craftsmen as visiting artists. His administration of the school was less successful, but with the aid of an efficient bursar it was steered without mishap through the early years of the 1939–45 war.

Gorton's appointment as Bishop of Coventry was due entirely to the influence of Brendan Bracken, the Minister of Information in Churchill's wartime coalition government to whom the Prime Minister often turned for advice on church affairs. Bracken had spent a month at Sedburgh School when Gorton was chaplain there and this was long enough for him to become an admirer and life-long friend. He persuaded Churchill that, after the wartime bombing, Coventry needed a different kind of bishop and Archbishop Temple readily agreed that Gorton fitted this bill.

His enthronement in February 1943 took place in the ruined cathedral, open to the sky and debris piled on all sides. It was a bleak prospect. Within a matter of days, however, Gorton had embarked on a tour of the diocese, meeting the clergy in their deaneries for a whole day, part of which was devoted to reading St Mark's Gospel in Greek. He urged them to continue to meet at regular intervals for study and mutual support. For those who desired more there was a fortnightly meeting at Bishop's House for reading, study and discussion. This continued for several years until an increase in general busy-ness made attendance less easy. Coventry's many factories also engaged his attention from the earliest days of his episcopate and, having got to know the managers and shop stewards, he secured their agreement to the appointment of works chaplains. About twelve of these were active at the time of his death.

The development of large new housing estates during the post-war years also claimed much of his time for the provision of church buildings and the appointment of lively clergy to pioneer new work, but he became impatient with the constraints on moving resources to places where they were most needed. On the other hand, he was very much against the amalgamation of small rural parishes, believing that most of these should be ministered to by specially recruited older men after they had attended a 12–18-month training course and served a curacy in a strong parish. Collaboration with the non-Anglican churches was another of his special concerns and it was his idea that the rebuilt cathedral should have an ecumenical chapel and that there should also be a Christian Service Centre involving all the churches.

Gorton got on well with every sort of person but he was essentially an individualist and not always easy to work with. His lack of formality and unpredictability endeared him to ordinary people and his intense pastoral love won a notable response from some who rarely ventured inside a church. But his lack of administrative skill was always a problem – it was not unknown for him to offer the same living to two different priests – and to those responsible for the ordering of great diocesan services or even small parish confirmations his detachment could be a nightmare. On one occasion he was missing from the tail of an outdoor procession making its way to a village church and was eventually tracked down to a small cottage where, in cope and mitre, he sat on the corner of the kitchen table talking to a white-haired old lady. He had quite forgotten that he was due to institute her new rector. Some of his appointments were strange, too, though he had a keen eye for brilliant, creative men for key posts.

In the end he burnt himself out and died in office at the end of November 1955. Soon after his death the Archbishop of Canterbury, Geoffrey Fisher, with whom he had nothing in common except great success as a headmaster, wrote – 'He has gone like a comet, leaving streams of colour and light and exhilaration behind, unto the consuming glory of God and his Kingdom.' Of how many bishops, from any background, could that ever have been said?

Geoffrey Fisher

Professor Donald MacKinnon's verdict on Fisher was less favourable – 'The history of the Church of England may yet recognize that the worst misfortune to befall its leadership at the end of the war was less the premature death of William Temple than his succession by Fisher of London and not by Bell of Chichester.' This may well be true, though there is generally agreement that the prophetic Bell lacked some of the gifts required in an Archbishop of Canterbury. The argument advanced at the time was that the Church's greatest need when the war ended would not be for prophecy but for first-class administration that would bring its organization and finances into the modern world. The Prime Minister, Winston Churchill, was easily convinced, since he had not the slightest intention of appointing to the primacy a bishop who had openly challenged the indiscriminate bombing of German cities.

In fact, Geoffrey Fisher, who moved to Canterbury (1945–61) from London (1939–45), having previously been at Chester (1932–39), achieved a great deal during his time as archbishop, though his reputation remains sullied by the priority he accorded to the revision of canon law. This occupied a large part of the agenda of the Convocations from 1947 to 1969 and, while Fisher regarded it as being one of the greatest achievements of his archiepiscopate, the result was subsequently ignored by a Church whose problems were of an entirely different character. That Fisher should have accorded such priority to the rule-book was in some way unsurprising. He had been an outstandingly good public school headmaster and there acquired a management style which he believed to be equally appropriate to the leadership of the Church of England. Never did he recognize that changes in the intellectual climate and the social order triggered by the war were presenting the Church with challenges that demanded far more than administrative action. In spite of three first-class degrees from Oxford, his mind was not of the speculative sort and theological issues were of no interest to him unless they related to some practical matter he had been dealing with.

One of the best things he did was to secure the rationalizing of clergy stipends. When he became archbishop there were wide disparities, related neither to responsibilities nor to need, and caused mainly by the accident of endowment. The Ecclesiastical Commissioners handled their investments with great caution and many of the clergy, still paid quarterly, were living in dire poverty. Fisher took this in hand, united the Ecclesiastical Commissioners and Queen Anne's Bounty to form the Church Commissioners, pooled all the parish endowments, instituted a new body to maximize income, and introduced stipend scales based on equality. The laity were also challenged to raise new money for stipends and, although a minimum income of £500 per annum did not make the recipients rich men, it provided the basis for a system that was recognized as just and capable of constructive development. Another outcome of the reform was the allocation of money for the payment of clergy and the building of churches in the many new housing areas that sprang up in the immediate post-war era.

Fisher also displayed considerable statesmanship in his leadership of the Anglican Communion. The inevitable dislocation and breakdown in communication caused by the world war left many of the provinces and national church bodies dispirited and without much sense of international identity. Fisher tackled this by travelling more widely than any of his predecessors and by his brilliant chairmanship of two highly successful Lambeth Conferences. And, as the pressure for political independence grew within the British Empire, he saw the need for the Anglican Communion to become a federation of self-governing churches with indigenous leadership. In this he was ahead of the politicians and many of the new autonomous churches contributed much to the peaceful transition of their countries to independence within the Commonwealth.

Fisher's other concern was with church unity. A Cambridge sermon in 1946 became a landmark by its attempt to break a deadlock in unity negotiations with the suggestion that the Free Churches should 'take episcopacy into their system'. It was a pragmatic, rather than a theological, approach to church unity very much in the Fisher 'commonsense' style, and his failure to recognize that important theological issues were at stake brought disappointment. Nonetheless the sermon put unity back on the Church's agenda at just the right moment and, although subsequent developments abandoned the Fisher approach, he must be credited with the initiative. His private visit to Pope John XXIII in 1960 (the first by an Archbishop of Canterbury since the Reformation) played a significant part in the thawing of Anglican/Roman Catholic relations.

Fisher, the youngest of ten children, was born in the rectory at Higham-on-the-Hill in Leicestershire. His father held this family living for 42 years, his grandfather for 36 years and his great-grandfather for 60 years – the latter having been instituted a year before the Boston Tea Party and dying in the year of the first Reform Bill. In some circumstances the young Geoffrey might well have extended the succession but after brilliant careers at Marlborough College, where he won many prizes, and at Exeter College, Oxford, where he took firsts in Mods and Greats and in theology, he became an ordained schoolmaster. His first appointment was as an assistant master at Marlborough but after three years there and aged only 27 he became headmaster of Repton School. This was a demanding assignment. Arriving on the eve of the outbreak of war in 1914, he immediately lost 60 senior boys and six masters who enlisted in the army. Discipline was lax. William Temple, his predecessor who recommended him for the post, had not been a great success and homosexuality was rife. Fisher immediately expelled two senior boys and began to rule with a very firm hand. Hard floggings were administered to the delinquent and he saw it as his responsibility to inculcate Christian standards through his own teaching of divinity and his sermons in the chapel. But he was a caring, genial man who got to know all the boys and proved to be a highly effective headmaster.

After eighteen years of schoolmastering, however, he felt the need of a change and wondered about the possibility of becoming a country parson, but he was pleased to be appointed Bishop of Chester and devoted to the diocese the same efficiency and enthusiasm that he had displayed at Repton. His friendly, avuncular style brought popularity and he was an effective fund-raiser. In 1939, however, his equilibrium was disturbed not only by impending war but even more by the offer of the Bishopric of London. His immediate reaction was unusual in a man noted for his matter-of-fact approach to problems and calm unflappability:

> As soon as I read the Prime Minister's and the Archbishop's letters I knelt down and wept like a child. The thing frightened me and, as I knelt in mute prostration before our Lord, the words which came as commentary were our Lord's, 'Father, if it be possible, let this cup pass from me.'

He believed that, while his gifts equipped him quite well for Chester, they were far too limited for London with its public life and constant demand for statements and pronouncements. He was also a stranger to London. In the end William Temple, then at York, persuaded him to accept because there was urgent need for a first-class administrator at London since the long reign of Winnington-Ingram had left the diocese in considerable chaos, particularly in matters relating to worship in the parish churches.

Characteristically, Fisher dealt with London's problems by issuing a set of Bishop's Regulations which decreed what was permissible in the realms of worship, marriage, divorce and other pastoral situations. The fact that most Londoners did not go to church seems hardly to have crossed his mind. But the disciplinarian was required also to be the supporter and encourager, for soon London was experiencing the Blitz and maintaining morale, as well as dealing with bombed churches and vicarages, was the highest priority. During his five years in the diocese he visited half the parishes, but details of his ministry at that time are scanty since, as his biographer Edward Carpenter to his chagrin discovered, virtually all the papers relating to his London episcopate have disappeared – probably destroyed in a bonfire lit by the wife of one of Fisher's successors.

When William Temple died unexpectedly in 1944 there were effectively only three candidates for the succession to Canterbury – Bell of Chichester, Garbett of York and Fisher – and, the first two of these having been ruled out for quite different reasons, the Prime Minister's choice could hardly have been more simple. This time Fisher had no qualms about accepting, though he was in no sense a national figure and knew that when the war ended both church and nation would be faced with massive tasks of reconstruction. Neither was he any longer inhibited by the demand for public pronouncements. During his Canterbury years he could not keep quiet. Shortly before the end of the war he declared that the victors must not be unjust to their former enemies and he supported a House of Lords motion for 'the progressive establishment of a United Europe'. His statement, following the use of atomic bombs on Japan, that it might be within the providence of God that the human race should destroy itself, was strongly contested by many other church leaders.

Fisher was the last archbishop to assume that his position entitled him to speak directly to the Prime Minister and other senior politicians about the morality of their decision-making and he was the last archbishop to whom politicians conceded that right, though this was not done without grumbling. During the 1956 Suez Crisis he attacked the Eden government's policy in the House of Lords and the introduction of Premium Bonds also aroused his displeasure – 'an irresponsible transfer of wealth'. Prime Minister Harold Macmillan's boast that the nation had 'never had it so good' was roundly denounced, as also was his own action in inviting Archbishop Makarios, the rebellious Greek Cypriot leader, to the 1958 Lambeth Conference and then carelessly describing him as 'a low character'. Five years earlier, however, his handling of the coronation service won universal praise. The choice of new bishops occupied a good deal of his time and during his Canterbury years over 50 diocesan bishops and 26 suffragan bishops, some of whom became diocesans, were appointed. Since politicians were becoming much less interested in episcopal appointments, Fisher's influence was much greater than that of any of his predecessors, though he did not always get his own way. He favoured pastors, rather than scholars or prophets, and generally went for 'safe' men who were unlikely to challenge his ideas, though one notable exception to this was his suggestion of Mervyn Stockwood for Southwark in 1959. During the latter part of his reign, however, many of the bishops became frustrated and critical of the amount of time taken at their meetings by small administrative matters. They also resented being treated as if they were public school housemasters subject to an increasingly talkative and dictatorial head. 'If I take the trouble to dress properly, I expect the same of you' was his response to the suggestion that it might not always be necessary for church dignitaries to wear apron, breeches and gaiters at London meetings.

In the end one of his chaplains had the courage to tell him that he ought seriously to consider the possibility of retirement. Which he did, and resigned in 1961. He then spent another eleven years ministering in a small rural parish in Dorset where he was a greatly loved figure, but from where, disregarding convention and loyalty, he conducted a tiresome campaign against a scheme for Anglican/Methodist unity. It seemed that he could not forget that he had once been his successor's headmaster.

The ordained headmaster has survived even into the twenty-first century but none of their small number is a powerful public school figure who might in another age have become a strong diocesan bishop. Having said Goodbye to this particular sort of bishop it is however important to consider whether or not some future bishops might be recruited from fields which are neither educational nor ecclesiastical. There are plenty of precedents for this from the past. St Paul was a tent-maker, Ambrose, the saintly Bishop of Milan in the fourth century, was chief constable of that city before being pressed into episcopal service. William of Wykeham was an architect before his appointment as Bishop of Winchester in 1367.

Such precedents are not a sure guide for the present episcopal ministry of the Church, but in an age when many of the functions previously exercised by the Church have been taken over by organs of the state it seems worth considering whether some of the Christians who now provide leadership in those spheres might not transfer their skill and experience to the leadership of the Church. A county Director of Social Services has a large responsibility for the welfare of individuals, leads a large staff and is well accustomed to making strategic decisions to meet need. Might not such a person, with further training in theology and the provision of a theological consultant make a good bishop? The administrator of a large hospital or a university, or of a major charity, might do equally well, and leadership of the right sort in industry or commerce could also have much to offer.

All of which presupposes a different form of episcopate from that currently exercised. There would be little point in withdrawing men and women from influential lay ministry in the secular sphere in order to carry out most of the tasks that now fall to a diocesan bishop. But if, as I propose in the final chapter of this book, the bishop is released to become a pioneer leader in the Christian mission a variety of non-ecclesiastical skills and experience will be an important qualification for episcopal office.

9

The church reformers

Like all living organisms, the Christian Church has survived because of its capacity to change and to adapt to its ever-changing environment. The first-century pioneers of Christianity would be astonished, and almost certainly be appalled, by the shape of the Church's life and many of the patterns of its witness today. But they would not be surprised to find it different from what they had known, because they were conscious of sharing in the life of a faith community designed to be flexible enough to respond to God's promptings and pressures in the years to come. Hopefully they would recognize in the Church of the twenty-first century what they had experienced in the foundation gospel message and the sacraments of Baptism and Holy Communion. The intervening years have seen the Church grow to be a world community of about 1,700 million adherents who express their faith through membership of 25,000 different Christian denominations, having survived long periods of somnolence, corruption and persecution, as well as long periods of extraordinary creativity and powerful influence.

With some notable exceptions, bishops have not been at the forefront of change in the Church. Indeed, more often than not, they have presented an obstacle to change. In this they have not differed markedly from the leaders of other institutions in which that which is most valued is protected rather than put at risk. Thus would-be church reformers have normally been confronted by a solid wall of episcopal opposition which was broken down or bypassed only after many years of heroic endeavour.

By the time the Church of England entered the nineteenth century it was once again in urgent need of radical reform and renewal. The degree to which lethargy and corruption had weakened its witness in the previous century has often been exaggerated, but there can be no doubting that the extraordinary changes in society initiated by the Industrial Revolution, and the questioning of traditional religious faith initiated by the leaders of the Enlightenment from the late seventeenth century onwards, had left the Church far behind and for some years more or less helpless. The Evangelical Revival in the eighteenth century and the

Tractarian Movement in the nineteenth both represented a return to roots – Scripture in the first and Tradition in the second – and both provided the Church with renewed dynamism.

But the process of reformation in the Church's organization, which gathered pace throughout the nineteenth century, was part of a great and remarkable burst of social and economic energy that secured the passing of the first Reform Bill in 1832 and brought about the transformation of virtually every part of English society during the reign of Queen Victoria.

Edward Stanley

Edward Stanley was one of the great episcopal reformers and although he spent only twelve years as Bishop of Norwich (1837–49) – the diocese then comprising not only Norfolk, but also the eastern half of Suffolk – he is said to have changed the religious life of East Anglia. He was a friend of Dr Arnold, the reformer headmaster of Rugby School, and was himself an undoubted liberal in both politics and religion. Not long after his appointment to Norwich he upset many of his fellow bishops with a speech in the House of Lords in which he advocated the relaxation of the Clerical Subscription Act, claiming that few of the clergy subscribed *ex animo* to the Thirty-Nine Articles of Religion and that in any case the Church of England had 'a sort of elasticity' which enabled it to accommodate people with different understandings of the Christian faith. It was an unprepared speech and he was accused of libelling the parish clergy.

Born in 1779, the son of a baronet, Stanley had hoped originally to enter the Royal Navy, but this was forbidden by his father and he went instead to St John's College, Cambridge. He arrived with knowledge of neither Latin nor Greek and with little mathematics, but he worked hard and finished as a maths Wrangler. After a short curacy in Surrey he was presented in 1805 to the family living of Alderley, in Cheshire, where he remained for 32 years. He was a diligent pastor and devoted much time to raising the standard of the schools in the locality and starting infants' schools. Mechanics institutes and temperance societies were also formed, as well as a clerical society to encourage the clergy of the neighbouring parishes to engage in regular study. He sought to mitigate the harsh effects of the unpopular 1834 Poor Law Act by offering to serve as chairman of the local Board of Guardians.

Besides all this Stanley broke new ground by engaging in the study of geology, mineralogy and ornithology and published a two-volume *History of Birds – their Nature, Habits and Instincts*. While most of the bishops were busy opposing the 1832 Reform Bill, he proposed a petition for the inclusion of the Church in its proposals. This got nowhere, but the beginning of church reform was not long to be delayed and Stanley's liberal outlook was also expressed in a series of pamphlets in which he argued for an ending to the hostility between Protestants and Roman Catholics.

The Prime Minister, Lord Melbourne, first offered him the newly formed Bishopric of Manchester, but he declined this on the grounds that his experience was limited to rural life. So he went instead to Norwich, succeeding Henry Bathurst who had died in office aged 93 and left the diocese one of the worst in the country for pluralism, lack of services and general neglect. Anything he did was bound to be an improvement and, starting as he meant to go on, Stanley asked that Dr Arnold be allowed to preach the sermon at his consecration in Lambeth Palace chapel. This was refused by Archbishop Howley on the grounds that it would upset the clergy, but Stanley refused to invite anyone else, so one of Howley's chaplains preached.

The enthronement in Norwich Cathedral was a lively affair that aroused wide interest and much controversy. The mayor and city council, together with the diocesan clergy, were invited and their number was augmented by 1,200 children from Norfolk's charity schools. Each of these contingents carried a banner bearing the name of the school and a good time was had by all, except some local Tories who, because it was the time of a general election, accused Stanley of using the occasion to drum up support for the Whig Lord Melbourne. There was trouble too over the sermon, for the new bishop said *inter alia* that conscientious dissent from the Church of England was neither sinful nor schismatic and that education was so vital to individuals and society that its development must be welcomed even when the motives were not specifically religious. Some described the sermon as heretical and at a welcoming dinner after the service the Reverend Lord Bayning, who proposed the new bishop's health, deliberately neglected to follow the custom of requesting that the sermon be published. An archdeacon thereupon publicly rebuked the Reverend Lord for his neglect, but this only made matters worse for the response was a declaration of disagreement with the preacher and this won loud applause from many of the other guests.

Following the example of Herbert Marsh of Peterborough, who had revived the ancient office of Rural Dean, Stanley appointed no fewer than 70 of these officers who were invited individually to the Bishop's Palace for a meal and to report on the state of church life in their deaneries. As a result of this a number of delinquent clergymen were removed. The rural deans were also used to convey the bishop's wishes to the parishes and Stanley himself, aided by the new railways, visited many of the parishes. His predecessor had conducted mass confirmations at seven-yearly intervals at the main centres of population, but now there were annual confirmations and the parish clergy were instructed to prepare the candidates carefully. Higher academic standards were demanded of ordination candidates. In the course of twelve years 173 parsonages were built to facilitate the residence of the clergy in their parishes and a large number of schools were established. Stanley inspected the schools personally to ensure that adequate standards were reached and maintained and he continued to demonstrate his concern for the humane administration of the Poor Law.

Having taken the diocese by storm, it is hardly surprising that Stanley's reforming zeal provoked opposition during his early days, but gradually the opponents were won over and eventually he had everyone's admiration and affection. He was a regular attender of the House of Lords and proved to be somewhat to the left of most Whigs. At a meeting in Exeter Hall, London, in 1846 he proposed the setting up of socialist villages along lines suggested by J. M. Morgan, a disciple of Robert Owen. These were to comprise 300 to 400 families, with capital provided by a Church of England Self-Supporting Village Society, but since the capital repayment was to be spread over 150 years there were few investors and in the end nothing came of it.

In 1848 Stanley was one of the handful of bishops who shared with Archbishop John Sumner in the controversial consecration of the liberal Renn Dickson Hampden to the Bishopric of Hereford, but in the following year he died suddenly while on holiday in Scotland. The crowds at his funeral were said to be larger than any witnessed in Norwich since the Middle Ages. His son, Arthur Penrhyn Stanley, was a notable reforming Dean of Westminster.

Charles James Blomfield

Charles James Blomfield, Bishop of Chester 1824–28, then of London 1828–56, shared Stanley's reforming zeal and during the years 1834–46 he and the Prime Minister, Sir Robert Peel, changed the life of the Church of England more radically than at any other time since the Reformation. Such a reform was sorely needed.

In 1832 Blomfield wrote to the Archbishop of Canterbury, William Howley, 'It is impossible that the Church (insofar as it is a human institution) can go on as it is.' Throughout the 1820s pressure for reform of the Church's finances, the exercising of patronage, and the organization of dioceses, cathedrals and parishes mounted and the archbishop had introduced three modest reform Bills in the House of Lords in 1831. But all were lost because the peers recognized their inadequacy. The Prime Minister, Lord Grey, thereupon appointed a Commission, of which Blomfield – who had suggested the idea – was a member, to collect statistics and these revealed that no fewer than 4,883 benefices were worth less than £200 per annum. Among the rest were some of very considerable wealth, while many of the bishoprics and cathedrals provided their occupants with a life-style equivalent to that of a modern millionaire. In 1834 Peel, who had succeeded Grey, appointed another Commission, of which again Blomfield was a member, to make proposals for the re-arrangement of the dioceses, the equalization of episcopal stipends, the augmentation of poor benefices and an increase in the number of clergy. This body was permanently constituted as the Ecclesiastical Commission in 1836 and became responsible, with increasing power, for the administration of the Church of England's financial assets.

Blomfield was the main driving force behind this reform. Archbishop Howley cautiously supported the main proposals but was happy to delegate the implementing of them to the Bishop of London. The Archbishop of York, who was also on the Commission, once remarked, 'Till Blomfield comes we all sit and mend our pens and talk about the weather,' while Sydney Smith of St Paul's described his bishop as 'a man of very great ability, humane, placable, generous, munificent, very agreeable, but he has an ungovernable passion for business and a constitutional impetuosity'.

Blomfield's reforming zeal did not however extend to other church and social matters, for he was at heart a conservative. Soon after his translation from Chester to London he asked for the pleasure-ground in St James's Park to be closed on Sunday mornings and he opposed the opening of all places of amusement on Sundays. An invitation to dine with the King one Sunday was declined. When the first Reform Bill was thrown out in 1831 by a majority of 41 – twenty-one bishops being among them – Blomfield was noticeably absent. At his suggestion a government statement about an outbreak of cholera in 1832 was prefaced with a declaration that the pestilence had been sent by God.

Blomfield, the son of a schoolmaster, was born in Bury St Edmunds in 1786. He went from the local grammar school to Trinity College, Cambridge, where he worked himself to the bone and won so many prizes that his education cost his father virtually nothing. He was elected to a fellowship in 1808 and began the publication of a series of classical studies. In 1810 he was ordained by the Bishop of Bristol who, conveniently, was also Master of Trinity College, and after a few months as a curate became Rector, sometimes in plurality, of parishes in Lincolnshire, Buckinghamshire, Suffolk and Essex.

He was a diligent parish priest but the death of his wife a year after their move was a serious blow, though he remarried twelve months later and subsequently had eleven children. In 1820 Lord Bristol – a friend of his father – drew the attention of his brother-in-law, Lord Liverpool, the then Prime Minister, to Blomfield's abilities and in the following year he was appointed to the Crown living of St Botolph's, Bishopsgate, in the City of London. The income was £2,000 (about £56,000 in current money) per annum, and he retained his Essex parish, residing there for three months of the year and, when absent, requiring the curate to send him 'in the vegetable basket' a weekly report on the parish. At St Botolph's, where he ministered to a population of 10,000, his sermons attracted large congregations and he started one of the earliest infants' schools. His responsibilities were increased in 1822 when he was made Archdeacon of Colchester and two years later he published *A Manual of Family Prayers* which had a huge circulation in England and America.

In the same year Blomfield was appointed Bishop of Chester, which was not quite the episcopal post for which he had been hoping. A huge diocese, covering Cheshire, Lancashire and Westmorland, the population in and around Manchester was increasing at a phenomenal rate, but it was one of the worst paid bishoprics. He was therefore allowed to retain St Botolph's, though the journey from Chester to London took five days. Despite his misgivings, he set about the task with characteristic vigour and in his primary charge to the clergy in 1825 called attention to problems that were by no means confined to the Diocese of Chester:

> The poverty of benefices, and the consequent non-residence of incumbents, neglect of churches and glebe houses, and destitution of clerical families; the indifferent character and inadequate salaries of curates; infrequency in the celebration, and irregularity in the performance, of the sacred offices of the Church; the incapacity and negligence of churchwardens; the intrusive zeal of some of the more active clergy and the prevalence of unclerical dress, pursuits, and amusements among others; the use of sham titles, and untrue or careless testimonials to candidates for Orders; the short stay of bishops in the see, owing to its inadequate endowment; and, lastly, as the natural consequence of all the rest, the general obloquy now heaped upon the Church, which is the more stinging because it is in part deserved.

The rest of Blomfield's life was to be devoted to the eradication of these abuses in the Church as a whole and he was not long in displaying a firm hand in Chester. The educational requirements for ordination were raised and all Irish candidates, whose standards had been particularly low, were now refused. Recent Acts of Parliament relating to clerical discipline were strictly enforced; fox-hunting, drunkenness and secular occupations were absolutely forbidden, and clear instructions were given about the conduct of worship. The Book of Common Prayer and its rubrics were to be strictly adhered to: 'If there be any direction for the public service of the Church with which a clergyman cannot conscientiously comply, he is at liberty to withdraw from her ministry but not to violate the solemn compact he made with her.' A young deacon who was reported to be using the sign of the Cross was told in no uncertain terms that he would not be ordained to the priesthood unless he desisted.

Blomfield was very active in the diocese with, someone said, 'an eye for everything and an ear for everybody'. Long neglected Manchester required special attention and huge crowds assembled whenever he preached in the rapidly expanding city. In the course of a ten-day tour of parishes he covered 200 miles and confirmed 8,000 people. Three more expeditions were completed during the next two months, whereupon he retired to his London parish for a Christmas rest. Not all of the Chester clergy were pleased to have so active a bishop who was described by one of them as 'meddlesome, hasty and tyrannical'. Soon after becoming a bishop his portrait was painted and someone remarked that it represented him with a decided frown. 'Yes,' he replied, 'that portrait ought to have been dedicated, without permission, to the non-resident clergy of the diocese of Chester.'

In the House of Lords he was an impressive speaker and a formidable debater. His maiden speech was, to the great displeasure of the Duke of Wellington, devoted to an attack on the proposal for Roman Catholic emancipation (a subject on which he later changed his mind) and, although this incurred the wrath of its proponents, a zealous Cheshire Protestant rewarded him with an enormous cheese. He explained to those who objected to his speech: 'Whatsoever measure threatens the Established Church with a diminution of its property, its privileges and its security is justly regarded by us as hostile to the interests of religion itself.' On the other hand, he voted in favour of the repeal of the Test and Corporation Acts and favoured Dissenters being allowed to have weddings in their own churches. He also found the wearing of an episcopal wig uncomfortable and asked the Bishop of Chichester to raise the matter with the King. But George IV was too conservative in outlook – on some things, anyway – to permit such latitude and wigs had to be worn by bishops a little longer until William IV allowed them to be dispensed with.

In 1828 the death of Archbishop Manners Sutton led to the translation of William Howley from London to Canterbury, and the Duke of Wellington, who cared more for ability than political allegiance, appointed Blomfield as his successor in the capital. The duke was in a hurry and required him to move quickly. The letter offering him the bishopric arrived in Chester one Friday afternoon when Blomfield was arranging to start another tour of his parishes on the following Monday morning. But the horses went south rather than north and the new Bishop of London started almost immediately on a gargantuan task that was to occupy him for the next 28 years.

The population of the County of Middlesex had increased from 818,129 in 1801 to over 1.25 million in 1828, but although some monumental church buildings, paid for by the government, had been erected soon after the Battle of Waterloo, the provision of churches for the overwhelming majority of the poor had hardly increased at all. It was this fact, together with his Chester experience, that moved Blomfield to spearhead the reforms that led to the setting up of the Ecclesiastical Commission. Much of his time was absorbed by this development, but London itself could not be neglected and in 1836 he launched an appeal for a fund to provide new church buildings, schools and endowments. He pointed out that 34 parishes had a combined population of 1,137,000 but the seating capacity of their churches was no more than 101,682 and most of this was located in parish chapels which provided no satisfactory base for pastoral and evangelistic work. Another four parishes had a combined population of 166,000, with only eleven clergy and church capacity of only 8,200. The task before the Church, he declared, was to reclaim the population from 'practical heathenism' and to 'increase the stability of the Church and to promote the cause of social order and religion'. Like his other episcopal colleagues who favoured reform, he was motivated as much by the fear of social unrest leading to revolution as he was by the demands of Christian mission.

The immediate aim was to build 50 new churches and by the end of the first year of the appeal £106,000 had been raised from the rich. But then the gifts began to tail off and associations were formed to encourage local giving. In his 1846 charge Blomfield reported that 44 new churches had been completed, ten were in course of building, two were about to be started and grants had been voted for another seven. This was however still not enough, he declared. At least 400 new churches were needed, since 'more than a million souls are unprovided with the means of grace'. By 1854 £266,000 had been raised and nearly 200 churches built, but he was disappointed that the wealthy did not contribute more. Yet even at the time of their building there were some who questioned the wisdom of his policy. His mind-set was that of an earlier agrarian era in which the provision of a parish church was sufficient to encourage the majority of the members of a village community to share in regular worship. But it was soon noted that London's new churches were often not filled to capacity, and there were those who believed that in a desperate missionary situation the provision of more clergy and lay missioners was the higher priority. By the end of the century many of Blomfield's churches would become millstones around the Church's neck and an impediment to mission. He had not recognized the extent to which the movement of the population from the rural areas to the great industrial cities had created conditions in which alienation from the Church and eventually a secularized outlook would become normal.

Blomfield had many other things on his mind and of these the consequence of the Tractarian Movement proved to be the most troublesome and time-consuming. He had not the slightest sympathy with the Church of Rome which he believed to be 'in a state of schism, if not of apostasy; she has forsaken the true faith and defiled herself with superstition and idolatry'. It followed from this that any move within the Church of England that appeared to be in a Romeward direction was to be firmly resisted. On the other hand, he conceded that the Tractarians had called the Church's attention to certain neglected elements in its life and he took seriously the clergyman who wrote to him and complained that the average church service was 'blank, dismal, oppressive and dreary'.

His campaign for greater efficiency in the Church's life was not confined to England. As Bishop of London he had jurisdiction over all Church of England clergymen who had no bishop of their own. The expansion of overseas missionary work during the nineteenth century increased the number of these considerably since there were in 1840 only five colonial bishoprics. As a result of Blomfield's initiative five more were created and a fund was established for the endowment of others.

While on a visit to the Queen at Osborne House in 1847, Blomfield had a fall which did not at first seem to have caused more than the bruising of his head. But paralysis of the right side of his face followed and required him to be off duty for five months. When he returned his mental vigour and business capacity seemed undiminished, but never again was he fully himself. Nonetheless he remained in office until 1856, when a Bill to facilitate the retirement and fix the pensions of Bishops of London was rushed through Parliament. By this time he was helpless and died in August of the following year.

Samuel Wilberforce

What Blomfield started, Samuel Wilberforce (Bishop of Oxford 1845–69, then of Winchester 1869–73) continued and developed with no less zeal. Archbishop Tait said that he 'changed the face of the Church of England'. Burgon described him as 'the remodeller of the episcopate', and one of the bishops who entered into his inheritance complained, 'He left us with no time to do anything.' Certainly the combination of vision, hard work and administrative skill which he applied to the over-large and hitherto sleepy Diocese of Oxford effected remarkable changes. Confirmations and ordinations were conducted with greater dignity; rural deans were instructed to convene regular chapter meetings, which the bishop himself would address from time to time; a theological college was opened at Cuddesdon and a teacher training college at Culham; over 100 new churches were built, while another 250 were either rebuilt or restored; many church schools and vicarages were erected; the stipends of the poorer clergy were improved; and over £50 million in today's currency was raised to finance these projects.

The son of William Wilberforce, the great emancipator of slaves, he shared his father's concern for the poor and the oppressed. Although a Tory, he was highly critical of the new industrial society which, he said, made men greedy, selfish and unequal. It was only to be expected that the workers would form organizations to fight for an improvement in their lot. So he urged the clergy to become involved in social reform and work for better sanitary laws, prison reform, a more humane Poor Law and the abolition of blood sports. He himself led the bishops who shared in the battle for the repeal of the Corn Laws in 1846, and of all the bishops of his time he had the clearest insights into what was happening in a rapidly changing society. And he believed that the dangerous social dislocation created by the huge gap between rich and poor was due to the failure of the complacent Church during the Georgian era. What is more, he often declared, the contemporary Church was doing nothing to bridge the gap; indeed it only reinforced the class structure. Yet Wilberforce was no radical social reformer. He simply wanted the nation to recover the values and the stability of its pre-Industrial Revolution past – which was of course impossible.

He was one of several Victorian church leaders who coped with tragic bereavement by throwing themselves into unceasing activity in the cause of reform, and in his case zeal was enhanced by unusual eloquence. It was inevitable that such a bishop should make enemies, and some of the enmity was due to what appeared to be unbridled ambition and a degree of intellectual evasiveness that caused him to be known as 'Soapy Sam'. His reputation was badly damaged by a speech in 1860 at a meeting of the British Association for the Advancement of Science held in Oxford. The subject under discussion was Darwin's recently published *Origin of Species* and in a misplaced joke Wilberforce enquired of the evolutionists: 'Is it on your grandmother's side that you claim descent from the apes?' In the audience was the scientist T. H. Huxley who rose to his feet and declared in a quiet dignified voice, 'I would rather be descended from an ape than from a man highly endowed by nature and possessed of great means of influence, and yet who employs these faculties and that influence for the mere purpose of introducing ridicule into a grave scientific discussion.' The cheers that followed indicated clearly that Wilberforce had seriously misjudged his audience.

He was born in 1805, the year of the Battle of Trafalgar. Like many evangelicals of that time his father, much involved in national affairs, was opposed to public schools, regarding them as hotbeds of vice, so young Samuel was educated privately until he went to Oriel College, Oxford, as a commoner in 1823. In spite of devoting much time to hunting, he took a first in mathematics and a second in classics, and in the infant Oxford Union cultivated the art of extempore speech taught him by his father. In 1828 he was made deacon and immediately appointed curate-in-charge of Checkendon, near Henley-on-Thames. After two years there he moved to become Rector of the small, attractive parish of Brighstone on the Isle of Wight. There he remained for ten years, earning a fine reputation as a zealous parish priest, a good organizer and an eloquent preacher. His diary recorded on 18 January 1831 – 'A good Audit Dinner. 23 people drank 11 bottles of wine, 28 quarts of beer, 2½ of spirits and 12 bowls of punch; and would have drunk twice as much if not restrained. None, we hope, drunk.'

In 1839 his cousin, Bishop Charles Sumner, broke his rule that only evangelicals were to be given appointments in Winchester diocese and made him Archdeacon of Surrey, adding to this in the following year a lucrative Canonry of Winchester Cathedral. At about the same time he moved from Brighstone to Alverstoke – a richer living near Portsmouth. Appointment as a chaplain to the Prince Consort marked the beginning of his influence at the Court.

But then tragedy stuck. In March 1841 his wife Emily died. They had fallen in love when he was fifteen and she only thirteen, and he was devastated by her death, though the inheritance of her estate turned him into a wealthy landowner. In 1843 he became Sub-Almoner to Queen Victoria and two years later, at her request, was appointed Dean of Westminster. But after only five months at Westminster he became Bishop of Oxford – the Prime Minister, Sir Robert Peel, describing him as 'the divine best entitled by professional character and merit to preferment'. Wilberforce accepted gladly but then wrote, 'I had wished for this and now that it comes it seems awful.' Nonetheless he buckled in and achieved wonders.

He also continued to play a prominent part in the national life of the Church. The Tractarians came to regard him as their leader, though he was fiercely opposed to any tendencies towards Romanizing and described the Roman Catholic Church as 'that great Cloaca into which all abominations naturally run'. His views on other subjects were also singular. He said that he never entered a railway carriage without reflecting that he might never leave it alive. Attendance at the theatre or opera disqualified a man from ordination. Family pews were defended on the grounds that they helped families to worship together 'in due order'.

As Lord High Almoner, Wilberforce served as chaplain to the House of Lords and was also active in its debates, confining himself mainly to church matters but deploying his eloquence on political and social questions when he believed Christian comment to be called for. He became a close friend of Mr Gladstone and when in 1862 the Archbishopric of York became vacant Gladstone strongly supported his translation, adding for good measure, 'Those who think he meddles too much in London would gladly see him removed to a spot where he would no longer be within an hour of the Metropolis.' But Palmerston, the Prime Minister, did not like his High Church views, so Wilberforce was disappointed, as he was destined to be six years later when the Archbishopric of Canterbury fell vacant. It was generally expected that Wilberforce would go to the primacy on the death of Longley, but he had been too critical of Disraeli and the appointment went instead to A. C. Tait. Had Longley's bronchitis lasted for another six weeks, by which time Disraeli had been succeeded by Gladstone, Wilberforce would almost certainly have been preferred to Tait.

It was then anticipated that he would succeed Tait at London, but the consolation prize had to be Winchester, from which Sumner eventually retired in 1869 after 40 years in office. Although Sumner had been a reformer, his zeal had flagged considerably during his later years and fast-developing South London, which was still in Winchester diocese, was virtually untouched by the Church. Wilberforce recognized that this would make heavy demands on his time and energy and, soon after his arrival in his new diocese, announced that he would take on no outside work. He kept to this for a time, but he was a national figure and before long was on his travels again. An immediate problem was the lack of an episcopal residence, because Sumner was still living in Farnham Castle as part of his retirement deal and Wolvesey Palace in Winchester, having been deemed unsuitable for geographical reasons and for want of drains, was let to a new teacher training college. This left Wilberforce only with Winchester House in London and it was from there that he ruled the diocese. It turned out to be an arrangement that suited him well, for he was bound to spend much time organizing new parishes and buildings in South London, and the House of Lords continued to claim much of his time.

During the year following his enthronement at Winchester, however, he had two heart attacks, the second of which was at first thought to have been fatal. But he recovered and continued to drive himself ceaselessly. An account by a local vicar of a visit to Ringwood Deanery in Hampshire in February 1871 tells a not untypical story:

> The Bishop spent a week among us in this Deanery. He came to hold an Ordination at Ringwood, to confirm in several churches, to be the life and soul of parochial missions held simultaneously in the four towns and some of the villages of the Deanery, and to make acquaintance with our leading laymen by staying at as many of their houses as time would permit. The list of engagements I arranged for him under these various heads – episcopal, social, evangelistic – is now before me and is simply appalling. He had stipulated that we should spare him after-dinner work; but this was not always practicable, and he was frequently in harness morning, noon and night.

The amount of work he accomplished was phenomenal. The development of the railway enabled him to travel more easily, though many of his journeys were still undertaken by coach or on horseback. On the map he carried with him he underscored in red the parishes in which he officiated and it was not long before the original map was almost completely obliterated by red marks. And he was a great letter-writer. On his first visit to the Channel Islands in August 1870 he travelled via France and on arrival in Jersey the governor handed him 160 letters which had been forwarded from London. All received a personal handwritten reply. He would not employ a secretary because he wanted his letters to be personal and on train journeys often made use of a small mobile desk, dating these letters from 'The Train'.

On the national scene he was responsible for piloting through Parliament a Bill that enabled the clergy to resign from their parishes if incapacitated by age or infirmity, and he also proposed in the Convocation of Canterbury the setting up of a committee to carry out a revision of the Authorized Version of the New Testament on conservative lines. On 19 July 1873 however he was in his London house feeling lonely, worn out and depressed, and after spending some time writing in the Athenaeum readily accepted the invitation of Lord Granville, the Foreign Secretary, to travel with him by train to Leatherhead and then ride together on the Surrey downs. This he was greatly enjoying when the horse he had been loaned stumbled causing its rider to turn a complete somersault and be killed by the fall. The news of his dramatic death captured the headlines of the national newspapers and *The Times* declared his loss to be near irreparable. In a remarkable tribute, Mr Gladstone wrote:

> I ask whether it is an exaggeration to say that the name and character of Bishop Wilberforce ever must stand high among the whole army of diocesan Bishops; not of this country only, but of the whole Christian

world, and not of this generation only, but also of the generations that have preceded it. I desire, at least, to avoid using the language of exaggeration, but there is no word adequate to describe the incessant, the unflagging labours of the Bishop throughout the 28 years for which, as his epitaph with noble simplicity records, he was a Bishop in the Church of God.

The size of the monument erected in his memory in Winchester Cathedral, where it occupies the greater part of the south transept, would doubtless have pleased him, but he may not have liked the verdict of Owen Chadwick, written a century later – 'He almost failed to attain his destiny because he saw it too clearly and pursued it too consciously.' T. H. Huxley was more cruel: on hearing of his old adversary's death, he said 'For once, reality and his brain came into contact and the result was fatal.'

Leslie Hunter

There was no-one in the Wilberforce mould during the twentieth century, though there were some bishops who saw the need for church reform and devoted much of their episcopal ministry to the cause of change. The most wide-ranging and prophetic church reformer among them was Leslie Hunter, Bishop of Sheffield 1939–62. When Archbishop Temple died in 1944 his mantle of Christian social concern and church reform fell on Hunter, who had none of Temple's charisma and was only an indifferent speaker. Small of stature, slightly built, and with thick brows over his brooding eyes, his appearance was formidable – sinister, even. Moreover he was sharp-tongued and certainly not a man to pick a quarrel with. Neither did he have easy social graces – encounters with him were apt to be punctuated by long silences. His wife explained: 'If he has nothing to say, he says nothing.' Yet no other diocese in the Church of England was in his time – or since – more forward-looking. He attracted clergy of unusual ability to work with him, and his loyalty to them and support of their varied ministries won their lasting gratitude and affection.

Arrival in Sheffield less than a month after the outbreak of war confirmed in his mind what he knew already, namely that the industrial working class was alienated from the life of the Church. There could be no doubting this – the facts and figures, not least in Sheffield, spoke for themselves. The primary concern of Hunter's 23-year-long episcopate was with this problem, and his vision was expressed succinctly in a 1946 Oxford lecture:

The Church of England should be a Church of the people – a home where the poor, the sensitive, the exploited and the revolutionary, as well as the conservative, are at home.

Born in 1890, Hunter was the son of a famous Scottish liberal Congregational preacher, but Alpine holidays brought him into contact with Anglican chaplaincies and an appreciation of Anglican worship. At New College, Oxford, he took a first in theology and during his time there was greatly influenced by the theology of F. D. Maurice and the friendship of Baron von Hügel – a Roman Catholic scholar and mystic. On coming down from Oxford in 1913 he was confirmed in the Church of England and joined the staff of the Student Christian Movement, first as its Travelling Secretary for Theological Colleges, then as its Bible Study Secretary. Like many of his generation, the influence of the SCM remained with him for the rest of his life.

In 1915 he published his first book *The Artist and Religion* in which he reflected on his work among student artists and his own one-time ambition to become a painter. In the event, he became a brilliant pianist, specializing in the music of Mozart. During 1916 he spent several months with the YMCA in France, ministering to soldiers, and in the same year was ordained. He now became involved in an interdenominational enquiry into the religious faith and practice of ordinary soldiers which, when published in 1919, revealed the huge gulf between the Church and working-class soldiers. He remained with the SCM until early in 1921 when, out of the blue, he received a letter from the Vicar of St Martin-in-the-Fields, Dick Sheppard, inviting him to join his staff, with special responsibility for the chaplaincy of the nearby Charing Cross Hospital. He accepted and was immediately captivated by Dick Sheppard's personality and ideas, but his stay at St Martin's was short, for in March 1922 he became a canon of Newcastle upon Tyne Cathedral. His brief was, besides routine cathedral duties, to engage in work with students and other young people, which he did, but he was also drawn by the acute poverty of post-war Tyneside – particularly bad housing and ill-health – to become involved in social work. A visit to Newcastle by the Cathedral Commissioners elicited from him the opinion that 'weekday Evensong is an unjustifiable waste of time'.

There was little opportunity to waste time in the parish of Barking, to which Hunter moved in 1926. Once a small country town, Barking now had a population of over 50,000 and had been incorporated into East London. Although 80 per cent of the parishioners went to the ancient parish church or to one of the three mission churches for their marriages and baptisms, only 1.6 per cent were on the electoral roll as regular churchgoers. Hunter, who had a large staff of curates, threw himself into what he saw to be a missionary task and became deeply involved in the life of the whole community, making housing, smoke-abatement and unemployment his special concerns. He introduced the Parish Communion as the main act of Sunday worship (an unusual innovation at that time), published a first-class parish magazine, and carried out an extensive restoration of the parish church. But, lacking the common touch, he found it difficult to get alongside ordinary people and after four years was driven by ill-health to resignation. Part of his time of recuperation was spent in the writing of *A Parson's Job* (1931) which, although based on limited personal experience, offered a wide and inspiring insight into parish life in industrial areas. He was the first to advocate team ministries for such areas.

In 1931, his health partly recovered, Hunter returned to the North-East as Archdeacon of Northumberland. Besides the care of his large archdeaconry, which covered the southern half of Northumberland including Tyneside, he was again active in the life of the cathedral, using it as the base for much educational work. The parish clergy tended to have mixed feelings about him for, although he strongly supported them he was not always able to conceal his impatience with their reluctance to move in new directions. Dark features and the traditional sombre garb of a dignitary led some to describe him as 'the black archdeacon'.

In the social field, he remained concerned about unemployment – 75,000 Tynesiders were out of work in 1935 – and as chairman of the Tyneside Council of Social Service he led a long-remembered major effort to alleviate the distress this created. In a letter to *The Times* in support of the 1936 Jarrow march he pointed out that this was a clear expression of a whole community's deep sense of frustration and despair. He added:

> The march from Jarrow ought therefore to impress those who live in happier areas that, while there has been much talking and some window-dressing on the part of the Government, little has yet been done to share or to remove the burden – while depression and unemployment remain on a vast scale.

He was a delegate to the 1937 Oxford Conference on Church, Community and State, and during the late 1930s was much involved in a campaign which advocated radical reform in the deployment and payment of the clergy. He had launched this campaign and wrote most of its two publications – *Men, Money and Ministry* (1937) and *Putting our House in Order* (1941) – but another 30 years were to pass before their proposals were implemented.

'Oh no! Not Sheffield!' was his wife's response when in 1939 a letter from the Prime Minister, Neville Chamberlain, was opened. Neither of them wished to go there, but friends urged acceptance and the ministry that followed proved them right. Hunter inherited a somewhat slack regime and the Church's links with civic life and the steel industry were insignificant. Hunter immediately initiated a thorough reorganization of the diocese, including an executive body with several lay members and a board of women's work. Gifted young clergy were brought in to tackle tough jobs, but heavy wartime bombing of Sheffield and the loss of many able priests to services chaplaincies delayed root-and-branch renewal. Six churches were destroyed and twelve churches and 40 vicarages damaged. Nonetheless, over £200,000 of capital was raised in 1944 and this sustained the work of the diocese over the next decade.

Hunter defended the rights of those who had conscientious objections to military service and described the indiscriminate bombing of German cities as 'sickening', though he recognized the military necessity. 'Humbug' was his verdict on the official explanations put forward to justify the dropping of atomic bombs on Hiroshima and Nagasaki in 1945. When the end of the war came within sight he began to look ahead to the rebuilding of church life in Germany, and in 1946 went with Bishop George Bell on the first official visit of churchmen to the British Zone of Germany. Thereafter he devoted much time to the welfare of German prisoners-of-war in Europe, and also of Europe's many refugees. Antisemitism was, he believed, a persistent evil that Christians should do everything to eradicate.

In the *Diocesan Review* for August 1949 Hunter looked back over his ten years in Sheffield and outlined a strategy for the decade to come – (1) More committed Christians needed to share actively in the life of industry and the local community; (2) More men and women to be recruited to the full-time service of the Church; (3) Money to be raised for more ordinands 'in order to penetrate, influence and evangelize the 90 per cent of people outside the Church'; (4) The laity to be stimulated to show more concern for the work of the Church outside their own parishes; (5) Greater concern for the development of Christian groups outside the parochial system – in spheres such as trade unions, hospitals, universities and schools; (6) More assistance in church administration to increase the efficiency of the diocesan office and facilitate local mission. Announcing this strategy was predictably easier than carrying it out in a Church where attitudes and structures were still largely resistant to change. Back in 1940 Hunter had said in a diocesan festival sermon:

For the Church to go forward unplanned, unco-ordinated, with its economy still in the stagecoach era, will be a betrayal of the cause committed to us . . . Absolute freehold and indefensible inequalities

between benefices have tended to produce a temper which is at vari-
ance with the idea of Christian community in the New Testament.

By the time of his retirement 22 years later most inequalities of stipend
had gone, but the parson's freehold remained a major obstacle to effective pastoral reorganization, even though he had succeeded in establishing a few team ministries. On the positive side, however, the opening
in 1953 of a diocesan conference house for the primary purposes of considering church and society issues, and in 1961 a youth training centre
to organize courses for young industrial workers, were major achievements. And nowhere in the Church of England was there greater awareness of the nature and magnitude of the missionary task that needed to
be tackled.

Here the partnership between Hunter and Ted Wickham proved to be
of critical importance. From the outset of his episcopate Hunter sought
to build bridges between the Church and industry, only to find most
of his efforts rebuffed by shop-floor workers who, with good reason,
were distrustful of the Church. In 1944 however he created the opportunity to appoint Wickham for a period of two years to discover if
there might be a full-time job for a priest on the shop-floors of the
major steel works. Ten years later the Sheffield Industrial Mission had an
international reputation and other dioceses also had industrial missions,
though none on the scale of Sheffield.

Wickham's brilliant leadership was responsible for this, but it could
not have been accomplished without Hunter's firm backing. He prepared
the way, raised the initial funding, kept in close touch with developments
through frequent meetings with the mission team, defended it against
attack from within the Church, and offered constant encouragement as
well as searching questions. This association continued informally after
his retirement, but it could not save the mission from the destructive
influence of his pietist successor.

With the passage of the years Hunter became increasingly involved
in the life of the wider Church and at some periods as much as one-
third of his time was spent away from the diocese. His vision and gifts
were sorely needed elsewhere. William Temple College, Rugby, which
he played a large part in founding as a centre for the study of church
and society issues, then serving as its chairman, had a large claim on
his time. So did Christian Reconstruction in Europe, which later became
Inter-Church Aid and Refugee Service, then Christian Aid. He gave a
decade to the chairmanship of the Church of England's Board for Wom-
en's Work and was largely responsible for the setting up of a Board for
Social Responsibility, with a strong Industrial Committee. In the Church
Assembly he supported liturgical change, the introduction of synodical

government and proposals for Anglican–Methodist reunion, though he said it was unlikely that any of these would assist the Christian mission in a secular society. On the eve of his retirement he concluded, sadly – 'The Church of England is not yet organized to be the Church militant on English earth.' He took his membership of the House of Lords very seriously and of the 41 debates in which he took part eleven were concerned with international relations. The advent of the Welfare State won his approval, though he was often at pains to stress the importance of the voluntary principle.

Retirement when he became 70 was by no means the end of his work and influence, and it turned out that another 21 years of life lay ahead of him. He continued to chair various committees, served on a commission on Crown Appointments in the Church of England, and added to his literary output (he had already written eleven books) by editing a well-received book on the Scandinavian Churches, of which he had considerable first-hand knowledge, and a volume of essays *The English Church: A New Look* in which he urged the more effective use of retired bishops.

During the last 30 years much time has been devoted to the revision of the Church's forms of worship and, following the publication in 2000 of *Common Worship*, it will be a relief to everyone, apart from the professional liturgists, if time is now given to absorption of the changes. Familiarity is a vital aspect of all forms of devotion – corporate and personal. During the primacy of Archbishop George Carey some attention has also been given to the Church's central administration with an Archbishops Council established to provide a sense of direction and to formulate policy. This has proved however to be an undistinguished and uninspiring body that commands little confidence in the Church as a whole, and it is fortunate that its ventures into the realm of policy-making have been few in number.

The truth is that the most significant and urgent reforms are required at diocesan, rather than national, level and in the role of the episcopate. These two must go together, but it is difficult to see how radical changes can be made in the better use of the reduced, but still considerable, resources available to a diocese without the dynamic leadership of a bishop who is free from many of his present administrative chores and pastoral demands and given time to think, consult and plan. For, although important twentieth-century changes have given the whole Church a stronger voice in decision-making, the Church of England remains an episcopal church and the temperature of reform, and much else, in a diocese is still controlled by its episcopal thermostat. Unless the bishop sees the need for change and leads the way towards change it will not happen. In this the Church differs little from other institutions.

It is essential therefore that those appointed to bishoprics be flexible enough to embrace change gladly and have the insight and energy to lead their diocese in the direction required for the expression of the Christian faith in today's ever-changing world. No more than in the realms of politics and business can the Church progress, or even survive, without such leadership. Many, perhaps all, of the Church of England's present bishops recognize the need for change in the way in which their own ministry is exercised. They are unlikely to agree on what these changes should be and not all have the insight, courage and drive to embark on a programme of radical reform.

This should not however inhibit the initiation of such a reform in those dioceses where the bishop is willing and able to provide the necessary leadership. Indeed, there is much to be said for an experimental approach in a handful of dioceses from which the rest can eventually learn. Some of the reforms urgently needed are discussed in the final chapter of this volume, but it is to be expected – and hoped – that there will be variety from diocese to diocese, since situations vary, as do the people involved in them.

Critical to success, however defined, in all church reform is an outward- rather than an inward-looking approach. Archbishop Geoffrey Fisher's commitment to the revision of canon law in the 1950s was a disastrous waste of time and a diversion from the real task facing the Church in the immediate post-war era. Most of the real reforms proposed belatedly in the 1960s were then frustrated in their true intentions because, having initially been opposed by the conservatives in the Church, they were eventually embraced by them and modifed to suit the supposed requirements of a Church which had averted its gaze from the more fundamental changes taking place in the world it was called to serve. At the present critical moment in world history it is not easy to propose further reform of the internal life of the Church, but it is difficult to see how the Church can contribute much of significance to human affairs unless some of these changes are made.

The world can never determine the whole of the Church's agenda since the Christian community has a gospel to proclaim, but any movement for reform which does not take account of the life of the community outside the church door is doomed to failure. Worldly as well as devout bishops are therefore needed and, since God is as active in the world as he is in the Church, there is no conflict between these twin aspects of episcopal ministry.

10

The social reformers

The notion that bishops and other church leaders have no business to be involved in the social, economic and political concerns of their nation is a modern one. The earliest Christians inherited the Jewish beliefs about the unity of religion and society, although their minority position in the ancient world gave them little opportunity to express these beliefs, apart from refusal to take part in war. But after the conversion of the Emperor Constantine in the fourth century Christian bishops became much involved in the administration of the Roman Empire. St Augustine, who was Bishop of Hippo in North Africa in the fifth century, emphasized in his great work *The City of God*, written shortly after the sack of Rome, that although Christians were involved in a pilgrimage to a better world, in which they would be closer to God, they must not neglect their responsibilities for the governance of the present world.

In Anglo-Saxon England most of the kings were Christian and many employed bishops as court advisers. Alfred, one of the greatest of all English kings, governed in accordance with his deeply held Christian convictions and gave his bishops an important role in society as well as in the Church. So this continued throughout the Middle Ages. Church and state were totally integrated and the model of the human body, with its separate but dependent organs, was often used to illustrate the closeness of the relationship. The bishops of the Reformation era were at the heart of both the religious and the political turmoil, and the execution of Archbishop Laud in 1645 was as much for political as for religious reasons, since it was still impossible to separate the two in the life of the nation.

After the Commonwealth experience however political theory became increasingly secularized and church and state were officially separated, with the Church reduced to a subordinate position. The Establishment remained however and episcopal appointments, made increasingly by politicians, were designed to guarantee support for the government. No-one doubted that bishops had a political role and it seemed natural that they should spend as much time in the House of Lords as in their dioceses. During the eighteenth century the development of politico-economic ideas was largely the work of clergymen. William Fleetwood, a fellow of King's College, Cambridge, who later became a notable Bishop of Ely, wrote the first scientific treatise on price, while T. R. Malthus, a curate at Albury in Surrey, was also a professor of economics. The philosopher-bishops George Berkeley and Joseph Butler had much to say about the relationship between politics and morality, and the universities continued to see the quest for truth as embracing every aspect of life, with no division between the secular and the sacred.

Throughout the eighteenth and early nineteenth centuries the bishops, closely linked to the aristocratic element in society, emphasized in their preaching the hierarchical character of society and sought to demonstrate that this was God-given. Sir George Pretyman Tomline, Bishop of Lincoln 1787–1820, then Bishop of Winchester until 1827, but better known as secretary and adviser to William Pitt the Younger, said on the eve of the French Revolution –

> Subordination of ranks, and the relation of magistrate and subjects, are indispensably necessary in that state of society for which our Creator has evidently intended the human species . . . Whoever weakens and threatens the existing social and political structure by his words or by his actions sins against the ordinance of God.

Long after this understanding of the social order had come under serious political challenge in Britain most of the bishops continued to defend it. Thus 21 out of 26 of them were among the 40 members of the House of Lords who defeated the Reform Bill in 1831. Only two voted in its favour and rioting mobs assailed bishops in the streets, burnt effigies of them and attacked their palaces. When the Bill returned to a newly elected Parliament in 1832 more bishops had discerned the writing on the nation's wall and eleven of them now supported it, but twelve still voted against reform.

As the nineteenth century advanced, however, and the bishops became more involved in their dioceses there came a growing concern for the plight of the poor, particularly in the new industrial towns and cities. At first this concern arose primarily from dismay at the extent to which the appalling social conditions hindered the work of the Church among the labouring classes. Men, women and children who worked fourteen or more hours a day for six days a week were too exhausted to attend church on Sundays. Families living in overcrowded tenements, without sanitation and open to the constant threat of disease, did not respond readily to the ministrations of their parish clergyman who lived comfortably in a fine rectory and, all too often, was afraid to visit them for fear of exposure to deadly infections. Methodism was far more successful in enlisting their support.

Later some of the bishops urged their clergy to work for the physical as well as the spiritual improvement of their parishioners and to become involved in movements for better working conditions, housing, sanitation and education. Christian charity demanded no less than this; so also did the fear of revolution. The more discerning bishops noted that poverty and a growing sense of injustice were providing the Chartist and Socialist movements with an ever-increasing supply of recruits and that these movements were seeking not greater generosity from the rich but rather a radical reordering of society. Such a reordering was not on the agendas of the bishops who were afraid of the possible influence in Britain of the anti-religious revolutionary movements at work in continental Europe and hoped that Christian charity and a modicum of social reform would enable the nation to return to the stable, contented social order of the pre-Industrial Revolution years.

James Fraser

There were however a few exceptions, including James Fraser, Bishop of Manchester 1870–86. Manchester was at that time among the most important and most difficult of dioceses. The city was at the heart of Britain's new industrial life. Throughout the century its population had grown at a phenomenal rate, creating a multitude of new and seemingly intractable social and religious problems. The Church of England was much too late in facing the challenge to its ancient agrarian parochial system presented by the inhuman factories and mills and the soulless streets and tenements. It was not until a new Diocese of Manchester was created in 1847 that more than a handful of new churches were built. The first bishop, James Prince Lee, did something to remedy this, but his autocratic style did not win the hearts of Lancashire's toiling masses.

For his successor the Prime Minister, W. E. Gladstone, did what no modern Crown Appointments Commission would ever dream of doing: he went to the small Berkshire village of Ufton Nervet where for the last four years a burly, red-haired and somewhat impetuous priest was faithfully and happily exercising a strong pastoral ministry and farming his glebe. True, James Fraser had taken a first in classics at Oxford and for seven years been a fellow of Oriel College. In his previous Wiltshire parish he had accepted responsibility for the supervision of ordination candidates in Salisbury diocese and also served on a Royal Commission on Education. More recently he had served on another commission which investigated the Employment of Children, Young Persons and Women in Agriculture. But of industrial England he knew nothing and his experience of leadership in the Church extended no further than that required by two remote rural parishes. Yet at the time of his death, fifteen years after accepting with great trepidation Gladstone's offer, Fraser was the best-known and most highly respected man in Lancashire. On the day of his funeral many businesses in Manchester closed, the Cotton Exchange, for the first time ever, ceased trading for several hours, many thousands lined the streets as MPs, mayors and magistrates from all parts of Lancashire went in procession from the town hall to the cathedral. Later a statue, paid for by public subscription, was erected in his memory in Albert Square. He was one of the nineteenth century's greatest bishops.

Gladstone chose him because of his interest in and mastery of education – one of the controversial issues of the time; and his hesitancy, mainly because of feelings of inadequacy, having been overcome through the unanimous advice of nine friends, he wrote a long and remarkable letter of acceptance to Gladstone in which he outlined his personal beliefs and aspirations:

> As little of a dogmatist as it is possible to be, I yet see the use, and indeed the necessity of dogma; but I have always wished to narrow rather than extend its field, because the less peremptorily articles of faith are imposed or defined the more hope there is of eliciting agreements rather than differences. Especially have I been anxious to see the Church adapt herself more genially and trustfully to the intellectual aspirations of the age, not standing aloof in a timorous or hostile attitude from the spirit of scientific enquiry, but rather endeavouring (as is her function) to temper its ardour with the spirit of reverence and godly fear. And, finally, my great desire will be, without disguising my own opinions, or wishing one set of minds to understand me in one sense and another in the opposite, to throw myself on *the heart* of the whole diocese, of the laity as well as of the clergy, of those who differ from the Church as well as those who conform to her. I have a high ideal of what a bishop of the Church of England ought to be, and though I am never likely to attain to it, I can at least keep it steadily before my eyes and reach after it.

This is precisely what he did. Possessed of enormous energy, he threw himself into the task and maintained its momentum for fifteen years. One of the conditions of accepting Gladstone's offer was that he would not be required to live in distant Mauldreth Hall, and, having established himself in a modest rectory in the Cheetham district of Manchester, he invariably travelled about the city on foot, carrying his robes in a blue case and whenever time permitted pausing to speak to others on the streets. In his early days he achieved fame by seizing and stopping a runaway horse and cart, and was loudly cheered for his effort when he arrived late at a mass meeting about compulsory education.

In his first speech to the diocesan conference he said, 'Our Church must show that in her wide and tolerant bosom every legitimate form of Christianity may find a home.' It took him only a few weeks to decide that if ever the Church was to fulfil its mission it must engage much more closely with the working class and the poorest in society. The degree of poverty he encountered was reflected in an address he gave to working men's wives in 1873:

> You must not allow any child of nine or ten, when he brings home his wages, to see that you spend them all on yourselves and let him go half-starved. This I know is done in numberless cases.

He became involved in virtually every organization concerned with social work and the improvement of the human lot and was in constant demand for sermons and speeches, often as many as six or seven in a day. In 1874, when arbitrators failed to agree over a wages claim by painters against their employers, he was called in to act as umpire and made an award which both sides accepted. During a cotton strike in north-east Lancashire in 1878 the operatives proposed that the bishop should adjudicate, but the employers refused. A dispute involving agricultural workers led him to ask in a published letter:

> Are the farmers of England mad? Fair wages will have to be paid to the labourer. If farmers can't afford fair wages at present, rents must come down – an unpleasant thing no doubt for those who will spend the rent of a 300-acre farm on a single ball, or a pair of high-stepping horses, but nevertheless inevitable.

This brought him a mountain of letters – some abusive, others grateful – and a public rebuke from his neighbour, the evangelical Bishop J. C. Ryle of Liverpool. He strongly supported the infant trades union and co-operative movements and there was no subject on which he did not have an opinion. Within a short time of his arrival in Manchester he was recognized as a leader whose views could not be ignored. A friend wrote, 'He's like a chestnut horse and never wants whip or spur. He seems to enjoy as a luxury bursting the trammels which should hedge a Bishop.' After a speech in the House of Lords supporting the admission of Nonconformists to Oxford and Cambridge colleges another friend, Dean Stanley, said, 'Well! You do verge on the imprudent more than any man I know.'

Fraser was born in 1818 in the Gloucestershire village of Prestbury to which his father had retired, having made a lot of money as a merchant in India. When he was only fourteen, however, his father died and by this time the Indian profits had been lost on unwise speculation and the family was left very poor. Young James was sent to Staffordshire to be brought up by his solicitor uncle, and at Shrewsbury School won a scholarship to Lincoln College, Oxford. There he had little money to sustain much of a social life and was driven to a spartan existence and the ways of a recluse. Relief came with appointment to an Oriel fellowship and his income now allowed him to indulge his passion for riding, but, having decided that field sports were not desirable for anyone in Holy Orders, he spent a final fortnight hunting in Leicestershire before his own ordination in 1846.

On becoming a priest in the following year he accepted appointment to the college living at Cholderton – no-one else wanted it – while retaining his fellowship to augment the meagre benefice income. The parish, on the northern edge of Salisbury Plain, was no more than a hamlet, but Fraser kept himself busy. He completed the building of a new church, which had been started by his predecessor, added a new coach house to the rectory, enlarged the stable and built a schoolroom. Bishop Hamilton of Salisbury also found him things to do as one of his examining chaplains. The Royal Commission on Education which he joined in 1858 involved the surveying of schools in several counties and his report, which won high praise, brought him to the attention of Gladstone and other members of the government.

After twelve years at Colderton, he moved to another Oriel living – Ufton Nervet – a small hamlet about eight miles east of Reading. There he built a new church to replace the decayed mediaeval building and in 1865 was invited to serve on a commission charged with reporting on the educational system and schools of the United States. The voyage to New York took just under nine days and he was away from April to October. His report, submitted in 1886, enhanced his reputation as an able man and in December of that year he was offered the Bishopric of Calcutta. This he declined on the grounds that he felt too old at 48, that the climate would not suit him, that he was providing a home for his mother and that he was no linguist. From July 1868 to January 1869 he was involved in a commission on rural employment and his report emphasized the importance of breaking down distinctions of caste in rural communities. He also called attention to an experiment in co-operative farming and the setting up of a co-operative store, both of which greatly impressed him.

Although Fraser's liberal outlook sometimes led his enemies to describe him as a latitudinarian, he was in fact a High Churchman of the pre-Tractarian era. He was much influenced by the thought of the sixteenth-century divine Richard Hooker, and shared his vision of the Church of England as the Church of the whole nation, occupying a position between the extremes of Roman and evangelical polity based on tradition evaluated by sound learning. During his years at Manchester he enjoyed very cordial relations with the Dissenters who, towards the end of his life, described him as 'The Bishop of all the denominations', but he left them in no doubt that they ought to belong to the Established Church. Equally he was ready to protect Tractarians from persecution, provided they kept within the law, though he had little sympathy with either their theology or their forms of worship and told his diocesan conference, 'If the law requires me to wear a cope, though I don't like the notion of making a guy of myself, I will wear one.'

In his first speech at the Convocation of York in 1871 he supported a motion proposing the disuse in worship of the Athanasian Creed. 'This Creed illustrates in a remarkable way', he declared, 'the manner in which the wit of men has endeavoured to give, out of its own resources, a definiteness beyond what is given in Holy Scripture to religious ideas, by putting them in theological terms.' The motion was carried in the House of Bishops but lost in the House of Clergy, and later he told a meeting of clergy – 'It was an evil day when the Church added to the Apostles' Creed curious reticulations of faith . . . One great secret of Christ's influence was that he turned men's thoughts away from the discussions of the Rabbis.'

In view of Fraser's liberal outlook and general tolerance it was ironic that he should have been involved in two noisy controversies – one liturgical, the other doctrinal – which he believed required him to take a firm line, and the first of which led to one of his clergy being committed to prison. In both instances he came under severe pressure to enforce the law and in the end felt that he lacked the power to do otherwise, though he made his own position clear in a response to a group of Protestant protesters – 'These broils in parishes, partly the offspring of folly, partly of obstinacy, fill me with anxiety and distress, and make me wish again and again that I had never left my quiet little village in Berks, where such anxieties were utterly unknown.' Significantly, his involvement in these controversies, one of which became a national cause célèbre, did not affect the high regard in which he was held throughout the diocese. The more powerful and abiding memory was of a bishop whose concern for the Christian mission led him to give lunchtime addresses in factories, mills and railway works, and whose compassion for the poor led him to spend time with boatmen on canals, scavengers and night-soil men. During his episcopate 99 new churches were built and 109 new parishes formed. He gave over £31,000 to charities and was contemplating retirement when he died suddenly.

Brooke Foss Westcott

Brooke Foss Westcott, Bishop of Durham 1890–1901, was of a very different stamp. He was one of the foremost nineteenth-century biblical scholars who left a permanent mark on New Testament studies with a number of classic commentaries and most of all with the epoch-making *Cambridge Greek New Testament* (1881) which he edited with his former pupil F. J. A. Hort. His scholarship was moreover blended with the insights of a mystic. Yet when at the age of 66 he became Bishop of Durham he soon established himself as the foremost among episcopal social reformers. He had become President of the Christian Social Union on its formation, shortly before he moved to Durham from the Regius Professorship of Divinity at Cambridge, and in his first letter to the clergy of the diocese, sent in advance of his enthronement, he undertook 'to face in the light of the Christian faith some of the gravest problems of our social and national life'.

He did not have long to wait before being confronted by a problem that was grave indeed. In 1892 the Durham coal owners, seeking to safeguard their profits during a period of falling coal prices, proposed a reduction of 13.5 per cent in the already meagre wages of the miners. This was strongly resisted and, when the offer of the miners to take a 10 per cent reduction was refused, the entire coalfield went on strike. In the absence of strike-pay and social security benefits, the consequences for the men and their families of a long stoppage could only be disastrous. Westcott stepped in and invited both sides to meet under his chairmanship in his home at Auckland Castle. The meeting lasted the best part of a day until a settlement of 10 per cent, as urged by Westcott, was agreed. The announcement made to a large crowd gathered outside the castle was greeted with cheers of relief and from then onwards Westcott could, in the eyes of the miners, do no wrong. It was the most important event in his episcopate, and he continued to support the miners by helping to form conciliation boards to deal with any future disputes and by pleading with the owners to provide them with better housing.

But although he spoke in Britain's main cities under the banner of the Christian Social Union and, soon after becoming a bishop, made at Hull a widely reported and much-challenged speech favouring some form of socialism, he was generally concerned more with principles than with specific political action. He believed it to be his duty as a bishop to act as a reconciler, rather than take sides, and to make Christians aware of their social responsibilities. His published collections of sermons and lectures which included *Social Aspects of Christianity*, *The Incarnation and Common Life*, and *Lessons from Work* were very widely read.

And for him Christian social responsibility involved support of the co-operative and trades union movements. Leaders of these and other socially progressive organizations were often invited to conferences at Auckland Castle. But he played little part in the work of the House of Lords.

Westcott was born in 1825 in Birmingham where his father was a manufacturer and also a lecturer in botany at the medical school. At King Edward's School, where he was much influenced by the headmaster, James Prince Lee, he was regarded as a shy, nervous and thoughtful boy, but out of school he saw a demonstration in support of the 1832 Reform Bill and also attended a Chartist meeting. Later he said that his interest in social and political questions dated from that time.

Having won most of the school's prizes, he went as a scholar to Trinity College, Cambridge, where he became top of the first class in classics, a mathematics Wrangler, and again won most of the prizes. He stayed on to teach and in 1851 was ordained by his former headmaster who was now Bishop of Manchester. In the following year he left Cambridge to become an assistant master at Harrow School where, although he proved to be an indifferent teacher, he remained for seventeen years. He was recognized as a scholar and a holy man and his influence on some individuals, including Charles Gore, was very great.

The fruits of his research were also remarkable – *A History of the Canon of the New Testament* (1855), *Characteristics of the Gospel Miracles* (1859), *An Introduction to the Study of the Gospels* (1860), *The Gospel of the Resurrection* (1866) and *The History of the English Bible* (1869). All displayed an awareness of the demands of the new critical scholarship, but Westcott's conclusions were less radical than those of many German scholars and the volume on the Resurrection reflected something of the mystical temperament that informed much of his later writing. He might well have left Harrow in 1861 to become Hulsean Professor of Divinity at Cambridge – a post he would have much liked – but he stood aside to allow it to go to his former pupil, J. B. Lightfoot, whom he believed to be the better equipped.

Movement came eight years later with appointment to a Residentiary Canonry of Peterborough Cathedral, but his absence from Cambridge lasted only just over twelve months for in 1870 he was offered, and accepted, the Regius Chair of Divinity. On this occasion Lightfoot stood aside for his former teacher and pressed hard for him to be appointed. For the next thirteen years Westcott successfully combined his duties in Peterborough and Cambridge. He enjoyed living in the cathedral close and recognized the need for the cathedral to be infused with new life. The Dean and Chapter was persuaded to have a daily 8 am Holy Communion in one of the side chapels and also to observe the Saints' days. He was assiduous in sharing in these generally thinly attended services and his mystical character was well expressed in the response to a question from his daughter whom he met one dark winter morning while returning from the cathedral to his home – 'Were there many there, father?' 'Yes, it was full.'

He also saw the cathedral as a centre of education and gradually trained his thin voice so that, in days long before the invention of sound reinforcement systems, his sermons and lectures could be heard in the large building. His thought was too dense for him to be able to attract large crowds, though a volume of sermons *The Historic Faith* ran to six editions and, as at Harrow, his combination of scholarship and spirituality made a great impact. During university vacations he took in a few pupils, one of whom was Henry Scott Holland who later, when a Canon of St Paul's, was the driving force of the Christian Social Union. In 1883, however, the dynamic Bishop of Peterborough, William Connor Magee, complained that he was neglecting his cathedral duties and asked for his resignation both as a canon and as an examining chaplain. Westcott was deeply hurt by this and resigned at once, but his distress was quickly relieved by Gladstone's offer of a conveniently vacant Canonry of Westminster.

Although the former dean, A. P. Stanley, had done much to enliven the abbey's life, there had never been any suggestion that members of the chapter should forsake their other interests and it was not difficult for Westcott's busy life in Cambridge to be accommodated. During his time as Regius professor the chair became a position of influence and power. Academic standards were raised, an honours degree in theology instituted, a divinity school built, and a training course for ordinands (later developed into Westcott House Theological College) started. His lectures, like his sermons, were often difficult to follow, but scholarship of a recognizably high order, saintliness and a magnetic personality drew the crowds and by the end of his time in Cambridge he was regularly lecturing to 300 and more. He was largely instrumental in the founding of the Cambridge Mission to Delhi and was among the first promoters of extension lectures for those who were unable to have a university education. Among these were many women, whose admission to Cambridge he always opposed, believing that they should have a university of their own.

Work on a revised text of the Greek Testament, which he had started almost thirty years earlier, was brought to completion in 1881 and appeared just five days before the publication of the Revised Version of the New Testament, on the translation committee of which he had served for the previous eleven years. Substantial commentaries – *St John's Gospel* (1881), the *Johannine Epistles* (1883) and *Hebrews* (1889) were immediately recognized as major contributions to New Testament studies and remained standard works for many years.

At Westminster, where he resided and preached during Cambridge vacations, Westcott felt very much at home and appreciated the Abbey's expression of the religious life of the nation. His sermons became increasingly concerned with the big social issues of the day, though they lacked none of the spiritual intensity that characterized all his preaching. Recalling the address he gave at the founding of the Christian Social Union in 1889, Henry Scott Holland wrote –

> No-one who was present will ever forget it. Yet none of us can ever recall in the least what was said. No one knows. Only we know that we were lifted, kindled, transformed. We pledged ourselves; we committed ourselves; we were ready to die for the Cause; but if you asked us Why and for What, we could not tell you. There he was; there he spoke: the prophetic fire was breaking from him. We, too, were caught up. But words had only become symbols. There was nothing verbal to report or repeat. We could remember nothing, except the spirit which was in the words: and that was enough.

Later that year he presided over a meeting of Anglicans and Free Churchmen, held in his house, and from which came a committee of the Christian Union for Promoting International Concord – a cause that was always close to his heart, though later he shocked many of its supporters by approving of Britain's part in the Boer War.

After he had declined offers of the Deaneries of Exeter and Norwich, it seemed likely that he would end his days at Cambridge and Westminster but following the sudden death of Bishop Lightfoot in 1889 Queen Victoria pressed for Westcott to succeed him. The Prime Minister, Lord Salisbury, strongly resisted this on the grounds that diocesan administration would waste his gifts as a scholar and that he was not a strong leader, though the real reason seems to have been that he was a Broad Churchman with socialist views. In the end the Queen's wishes prevailed and when, just a few months after Westcott's enthronement at Durham, the Archbishopric of York fell vacant she suggested him for the Northern Primacy. This time, however, the Prime Minister stood firm, pointing out that he was inexperienced and that his socialism would be even less acceptable in an archbishop.

Westcott's eleven years at Durham, which took him beyond his 76th birthday, were wholly successful. He was happy to leave his former pupil's recently created administrative structures unaltered and did not feel the need to raise more new money for church buildings. But he visited the parishes, was tolerant of the various shades of churchmanship to be found in their churches, and was friendly to the Methodists and other Nonconformists. His preaching, which had not always been fully understood in Cambridge and Westminster, was far above the heads of the congregations in the mining villages, but all felt improved by the hearing of the sermons. Efforts to improve the human lot could be certain of his support and he had a particular interest in education. Like Lightfoot, he always had six to eight Oxford or Cambridge graduates in residence at Auckland Castle preparing for ordination under his guidance. His own family of seven included five sons, all of whom were ordained.

The historic pre-eminence of the Bishop of Durham meant a great deal to him, but he hated riding in a carriage and when obliged to do so always sat facing the back and concealed from view. He replied to letters in his own hand and usually by return of post. Support of the miners and friendship with their leaders led to frequent requests that he should preach in the cathedral on their annual Gala Day. Just a few days before his death in 1901, when it was obvious to everyone that the end was near, he gave them a remarkable sermon on the text 'The love of Christ constrains us' (2 Corinthians 5.14). It ended:

> Take it, then, my friends – this is my last counsel – to home, and mine, and club: try by its divine standard the thoroughness of your labour and the purity of your recreation, and the Durham which we love – the Durham of which we are proud – will soon answer to the heavenly pattern. If Tennyson's idea of heaven was true, that 'heaven is the ministry of soul to soul', we may reasonably hope, by patient, resolute, faithful united endeavour, to find heaven about us here, the glory of our earthly life.

Following his death the Darlington Independent Labour Party recorded 'the deep sense of loss the cause of social reform has sustained, and the highest appreciation of the earnestness and zeal with which he sought to improve the social conditions of the masses'. A Durham parish priest described him as 'The humanest and kindliest of men.'

Charles Gore

Charles Gore, Bishop of Worcester (1902–05), Birmingham (1905–11), Oxford (1911–19) was one of the twentieth century's most notable churchmen. For almost 40 years he dominated the Anglican theological scene and had a considerable influence over the development of church life during a period of great social change. He was an Anglo-Catholic who emphasized the essential part played by the Church and the sacraments in the Christian scheme of salvation, but he had views on the Bible and the person of Christ that were for some years regarded by many as dangerous or even heretical. His convictions, expressed eloquently and always with transparent integrity, included radical social concern which led him to espouse socialist solutions to problems such as poverty and poor housing. His whole life was devoted to fighting causes, many of which involved quarrelling with friends, none of whom he lost as a result of the verbal battles. W. R. Inge, whose theological and ecclesiastical views could hardly have been more different, said, 'No more stimulating Christian teaching has been given in our generation,' and Hensley Henson, whose appointment as a bishop was strenuously opposed by Gore, said of his adversary at the time of his death, 'I judge him to have been the most considerable English Churchman of his time, not the most learned, not the most eloquent, but so learned, so eloquent, and so energetic that he touched the life of his generation at more points and more effectively than any of his contemporaries.'

Gore's appointment as Bishop of Worcester was greeted with Protestant objections, which delayed his consecration until some legal points had been sorted out. The *Review of Reviews* likened the appointment, in imagination, to that of John the Baptist being sent by Pontius Pilate to be bishop over Galilee during the reign of King Herod. Nothing daunted, Gore launched himself on a dynamic episcopate which began with refusal to live in Hartlebury Castle, the historic residence of the Bishops of Worcester, and ended with the revival of a scheme for the creation of a much-needed Diocese of Birmingham. Gore contributed the whole of his personal fortune – £10,000 left to him by his mother – to the financing of the new diocese and then opted to leave Worcester to become its first bishop. He was in his element in the burgeoning life and dominant Liberal politics of the city, establishing strong relations with the civic authorities and getting on well with the influential Free Churches. A considerable furore arose however when he forbade Henson to preach in Carrs Lane Congregational Church, though in the end Henson defied him and had the inhibition framed.

Translation to Oxford in 1911 was sensible enough on paper, for he had been a powerful religious influence in the university during the 1880s and 1890s, but he accepted the move against his better judgement and came to regret it. In a widely spread and conservative diocese he found it difficult to make an impression, and his relations with the university were now uneasy, though his mission to Oxford in 1914 made a great impact. His conducting of confirmations and, as always, his sermons were memorable. Much of his correspondence was conducted by postcard and he urged the clergy to do the same. Asked to do something or other, he would scribble the reply – 'Sorry, I can't. C. G.' In the end he resigned because he disagreed with the Representative Church Council's decision that baptism alone, without confirmation, should be the qualification required of those who would vote for the new Church Assembly.

Gore first appeared as a controversial figure in 1889 when he edited a volume of essays written by himself and six theologian friends who had been meeting informally for the past twelve years in what they called the 'Holy Party'. *Lux Mundi* aimed, said its editor, to 'put the Catholic faith in its right relation to modern intellectual problems', and the essay which caused most offence was the one written by Gore on 'The Holy Spirit and Inspiration'. In it he argued that the results of Old Testament criticism must be accepted and also that the true humanity of Christ must be recognized. But the real bombshell came in a footnote that seemed almost casual:

> Jesus never exhibits the omniscience of bare Godhead in the realm of natural knowledge; such as would be required to anticipate the results of modern science and criticism. Indeed, God declares his almighty power in his condescension, whereby he 'beggared' himself of Divine prerogatives to put himself in our place.

The reaction was widespread and violent, with the greatest distress being expressed by Gore's Anglo-Catholic friends who believed him to have departed seriously from Catholic truth and betrayed their cause. The volume ran to many editions and in the tenth of these Gore included a new preface in which he apologized for anything he had written which seemed to suggest that Christ was fallible. He went on to write two books in which he spelled out further what came to be known as the *kenotic* (self-emptying) theory of the Incarnation. But never again did he cross the boundaries of theological orthodoxy.

Gore was born in Wimbledon in 1853 and came from an aristocratic background. His mother was the widow of an earl and his paternal and maternal grandfathers were also earls. Charlie, as he was known in childhood, never quite lost the aristocratic touch, though his way of life as a priest and bishop was austere and he had a deep concern for the poor. During his early years his parents were relatively poor, but they managed to send him to Harrow where he was deemed to be one of the most brilliant pupils in the school's history. Brooke Foss Westcott, the New Testament scholar and future Bishop of Durham, was on the teaching staff at that time and influenced him greatly, as did the outstanding headmaster, H. M. Butler. His Anglo-Catholic faith, radical temper, vigorous style of speech and concern for social justice all had their beginnings at Harrow. A neighbour in Wimbledon, though a few years older, was Henry Scott Holland who became a notable Canon of St Paul's, then

Regius Professor of Divinity at Oxford. The two men enjoyed the closest of friendships until Holland's death in 1918 and influenced each other's thought considerably. Meanwhile, Gore's brother, Spencer, was becoming England's first lawn tennis champion.

Like Holland, Gore went as a scholar to Balliol College, Oxford, then in the heyday of its academic brilliance, and, having taken a double first in classics, won a prize fellowship at Trinity College, Oxford. There he taught philosophy, mainly Plato, but much of his time was spent in study of the Apostolic Fathers and in seeking to formulate a contemporary Catholicism which demonstrated continuity with the faith of the earliest Church and at the same time took account of new insights into truth. He believed that he was called to be a 'free thinker' as well as a devout Christian, but viewed in the broad context of the developing theology of his time his work was essentially conservative.

Following ordination in 1876, Gore had two university vacation curacies at Christ Church, Bootle, and St Margaret's, Princes Road, Liverpool, where work among the poorest of the poor confirmed his commitment to social justice. In 1880 however he was persuaded to become vice-principal of Cuddesdon Theological College, and during the next four years helped to renew the college's reputation as the foremost place for ordination training. He then became the first principal of Pusey House, Oxford, which aimed to offer within the university an Anglo-Catholic witness through worship, scholarship and pastoral care. It was during his nine years there that the *Lux Mundi* controversy erupted and his influence in Oxford was said to be comparable with that of John Henry Newman before he became a Roman Catholic. He also joined Scott Holland, Westcott and others in the foundation of the Christian Social Union which became a strong witness to the implications of the Christian faith in a society where the gulf between rich and poor was very wide. For Gore this was inspired partly by his belief that the Incarnation demonstrated the holiness of all life, and partly by the witness of the Old Testament prophets, with whom he had a close affinity.

He spoke in favour of socialism, in its general sense, at the 1908 Lambeth Conference and again at the 1910 Edinburgh Missionary Conference. In the following year he supported strikers at a factory in Reading and took the chair at a meeting in support of women's suffrage. He often spoke at co-operative movement conferences. The 1914–18 war he regarded as divine judgement on a rotten society, based on selfishness and the worship of money. He bought shares in a large London store in order to protest at its annual meeting against the company's employment policy. 'The first charge upon industry', he once declared, 'is a proper wage for the workers.'

Towards the end of his time at Pusey House Gore gave particular expression to his concept of Christian community by founding a brotherhood of celibate priests who held all things in common. This expanded to become one of the Anglican Church's major religious orders – the Community of the Resurrection – with its mother house at Mirfield in Yorkshire and much significant work in South Africa. It was in order to provide his brotherhood with a base, and to secure more parish experience, that Gore became Vicar of Radley, near Oxford, in 1893. But village life was not his *métier* and after twelve months the Crown sought to rescue him with the offer of the Deanery of Winchester. This he declined on the grounds that the post needed a financier and would not afford much leisure. So he accepted a Canonry of Westminster instead and between 1894 and 1902 his house in the Little Cloister of Westminster Abbey was an important centre of religious influence in London. Some members of the Community of the Resurrection lived with him and there was a constant stream of visitors who came for theological discussion, spiritual counselling and conferences on church and social reform. Following a meeting in the Jerusalem Chamber, attended by MPs and clergymen, he became chairman of a group that pressed the government for a Wages Board Bill that would provide a machinery for establishing minimum wages and settling disputes. His sermons in the Abbey attracted large congregations whose excitement was heightened when Henson, a colleague on the chapter for eighteen months and always a friend, appeared in the pulpit to 'correct' what they had heard the previous Sunday. Under Gore's influence the sacramental life of the Abbey was deepened and the beautiful mediaeval chapel of St Faith rescued from its use as a store. This was not unrelated to his book *The Body of Christ* (1901) which had many editions and was very influential through its emphasis on the centrality of the Eucharist in the Church's life and its formulation of a doctrine of the Real Presence of Christ in the Eucharist, without the concept of transubstantiation.

During his seventeen years as a diocesan bishop Gore wrote very little apart from *The Basis of Anglican Fellowship* (1914), which was a useful statement of Anglican comprehensiveness and a plea for the ending of party feuding in the Church, but in no sense a major work of scholarship. Diocesan responsibilities inevitably claimed much of his time and he was also a national figure, interested in many things and battling on several fronts in the twin causes of truth and righteousness. The wartime National Mission of Repentance and Hope enjoyed his support, as did the Life and Liberty Movement, but by the end of the war the ceaseless round of activity was beginning to affect his health. He was tired, anxious and frustrated. The appointment of Henson to the Bishopric of Hereford indicated that he was not winning the battle against liberalism.

There seemed every possibility of an unacceptable compromise being reached with the Free Churches over the sacraments and the ordained ministry, and the Anglo-Catholics now seemed preoccupied with 'smells and bells'. Few of the bishops appeared to him to be capable of dealing with the intellectual problems that would face the Church in the post-war world. All of which suggested that the Church of England would remain a loose coalition of rival interests with an equally loose relationship to the state, rather than the dynamic Body of Christ for which he had so long fought. His resignation in 1919 over the electoral qualification issue, accompanied famously by the waving of his fist at Lambeth Palace as he returned to Westminster, was an expression of deep disappointment. Much later, Archbishop Lang, after reading G. L. Prestige's *Life of Gore*, lamented that his prophetic gifts had ever been shackled by his becoming a bishop – 'The restraints brought out all his testiness and petulance. Yet what a noble life! It humbles me.'

But the resignation from the Oxford bishopric by no means ended his contribution to the Church's life. He took a small house in London, lectured at King's College and, freed from diocesan and other chores, wrote a widely read trilogy on Christian belief. He also played a major part in the editing of a two-volume *New Commentary on Holy Scripture* (1928), which had many editions, gave the Gifford Lectures, published as *The Philosophy of the Good Life* (1930), and when he was 76 produced a small book on *Jesus of Nazareth* (1929). Neither did he cease to express his mind on controversial subjects. At the Malines Conversations in 1923 and 1925 his criticisms of the Roman Catholic view of authority was much franker than ecclesiastical diplomacy demanded, and, although his involvement in the 1930 Lambeth Conference was confined to the conducting of a retreat for the bishops, he roundly denounced their approval of contraception and of a unity scheme involving Anglicans and Protestants in South India.

Gore's interest in the Christian mission in India went back to his time as vice-principal of Cuddesdon. In 1908 he let it be known that he would not be averse to translation to the vacant Bishopric of Bombay, but when the offer came he declined because there was so much unfinished business in Birmingham. In 1931 he undertook a long and exhausting visit to India – preaching, lecturing, conducting retreats and offering advice to the Oxford Mission to Calcutta and to the Cambridge Mission to Delhi. This proved to be too much. He collapsed and, although he managed to get back to London, he never fully recovered and died in January 1932. Shortly before his death he was visited by Archbishop Lang who found him only semi-conscious and heard him say, 'Transcendent glory.' Thousands of people filed past his coffin when it lay in Holy Trinity Church, Sloane Street, in Chelsea, before his funeral.

Reflecting on Gore's life, H. D. A. Major, a prominent liberal modernist, wrote:

> She who had been aptly described as the Conservative Party at prayer became as a result of Gore's influence, at least in the persons of her Anglo-Catholic clergy, the Socialist Party at Mass.

———————————

The service used at the consecration of bishops in the Church of England contained, until the advent of the Alternative Service Book in 1980, the following question addressed to the royal nominee:

> Will you shew yourself gentle, and be merciful for Christ's sake to poor and needy people, and to all strangers destitute of help?
>
> *Answer*: I will so shew myself, by God's help.

Why this or a modern equivalent question was omitted from the new ordinal is far from clear, though it is well known that most liturgists are more concerned with what happens in the sanctuary than in society. In marked contrast, the liberation theologians of Latin America have helped twenty-first-century Christians to see that faithfulness to the biblical revelation requires the Church to display not only wide social concern but also a distinctive bias to the poor. And this because God himself shows a like bias.

It is not yet possible to record that the Church of England has received this insight and adjusted its message and its life to express the Divine bias, though Bishop David Sheppard, during his years at Liverpool, and a few other bishops have made valiant attempts to push their colleagues in this direction. Nonetheless it seems likely that virtually all of today's bishops are broadly in favour of the reforming aims of the present Labour government – any reservation being confined to the few who are disappointed that these aims are not sufficiently radical.

During the long years of Margaret Thatcher's Conservative administration, when the Opposition parties were weak, the bishops and the General Synod Board of Social Responsibility were among the few agencies making any serious assault on the government's individualistic philosophy and its related undermining of the Welfare State. This led to strained relations between the Church's leadership and the Conservative Party, culminating in an absurd attempt by a 10 Downing Street spokesman to dismiss the 1985 *Faith in the City* report as Marxist. Under a Labour dispensation, in which the Prime Minister and several other members of the Cabinet are avowed Christian Socialists, the position is obviously different, but this does not leave the socially conscious Christian with nothing to do.

Tony Blair and his colleagues are not revolutionaries, which is not to say that they lack a revolutionary vision of an egalitarian society, but rather that they favour a pragmatic approach that will get some things done and enable them to retain power long enough to bring about significant changes in Britain's social order. This is a worthy aim and approach, but the compromises involved are dangerous and for the time being (how long?) leave too many people at the base of an unjust social and economic pyramid. Hence the need for the Church, through its episcopal and other spokesmen, to adopt a position of critical solidarity towards the government's policies while seeking to influence public opinion so that a more radical approach to serious social problems may become possible.

Among these problems, the plight of the asylum seeker and the refugee (the 'stranger destitute of help') has high priority, as has the linked issue of squalid urban housing. The creation of a truly multi-racial society and one in which privately funded health care and education no longer reinforce social and economic division is still a long way from achievement. Britain's relations with Europe and its responsibilities towards the developing world require bold and generous decisions. There is, as there will always be in a fallen world, much to challenge the Christian conscience.

All such issues do however raise questions of great complexity, the answers to which lie beyond the competence of a bishop who lacks adequate briefing by those with the necessary expertise and experience. Yet statements of the broad moral principles at stake are still worth making as a contribution to general debate, and much more use needs to be made of the many excellent reports produced by the General Synod Board of Social Responsibility. During the last fifty years considerable resources of professional expertise have been invested in the compiling of these reports, but all too often they have led to no more than an unsatisfactory debate in the General Synod, then been left to gather dust on bookshelves. Bishops need to get reports of this kind discussed, and where possible acted upon, in their dioceses if the Church's social concern is to have much credibility and influence.

This credibility and influence also requires the Church to be equally concerned about the use of its own human resources and money. The urgently needed reassessment of its mission strategy in England must not lead, at a time when money is short, to the neglect of the most deprived and socially challenging area of the country. The Church's presence in these areas at a time when most other social agencies have retreated to the comfortable suburbs has been to its great credit and bishops who are concerned about social reform will ensure that this not only continues but is also reinforced. Promotion of social equality also requires them to promote with greater enthusiasm ecclesiastical equality for women.

11

The missionaries

When Queen Victoria was crowned in 1837 Britain had no great colonial ambitions. The painful loss of the American colonies in the previous century had indicated that imperial expansion could be a costly enterprise, while the experience of India, where an apparently inexhaustible wealth was being extracted through the East India Company, suggested that in some places at least the benefits of colonialism could be obtained without direct government intervention. Yet, at the time of her death in 1901 Queen Victoria was Empress of India and ruled over a quarter of the world's population living on almost a quarter of the world's land surface.

The development and decline of the British Empire can now be seen as one of the more remarkable, as well as one of the most preposterous, happenings in human history, and it was due to the combination of several factors. By 1850 Britain was the world's leading industrial power and urgently needed more outlets for the sale of manufactured goods. The successful pillaging of India's wealth encouraged the exploration and exploitation of other parts of the world. The strength of the Royal Navy guaranteed freedom of the seas, thus facilitating exploration and trade, and eventually it came to be seen that large-scale commercial activity in Britain's favour required military and political domination.

Undergirding these practical considerations, and in some ways cloaking their more sinister aspects, was a powerful belief that the British way of life, expressed in the rule of law, public service and the Christian religion, would be beneficial to the people of distant lands. This led to a call to young men in public schools and universities to dedicate themselves to the building and service of a great Empire. It was an appeal to heroism which evoked an astonishing response in which religious conviction played an important part. Oxford and Cambridge men went overseas in their thousands, many of them meeting early deaths in inhospitable climates and some at the hands of defiant indigenous warriors. By the end of the nineteenth century it could be said that 'Blacks are now ruled by "Blues".'

The Church of England played a highly significant part in the development of the Empire. Clergymen – some only in their early thirties – were consecrated for new bishoprics in regions where the British flag was flying. Initially they confined their ministries to the British settlers, soldiers and government servants, and their aim was that of planting the Church of England – its liturgy, architecture and beliefs – on the distant colonial soil, but soon the work was expanded to include medical, education and missionary work among the indigenous populations. Some missionary work had in fact been undertaken long before Britain experienced its imperial dream. The Society for the Propagation of the Gospel was founded in 1701 and the Church Missionary Society in 1799, and in some parts of East and Central Africa medical missionaries, most notably David Livingstone, were on the scene well before the traders and the military. The Universities' Mission to Central Africa, founded in 1857 following an appeal made at Cambridge by Livingstone, aimed to promote 'true religion, agriculture and lawful commerce, and the ultimate extinction of the slave trade'. This demanded heroism and sometimes martyrdom.

Nonetheless it was the growth of Empire that enabled the Church of England to grow rapidly from a small, national Church to a worldwide Anglican Communion with dioceses, provinces, bishops and archbishops in almost every part of the globe. The first Lambeth Conference was held in 1867 and attended by 76 bishops; a Pan-Anglican Congress held in 1908 attracted about 7,000 clerical and lay delegates. During the early years of the twentieth century the title of a book by an American layman, John R. Mott, *The Evangelization of the World in This Generation*, became a catch phrase among enthusiastic missionaries and many in the now international Anglican Communion who attended a great missionary conference held in Edinburgh in 1910 shared this vision and hope. But the pattern of Christian missionary work was destined to take an unexpected turn. The Church which had grown with the development of the British Empire found itself deeply involved in the rapid decline of that Empire and its replacement with a multi-national, multi-racial Commonwealth in the years following the end of the 1939–45 world war. English missionaries played an important part in the education of those who were to exercise leadership in the new, independent countries, and also in preparing these countries for self-government. In this they were usually ahead of those responsible for the transfer of power, and in a very short time the leadership of the Anglican dioceses outside Britain was in indigenous hands.

George Augustus Selwyn

George Augustus Selwyn (Bishop of New Zealand 1841–68, then of Lichfield 1868–84) was just 32 when he was consecrated as New Zealand's first bishop. The eight years since his ordination had been spent as a private tutor at Eton and as an honorary curate in nearby Windsor, and when he sailed from Plymouth there were cries from the quayside, 'God bless you! Floreat Ecclesia! Floreat Etona!' During the four-month-long voyage he was taught Maori by a native New Zealander who was returning home, and on his arrival in the newly created diocese astonished the welcoming congregation by preaching and conducting the prayers in Maori. Twenty-six years later, when he left to become Bishop of Lichfield, New Zealand was a province of five dioceses, including the Bishopric of Melanesia which had been created as a consequence of his missionary work on the islands of the West Pacific.

By this time Selwyn was recognized as one of the Anglican Communion's foremost leaders and later he came to be seen as one of the founding fathers of the modern New Zealand nation. He combined a tough, decisive temperament with vision, strong pastoral gifts and outstanding courage. Whenever he entered a room, a certain 'spiritual electricity' was said to be felt and in the affairs of the Church this was accompanied by considerable organizing ability which enabled vision to be turned into reality. This was experienced vividly in the synodical structure which he devised for the New Zealand Church and which became the model for church government in many other parts of the world. For Selwyn this was in no sense a bureaucratic device, nor even an expression of democracy. Synods were for him an expression of the Church's spiritual character and in his second charge to the Diocese of New Zealand, given in 1847, he said 'I believe the monarchical idea of the Episcopate to be as foreign to the true mind of the Church as it is adverse to the Gospel doctrine of humility . . . The Bishop is the organ of the general sense of the Church.' He hoped that the title 'dignitary' would never be heard in New Zealand. He went to New Zealand because he believed that as a priest he was a man under orders: if asked by the Church's leaders to go to a particular place he must go. The islands of the Western Pacific were in fact placed under his jurisdiction as a result of a clerical error by someone responsible for drawing up the letters patent relating to his appointment but when it became clear that the Archbishop of Canterbury wished him to take on this additional responsibility he accepted without demur.

Selwyn, the son of a London lawyer, was born in Hampstead in 1809.

After Eton he secured a first in classics at St John's College, Cambridge, and was elected to a fellowship. Instead of teaching in Cambridge, however, he became a private tutor at Eton to the future Earl of Powis and, having been ordained, offered to serve as an unpaid curate of Windsor. Since the vicar, a pluralist, was residing at Datchet some miles away this left him effectively in charge of the Windsor parish and he was immediately confronted with a crisis in the form of a £3,000 debt which had been incurred through repairs to the parish church and over which a threat of court action for non-payment was hanging. Undaunted, Selwyn quickly raised this money and began to build up a strong church life, finding time to publish in 1838 a visionary pamphlet on the future of the English cathedrals. This broad vision was dedicated to Mr Gladstone, since he had suggested its writing, but it was given a hostile reception by the cathedral chapters, who did not wish to be disturbed, and by the bishops who were afraid that it would deliver too much of their own power to the chapters. So it never found acceptance, though it stimulated enough national discussion to mark Selwyn as a man of vision, ideas and missionary zeal. Hence the choice of him for the new Bishopric of New Zealand.

Church Missionary Society missionaries had been working among New Zealand's Maoris since 1814 and when the country was declared to be a British colony in 1840 the Westminster government pledged itself not to permit the extermination of the Maoris or the expropriation of their land. Selwyn strongly supported this policy and, having established his base on Maori territory, embarked on a six-months tour of the new diocese, by the end of which – in January 1843 – he had covered 762 miles on foot, 86 on horseback, 249 by canoe or boat, and 1,180 by ship. He then founded St John's College at Waimete, where he had his own modest home, and formed a community to express some of his cathedral ideals. On a site of 1,000 acres there was a school, a clergy training centre, a hostel for recently arrived young settlers, a hospital and a home for the aged and poor. It was open to all races and everyone, apart from the infirm, was required to contribute some physical work, thus enabling the college to become self-sufficient. A scheme for the proper deployment and payment of the clergy was well over a century ahead of similar proposals for the Church in England.

By 1848 Selwyn had preached in every village in New Zealand and over half of the 100,000 Maori population were now Christians. But the missionary work was increasingly hampered by the so-called Maori Wars which had started in 1845 and continued on and off until 1865. These had been provoked by the unwillingness of the New Zealand Company to honour the British government's land commitment. Disputes arising from seizures of land for settlers or purchase at only nominal prices led to violence, including murder, and eventually to armed conflict. Selwyn denounced the company and this led to unpopularity with the white settler community. He also sought to minister to both sides during the fighting and the *Auckland Times* of 18 March 1845 reported:

> Fearless in the very midst of the contest, Dr Selwyn sought to allay the heat of blood, and to arrest the fury of the field; afterwards unwearied at the bedside of the dying: – much more than this – he was the nurse, and the surgeon, and the servant of the sick as well as their spiritual attendant.

But in spite of his efforts and those of other missionaries the attitudes and actions of the white settlers caused a very large number of the Maori converts to become disillusioned with the Christian faith and return to their former beliefs.

Selwyn was however making good progress in the Pacific Islands. During 1851 he covered over 4,000 miles in the course of a four-months voyage, facing danger among the native inhabitants, most of whom had never before seen a white man, and establishing small Christian communities on several islands. He made seven such voyages during his time as Bishop of New Zealand and, in collaboration with the Church in Australia, formed the Melanesian Mission. The cost of this unceasing effort to his own family was reflected in a poignant letter to Lady Powis, written on the schooner *Undine* at sea on 15 April 1851 –

> I am just returning from a voyage of 4,000 miles to Stewart's Island, Otakou, Canterbury, Chatham Islands, Wellington, Nelson and New Plymouth, and am now within 100 miles of home, after an absence of four months. Our house, like yours, has been one of sorrow, for our dear little daughter, born in September 1850, has been taken from us. I had only known her for twelve days, and those full of business, so that I can scarcely call her features to mind; and 'When I shall meet her in heaven, I shall not know her.' We had hoped that she would have been the companion of her mother, and comfort her for the separation from her sons; but her lot is cast in a better state by Him in whom is the whole disposal: and we can rejoice in thinking of her as one of the spotless Innocents who follow the Lamb whithersoever he goeth. The loss is less to me than to her mother: for I cannot and must not look to children as a source of personal and domestic enjoyment: but we may rejoice, if it be God's will, in reports of their well doing under the care of the other parents and friends with whom they are so abundantly supplied.

In 1854 Selwyn made his first return visit to England chiefly for the purpose of obtaining authority for his diocese to be subdivided and for the Church in New Zealand to become self-governing. He also took the opportunity to preach four Cambridge sermons on missionary work and among the many who responded were John Coleridge Patteson, who was destined to be martyred in Melanesia, and Charles Frederick Mackenzie, who died of fever after an heroic ministry in Central Africa. On Selwyn's return to New Zealand four bishops (three of them Old Etonians and the fourth a former Eton master) were consecrated for the new Dioceses of Christchurch, Wellington, Nelson and Waiapu – the latter in Maori territory. A synodical constitution based on that of the American Church was adopted and, with the aid of money raised during the visit to England, plans were made for the creation of the Diocese of Melanesia. Patteson, who had been given charge of the mission to the Pacific Islands, became the first bishop of the new diocese in 1861.

Selwyn's next visit to England was for the 1867 Lambeth Conference at which he was described as 'foremost among the foremost men'. His contributions to the debates, in which he always emphasized the Church's missionary vocation, were heard with great respect and he expected to spend the remainder of his episcopate in New Zealand. Soon after the end of the Conference, however, he received a letter from the Prime Minister, Lord Derby, offering him the bishopric of Lichfield. This he declined, explaining that 'my heart is in New Zealand and Melanesia'. But he then came under strong pressure from Archbishop Longley to reconsider his decision and when, as a result of a personal interview with Queen Victoria, he was more or less commanded to accept Lichfield he felt that he had no real choice.

It was with a heavy heart that he returned to New Zealand to wind up his affairs there, and in January 1868 he was enthroned as Bishop of Lichfield – a diocese which then embraced Staffordshire, Derbyshire and half of Shropshire. He refused to live in the episcopal castle located some 25 miles from Lichfield and instead occupied the palace in the cathedral close. As in New Zealand, he threw himself into the work, embarking on an extraordinary programme of intense activity, and after addressing 44 rural deaneries on the subject of synodical government, held on 17 June 1868 a diocesan conference of clergy and laity – the first ever to be held in England. A year later however he was struck down by a heart problem and believed himself to be dying. In the event a two-months rest restored his health, though his constitution was now noticeably less robust. It soon became apparent to him that the diocese needed to be divided with a new one created for Derbyshire, and he argued that many more bishops were required. No diocese should have more than 500 parishes or more than 500,000 souls, and this should yield 5,000 confirmation candidates each year. But the division of Lichfield diocese did not take place until six years after Selwyn's death in office in 1884. His feast day in the Anglican calendar is 11 April.

John William Colenso

No nineteenth-century bishop caused a greater commotion than John William Colenso who became the first Bishop of Natal in 1853 and, although deposed by the Bishop of Cape Town in 1863 and solemnly excommunicated by the South African bishops three years later, retained his legal right to the bishopric until his death in 1883. By this time he was regarded by the Zulus as 'Father of the People'. A man of somewhat combative disposition, Colenso incurred censure soon after his arrival in Natal for not insisting that polygamists divorce their wives as a condition of Christian baptism. A few years later (1861) he published a commentary on the Epistle to the Romans which questioned St Paul's understanding of the Atonement and the sacraments, and denied the reality of eternal punishment. This led to disciplinary action by Bishop Gray of Cape Town who urged the English bishops to condemn the commentary, but they were unable to agree on an appropriate way of doing this and were content to inhibit him from preaching in their dioceses whenever he might be in England.

Worse was to follow: in 1862 he published *The Pentateuch and the Book of Joshua Critically Examined* in which he questioned the verbal inspiration of some parts of the Old Testament. This was the last straw and 41 English, Irish and Colonial bishops sent him a letter advising him to resign on the grounds that his views were incompatible with his ordination vows. The only result of this – for Colenso refused to oblige – was a national controversy in England and some humorous verse. *Punch* had Archbishop Longley writing:

> My dear Colenso,
> With regret,
> We hierarchs in conclave met,
> Beg you, you disturbing writer,
> To take off your colonial mitre.
> This course we press upon you strongly
> Believe me, yours most truly,
> Longley.

In the following year the bishops of the Canterbury Convocation condemned the Pentateuch book on the grounds that 'it involves errors of the most dangerous character' and Bishop Gray in distant Cape Town solemnly, but illegally as it turned out, deposed Colenso from the Natal bishopric. Concern about his beliefs and those expressed by the contributors to *Essays and Reviews* (1860) led to the convening of the first Lambeth Conference in 1867. Some of the anxiety undoubtedly arose from what the bishops perceived as a dire threat to the Christian faith posed by Darwin's recently published *Origin of Species*. It was also the case that Colenso, who had been influenced by F. D. Maurice, was no great theologian and presented his views in an unsophisticated fashion which encouraged rejection.

Colenso was born in humble circumstances in Cornwall in 1814 but he won a scholarship to St John's College, Cambridge, where his brilliance as a mathematician secured him the place of Second Wrangler and election to a fellowship. He taught mathematics at Harrow School for three years before returning to St John's as a tutor. In 1846 however he left Cambridge for the rich college living of Forncett St Mary in Norfolk where he exercised an exemplary pastoral ministry and spent much time studying theology before his appointment as Bishop of Natal in 1853. He arrived in the new diocese in the following year and after an extensive tour returned to England to recruit clergy and raise money. In his published journal *Ten weeks in Natal* he said that African culture was noble and that, given the proper opportunities, Africans would achieve as much as the members of other races. Missionaries should seek therefore to build on the indigenous culture and not attempt to replace it with European civilization. The gospel was to be preached not in order to convert the heathen but to set before him a pattern of love to follow. While not in favour of polygamy, Colenso argued that it should be regarded as part of the Zulu social order and not necessarily immoral.

This was a new, and for many an unwelcome, approach to missionary work which inevitably caused a furore in England as well as opposition from the South African bishops. When Colenso returned to Natal to establish a strong mission base at Pietermaritzburg from which to work among the Zulus, he immediately found himself in trouble for other reasons. His wearing of a surplice, the use of the prayer for the Church Militant and the taking of a collection at the Eucharist, led some English lay people in the diocese to describe him as a papist in disguise and to form a Church of England Defence Association to maintain Protestant principles. His effigy was publicly burned in Durban, though most of his ultra-Protestant opponents must have been reassured by a course of sermons in Pietermaritzburg Cathedral in 1858 in which he declared that Christ was no more present in the Eucharist than at other times, and that the sacraments were to be regarded simply as 'aids to devotion'.

Colenso – a remarkable linguist – was also engaged on a grammar of the Zulu language, a Zulu–English dictionary and the translation of the Bible into Zulu. For this work he employed a Zulu assistant and when the Genesis story of the Flood was reached the assistant asked some awkward questions about the narrative. Not wishing to undermine the general veracity of the Bible in the mind of his interlocutor, Colenso fobbed off these questions but they stimulated him to ask himself just what he believed about the Pentateuch. The result was a seven-part critical examination of the books which appeared between 1862 and 1879, and the first of which was to heighten the controversy caused by his other writings and utterances. The widespread belief that he had reneged on the Christian faith caused considerable alarm and a Windsor curate, S. J. Stone, responded by writing a hymn, 'The Church's One Foundation', with its reassuring verse:

> Though with a scornful wonder
> Men see her sore oppressed,
> By schisms rent asunder,
> By heresies distrest,
> Yet saints their watch are keeping,
> Their cry goes up, 'How long?'
> And soon the night of weeping
> Shall be the morn of song.

while Sir Henry Baker came to the defence of the Bible with his hymn 'Lord, thy word abideth'. Few of those who now sing these still popular hymns are aware of the feverish controversy that led to their writing.

Following his deposition and excommunication, Colenso denied Bishop Gray's jurisdiction and appealed to the Privy Council. The council, in a report occupying 400 pages, found in his favour on legal rather than doctrinal grounds, and the courts evacuated the sentence of excommunication of any legal effect, thus allowing him to retain the endowments of the see and also the cathedral. Darwin and the geologist Lyell were among those who contributed to his heavy legal costs and the scientific community was appalled at his treatment by the Church.

Colenso was absent from his diocese from 1862–65 and on his return a large crowd assembled to welcome him, though it was noticeable that few Anglicans were present. When he arrived in the cathedral the dean read out Bishop Gray's sentence of deposition and added, 'That sentence stands ratified in the presence of Almighty God' and, turning to Colenso, he added, 'Depart! Go away from the House of God.' But with the law on his side, he saw no reason to go, though he now regarded his main task as that of defending the Zulus against exploitation by the white settlers. He bitterly condemned the Zulu War of 1878–79 in which the power of the Zulu king was broken. By this time, however, a rival Bishop of Natal, W. K. Macrorie, had been in office for ten years and another cathedral had been built for him to use. Legally, Colenso was still the bishop and he had some supporters among the white population, but their number grew ever smaller and following his death in 1883 negotiations took place to incorporate them into the officially recognized diocese. The schism was not in fact formally ended until 1911. He died excommunicated but was buried beneath the altar of his small cathedral in Pietermaritzburg.

Charles Mackenzie

Speaking in the Senate House at Cambridge on 4 December 1857 to a crowded meeting of Oxford and Cambridge men, David Livingstone concluded with a challenge:

> I go back to Africa to try to make an open path for commerce and Christianity. Do you carry on the work which I have begun. I leave it with you.

The response was immediate; the cost was heavy. Within two years the Universities' Mission to Central Africa had been formed. A year later a young priest, Charles Mackenzie, was consecrated as the first Bishop of Central Africa and thirteen months after this died of malaria.

Mackenzie was born in Peebleshire in 1825. His father – a friend of Sir Walter Scott – died when he was only five and after attending Edinburgh Academy and a school near Sunderland he went to St John's College, Cambridge. Having discovered however that as a Scot he would be disqualified from a fellowship, he transferred to Gonville and Caius College where he proved to be a brilliant mathematician. He was duly elected to a fellowship, and became secretary of the Cambridge Board of Education and in 1852 a university examiner in mathematics.

In the previous year he had been ordained to a part-time curacy at Hartingfield, near Cambridge, and soon felt drawn to mission work overseas. On the advice of friends he declined an invitation to join the Cambridge Mission to Delhi in 1853 but two years later went with Bishop Colenso to South Africa. On their arrival he was appointed Archdeacon of Natal and spent the next eighteen months ministering to the English settlers in Durban and learning Swahili. He then moved 40 miles north to establish a mission post on the Umtali river where he worked among English settlers, soldiers and Africans. At a church conference in Pietermaritzburg in 1858 he spoke powerfully in favour of Africans having the same rights as Europeans in a proposed church synod but his plea was rejected and he left the conference. Ill-health then drove him back to England where by the summer of 1859 he was sufficiently recovered to be able to accept an invitation to become head of the newly formed UMCA which was seeking experienced leadership. A few weeks were then spent preparing other recruits and raising money, and on 2 October 1860 a great farewell service was held in Canterbury Cathedral.

Mackenzie was consecrated by the Bishop of Cape Town and other South African bishops on 1 January 1861 and authorized to minister 'to the tribes dwelling in the neighbourhood of Lake Ngasa and the River Shire'. He was believed to be the first bishop for a thousand years to be sent from England on a purely missonary assignment. In Natal he met David Livingstone, with whom he established a close relationship, though the two men did not always agree on strategy. Having sailed up the River Zambezi as far as its confluence with the River Shire, he marched with Livingstone to Magomero, where they established a fortified village. Magomero proved to be however a difficult and dangerous place from which to operate since the surrounding territory was the scene of constant tribal warfare from which the missionaries could not stand aside. On one occasion Mackenzie was observed holding his pastoral staff in one hand and a rifle in the other. The role of the missionaries in the conflict was later criticized in some quarters, but they claimed never to have acted in self-defence but only in the defence of defenceless Africans. Malaria was to be the greater danger to the Englishmen. Mackenzie arranged to meet Livingstone on Malo Island, at the confluence of the rivers Shire and Ruo, on New Year's Day 1862, but on the way his canoe overturned and the supply of quinine was among the provisions lost. Always careless of his health and already much troubled by heavy rain and mosquitoes, he pressed on, but was too late to meet Livingstone at Malo and died of fever on 31 January. A priest who was accompanying him died three weeks later, another member of the mission died on the next New Year's Day, and three months after this the doctor succumbed. Another layman became desperately ill and returned to England. The original mission team had been decimated.

Frank Weston

Two of Mackenzie's immediate successors were driven home by ill-health, another died of fever, and yet another was drowned, but in spite of this and many other setbacks, the work of the UMCA continued to expand and the discovery in the mid-1890s that mosquitoes were the carriers of malaria enabled some precautions to be taken and some lives to be saved. Bishop Frank Weston's death in 1924 was nonetheless the result of totally inadequate medical care. The most famous of Zanzibar's bishops, and a stalwart, uncompromising Anglo-Catholic, he was unfortunate enough to develop a carbuncle on his back and, without a doctor in reach, asked his boy cook to lance it with a kitchen knife. Fatal blood poisoning followed. The son of a militantly evangelical tea-broker, he was born in South London in 1871 and at Trinity College, Oxford, took a first in theology. As an undergraduate he felt drawn to the UMCA work in Zanzibar, but following his ordination in 1894 he first served curacies at the Trinity College Mission in London's East End and at St Matthew's, Westminster. He arrived in Zanzibar in 1898 and four months later published an open letter expressing his belief that the chief obstacle to missionary work was the Englishman's sense of racial superiority. This displayed at once his intellectual brilliance, his impulsive nature and what was to become a deep commitment to the African people. From 1904–08 he was principal of a large boys' school and during this time not only lived close to the Africans but also tried unsuccessfully to form a religious community.

In 1908 he became Bishop of Zanzibar and, having reorganized the diocese's mission stations, spent nine months of every year making long journeys on foot to these stations. The mission was making good progress under his deeply spiritual leadership; then came the explosion. In 1913 Weston learned that the bishops of the neighbouring East African dioceses, Mombasa and Uganda, had attended a conference in the Kenyan village of Kikuyu. Also present were representatives of the Presbyterian, Methodist and other Protestant churches who had agreed with the Anglicans on a loose form of federal unity based on acceptance of the authority of Scripture and the Nicene and Apostles' Creeds, and of the sacraments of Baptism and the Eucharist. Furthermore, at the end of the conference all had received Holy Communion at the hands of the two bishops.

Weston was greatly upset by this news and immediately communicated with the Archbishop of Canterbury, Randall Davidson, accusing his colleagues of 'the grievous faults of propagating heresy and committing schism'. He went on to demand 'a categorical recantation of the errors which they have taught in word and action'. A multitude of pamphlets and articles appeared, and in a letter to *The Times* on 29 December 1913 Bishop Charles Gore, an Anglo-Catholic, wrote: 'I doubt if the cohesion of the Church of England was ever more seriously threatened than it is now.' In the end the huffing and puffing was quelled by the outbreak of war, and in 1915 Davidson issued a diplomatic 'opinion' which satisfied neither side in the dispute.

Weston linked the events in Kikuyu with what he perceived to be a growing liberal tendency in the Church of England and this caused him to fall out with Bishop John Percival of Hereford who was seeking closer union with Nonconformists and invited them to receive Holy Communion in his cathedral – an action opposed by both the Convocation of Canterbury and the majority of his own clergy. Matters were made only worse by Percival's appointment of B. H. Streeter, a distinguished liberal New Testament scholar, as a Canon of Hereford – to which Weston responded by publishing on the door of Zanzibar Cathedral a notice indicating that he and his diocese were 'no longer in communion with John, Bishop of Hereford, and those who adhere to him'. Few people in either diocese were inconvenienced by this declaration.

From 1890 onwards most of Weston's diocese had been part of German East Africa and on the outbreak of war in 1914 he was isolated in Zanzibar and cut off from his mainland staff who were interned. He thereupon offered to recruit and command a corps of porters to carry supplies up-country and at one time he was in charge of 2,500 men, holding the rank of major. When the war ended he went to London for the 1920 Lambeth Conference and played a large part in getting the conference to issue an historic Appeal for Christian Unity based on a whole-hearted acceptance of Holy Scripture, the Nicene Creed, the sacraments of Baptism and the Holy Communion, and an episcopal ministry. Weston surprised many by his conciliatory attitude to the non-episcopal churches, though he was unwilling to modify his belief in the necessity of bishops consecrated in an apostolic succession. While in London he also took the opportunity to publish an attack on a circular about forced labour in Africa issued by the Secretary of State for the Colonies, Lord Milner. A joint memorandum signed by the leaders of all political parties led to the withdrawal of Milner's circular by his successor, Winston Churchill.

In 1923 Weston presided over, and dominated, the Second Anglo-Catholic Congress held in London's Albert Hall. Although basically shy and diffident, he was a brilliant orator who came alive on big occasions and had a magnetic influence over crowds. On his return to Africa he resumed his long journeys on foot, welcomed everywhere by Africans who treated him as one of their own. He died tragically, but as he always intended, in Africa, and long before his work was completed his many admirers regarded him as a saint – with good reason.

Joost de Blank

Joost de Blank, Archbishop of Cape Town from 1957 to 1963, did not spend long in Africa but he was the right man in the right place at the right time. Endowed with a highly complex personality, his autocratic flamboyant style often seemed out of place in a mid-twentieth-century bishop. His concept of his role as that of a prince archbishop was, many thought, just about the last thing required in South Africa as its race problem reached crisis point. Yet it was these very 'weaknesses', allied to very great courage, that enabled him to declare, in uncompromising terms which sounded throughout the world, that apartheid was inhuman, unChristian and fundamentally wrong.

Until de Blank's arrival in Cape Town the South African bishops, while having no truck with apartheid, believed that the best form of opposition involved them in working quietly behind the scenes to mitigate some of the worst excesses of racism. At the same time they tried to cultivate good relations with the Dutch Reformed Church in the hope that this highly influential community would one day come to see that the Christian gospel and apartheid were incompatible. But while this policy was being conscientiously pursued the position of non-whites was deteriorating rapidly and the Afrikaner government was about to withdraw South Africa from the Commonwealth and make it a republic, free from external interference. Probably only a new archbishop, coming from England and with no previous involvement in South Africa, could in this situation have spoken so plainly and so courageously. In his enthronement sermon he said:

It is my conviction that racial discrimination is a form of blasphemy, and that those who condone it or allow it without protest place their souls in eternal peril . . . Sin is sin, and has to be repented of and forsaken completely – here and now.

This was not what those who had elected him to the South African primacy expected, or greatly appreciated when they heard it, but the new archbishop became a beacon of hope to millions of black victims of apartheid, and never again could discretion be regarded as a credible form of opposition to a great evil.

A Dutch name and ancestry were useful in a country ruled by an Afrikaner minority. De Blank was born in Rotterdam in 1908 into a Dutch Reformed Church family and when his father moved to London to join the Unilever empire they attended the Presbyterian Church in Ealing. The young Joost eventually shed all Calvinist influence, however, as he moved through the City of London School to Queens' College, Cambridge, where he read English and law. Before going up to Cambridge he spent a year studying journalism and acquired skill as a communicator that never left him. Feeling drawn to Holy Orders, he went to Ridley Hall, Cambridge, and in 1931 became a curate in Bath. He now belonged to the Anglican evangelical tradition and, like many others of that sort, was attracted by the Oxford Group Movement – or the Moral Rearmament Association (MRA) as it was officially known. Indeed, after three years in Bath he moved to another curacy, at Bredon in Worcestershire, which left him free to become the MRA organizer for the West Midlands.

In 1937 de Blank became Vicar of Emmanuel Church, Forest Gate, in East London where he exercised a vigorous ministry in a parish of 12,000 people and gradually lost interest in MRA. At this time he was a pacifist but he changed his mind as the evil character of Nazism grew plainer and in 1940 enlisted as an army chaplain. During the North Africa campaign, then in Italy, he proved to be an able and popular chaplain, and although he did not go to France on D-Day he joined the British Liberation Army later as a senior chaplain. In November 1944, while attending a confirmation service in Antwerp, the building in which the service was being held was hit by a German V2 rocket and de Blank was one of only four members of the congregation who were not killed. He was however badly injured and left with a facial scar which thereafter gave him a somewhat sinister appearance. For the remainder of his life few days passed without his experiencing severe headaches.

On demobilization he joined the staff of the Student Christian Movement but this was not really his forte and in 1948 he became Vicar of St John Baptist Church, Greenhill, Harrow. This was already a strong parish – the previous vicar had left to become a bishop – and during the short space of four years de Blank, with the assistance of two curates, turned it into one of the most dynamic parishes in the Church of England. He had by this time long forsaken his evangelical allegiance and become closely identified with the Parish and People movement, particularly its emphasis on the centrality of the Eucharist and the need for the Church to be involved in every aspect of community life. These were heady days at Greenhill, with people queuing to join the large Sunday congregations and the vicar a leading figure in local life. His style was autocratic and he related more easily to men than to women – his mother, to whom he was devoted, lived with him – but his influence was great and extended further when his book *The Parish in Action* became a widely read guide to the renewal of parish life.

On his appointment as Bishop of Stepney in 1952 the same dynamism was soon felt in London's East End. Parishes were formed into teams,

rallies and congresses were organized, and de Blank was to be seen everywhere – a bustling figure in a purple cassock, who was impatient with
theology and determined to reinvigorate the depressed clergy and congregations of his area. And, to a degree, he succeeded. He was an entre-
preneur and showman, with flair for publicity and immense energy. So
much so, that when Bishop William Wand retired in 1955 many, including de Blank himself, hoped that he might succeed to the Bishopric of
London. But the Crown, far from being prepared to run this kind of risk,
appointed Bishop Henry Montgomery Campbell of Guildford who was
almost 70 and laboured on with no great distinction until he was 75.

A more important post awaited de Blank. In 1957 the Archbishop
of Cape Town, Geoffrey Clayton, suddenly collapsed and died. At that
time all the South African bishops had attended English universities and
been ordained in England, and they found themselves unable to agree
on the choice of a new archbishop from among their own number. So
they elected de Blank – to his own great astonishment, for he was not
even aware that an election was taking place. But he accepted the challenge and took Cape Town by storm. Following his enthronement in the
cathedral, over 2,000 people packed a welcome meeting in the city hall –
many failed to get in – and in his response he let them into what he called
a secret disability: he was 'colour blind'. A few months later he attacked
government policy and said that he would withdraw episcopal ministrations from any congregation that practised racial discrimination. This
brought him worldwide publicity and sharp attacks from members of
the Afrikaner government. But he was undeterred.

In 1959 he became president of the British-based Campaign against
Racial Discrimination in Sport, which touched a sensitive government
nerve, and following the Sharpeville massacre in 1961, in which 69
Africans were killed by the police, he demanded that unless the Dutch
Reformed Church abandoned its support for apartheid it should be
expelled from the World Council of Churches. This created a considerable stir, not least in ecumenical circles, for although the WCC was
strongly opposed to apartheid it was desperately anxious to keep the
DRC on board in the hope of influencing it for good.

Some of de Blank's episcopal colleagues and many white South African lay people were equally disturbed by his unequivocal stance, but
among Africans he was a hero and a light in the darkness. Large crowds
gathered to hear him speak in the cathedral or in meeting halls, and often
enough they heard a call to mutual penitence as the way to true reconciliation. In a letter to *The Times* of London on 1 March 1961 he described
apartheid as 'morally corroding, economically suicidal, politically senile
and theologically indefensible', but in the same letter he pleaded for
South Africa to be kept in the Commonwealth because he believed at that

time that more could be accomplished by sound argument than by what he called 'a senseless parade of passion'. As always, he lived at a frantic pace – dashing here and there, visiting parishes, organizing a church congress and a Ten Churches Appeal, talking to international visitors, addressing meetings, writing articles and frequently going abroad to speak about the South African situation. The spotlight was rarely off him and even when going to the theatre he would appear in a vivid purple cassock, accompanied by three or four young chaplains, also clad in startling colours. He needed ceaseless activity and seemed to enjoy it, but it could not last. In August 1962 he had a cerebral thrombosis and, after treatment in England, returned to South Africa in the hope of continuing his work there. It soon became evident however that the demands on him would never lessen and, since he was an 'all or nothing' man, he resigned from the archbishopric on the last day of 1963 at the early age of 54.

His final years were spent as a Canon of Westminster, where he felt like a caged lion, though he contributed much to the Abbey's life and carried out a multitude of preaching and speaking engagements throughout Britain. There was even a flicker of hope in his election in 1966 to the Bishopric of Hong Kong, but before he could take up this post his doctor, unsurprisingly, pronounced that he was unfit to take on its responsibilities and on 1 January 1968 he died. A memorial tablet near the main entrance to Westminster Abbey describes him as an 'Indomitable Fighter for Human Rights'.

———————————

The days of the overseas missionary bishop are now long past and in some of the former mission fields the Anglican Church is very much stronger than it is in England. Indeed there is sometimes talk of missionaries from these countries embarking on the reconversion of England, though it is unlikely that they would make a significant impact on our increasingly secularized society. Rather less ambitious, but worthwhile, is the Partnership in Mission scheme under which dioceses in England and in other parts of the world are linked and, by means of exchange visits, literature and prayer, provide each other with mutual insight, support and encouragement. Bishops are involved in this and a tropical suit has become an essential part of the episcopal wardrobe. The missionary societies still provide some overseas dioceses with financial help and specialists who undertake educational, medical and development work under local control.

The worldwide Anglican Communion, which was the remarkable result of the missionary work of the nineteenth century, is now about 70 million strong, with about 500 dioceses in 164 countries. After the Roman Catholic Church, it is the most widespread. The Lambeth Conference held every ten years, together with more frequent meetings of the Anglican Consultative Council and the primates, provides the link between the autonomous, self-governing provinces. The link is reinforced by common allegiance to the see of Canterbury and similar forms of worship.

In the autonomy of the provinces there lies however the beginnings of a serious problem. The 1992 Lambeth Conference found itself sharply divided over the issue of homosexuality. An increasing number of Christians in Western Europe and North America now believe that homosexual relations should be no barrier to church membership or entry to the ordained ministry. But for cultural as well as religious reasons this is quite unacceptable to many of the Anglican dioceses in Africa and Asia. And this division of belief is compounded by a different approach to the interpretation of the Bible. The African and Asian dioceses oppose any acceptance of homosexuality on the grounds that it is expressly forbidden by the Book of Leviticus and by St Paul. Evangelical fundamentalists among them regard homosexuality as an evil best dealt with by means of prayer and exorcism. But many English and North American bishops believe that the Bible needs to be handled differently and that a few words culled from Leviticus and the Pauline Epistles cannot be treated as ethically definitive for all time. If schism is to be avoided the leaders of the Anglican Communion will need to find a new formula to hold together unity and diversity.

An altogether more important issue concerns the relationship between Christianity and the other world faiths, and this is made all the more urgent by the rise of global terrorism and its association in some countries with grotesquely distorted versions of the Islamic religion. Most of the nineteenth-century missionaries were driven to heroic deeds because they had no doubt that the Christian faith alone offered the way to salvation and that the soul of 'the heathen, who in his blindness bowed down to wood and stone' was in mortal peril unless he was rescued by exposure to the Christian gospel. In the light of today's knowledge of the deeply spiritual character of the major non-Christian faiths and of the evident transforming effects for good they have on the lives of their believers, such exclusivity is no longer open to the Church.

During the second half of the nineteenth century Christians faced the challenge offered by the publication of Charles Darwin's *The Origin of Species* and, notoriously and disastrously, the bishops failed to offer the leadership then required. The challenge today offered by the presence of other religious believers in most parts of the world, including our own, is no less serious, and bold episcopal leadership in the direction of inter-faith understanding and sharing is now literally a matter of life or death.

12

The evangelists

The earliest bishops were the leaders of a missionary Church – of a community which had been called into existence to live in the light of Christian truth and to declare this truth to others in such a way that they would come to accept it for themselves. With some notable exceptions – Bishop Gregory of Neocaesarea, in modern Turkey, in the third century, was said to have converted practically the whole population of the city – bishops were not however in the forefront of this work of evangelism. This was entrusted to missionary priests and an order of evangelists, and it was understood that the whole Church had a missionary vocation. The primary task of the bishop was to keep this missionary vocation alive, to preside over worship, to teach the Christian faith within the Church and preserve it from heresy, to ordain other ministers, and to exercise pastoral care. The conversion of England during the seventh century was nonetheless led by bishops. Aidan, Cuthbert, Wilfrid, Chad and others, who were active in the North, were missionary bishops and although Augustine came from Rome as a monk he was soon consecrated as a bishop once his mission had gained a foothold in Kent. There were to be setbacks in the following centuries, but well before the Norman Conquest it was possible to regard England as a Christian nation. During the thirteenth century, however, the Dominican and Francisan friars made a considerable impact as itinerant preachers whose lively sermons often attracted people away from their dull parish priest. In the following century the Lollard preachers were concerned primarily with church reform and soon suppressed as heretics. Another 400 years passed before a Church of England priest, John Wesley, felt driven to lead a new missionary movement which in the end found it possible to survive only outside the life of the Established Church.

Wesley's missionary vocation came from an intense personal conversion experience and also from an awareness that the Industrial Revolution in eighteenth-century England was so dislocating in the established social order that a high proportion of the agricultural labourers who moved to the new towns were alienated from the life of the Church and no longer held any kind of Christian belief. The bishops were very much

slower to recognize this and when they did their response was the traditional one of building new churches and appointing clergy to minister
in new, territorial parishes. There was no awareness that systems and
methods which had been effective in stable, agrarian communities would
not serve as instruments of mission in the inhuman slums of urban areas.
By the end of the nineteenth century it was evident, though not widely
acknowledged, that the Church of England had made no significant
impact on the urban working class. The ministries of the Anglo-Catholic
slum priests were heroic and in many ways impressive, yet they had not
touched the fundamental problem.

Arthur Foley Winnington-Ingram

Among the bishops who recognized the need for evangelism was Arthur
Foley Winnington-Ingram, who became Bishop of Stepney in 1897 and
then occupied the Bishopric of London from 1901 to 1939. From almost
every point of view he was one of the most disastrous bishops ever to be
imposed on the nation's capital. Yet no Bishop of London has made a
greater impact on ordinary people. Archbishop Randall Davidson, who
was not given to enthusiasm or unconsidered utterances, said of him
during his Stepney years that he was 'the greatest spiritual force in the
Church of England since John Wesley'. Thousands of people crowded
into St Paul's Cathedral whenever he preached.

Winnington-Ingram's sermons, which so many found compelling,
were of a simple, homely sort – full of illustrations and anecdotes, often
of a sentimental character and delivered in a Cockney accent. He was
said to be very good at deathbed scenes and inasmuch as the sermons
had any identifiable theological content they were wholly orthodox.
He had in fact no interest in intellectual matters and W. R. Inge, who
was Dean of St Paul's and had many opportunities to see and hear him
in action, concluded, 'The mental processes of the Bishop are, for a
man in his position, of almost childish simplicity.' Yet he was in constant demand for inspirational addresses at church congresses and men's
rallies, during his long years in London he conducted many missions in
West End and North London churches, and until his later years he had
the power to draw large crowds of students whenever he preached in
Oxford and Cambridge. But attractive though his sermons were to some,
and often challenging to individuals, they made little impact on intellectuals and his sympathetic but not uncritical biographer, S. C. Carpenter,
admitted that 'he was not a man to sit down and think out new ways of
presenting the everlasting Gospel to the changing generations. He always
put the Gospel in the same old way.'

This inability to grasp the significance of what was taking place around him and to scrutinize the social order in the light of the gospel led Winnington-Ingram to adopt an attitude to the 1914–18 war which many felt to be deplorable and even un-Christian. Soon after the outbreak of war he became one of the country's most effective recruiting officers – 'We would all rather die, wouldn't we, than have England a German province' – and throughout the war years he equated the death of a soldier with the death of Christ on the Cross. He made numerous visits to the armed forces and early in 1915 Sir John French, the commander of the British Army in France, wrote – 'Dear Bishop, Five minutes of you cheers me up. Come out for ten days.' He went for Holy Week and Easter and conducted what he called a Mission to the British Expeditionary Force. Some 50–60 sermons and visits to 22 hospitals were supported by 10,000 cards containing private prayers for use by the soldiers. Two hundred men were confirmed. Later he wrote a letter to soldiers who were in hospital urging them to regard their time between clean sheets as 'a God-given opportunity for coming back to God, and making God your friend for life'. He convinced himself that a mighty religious revival would emanate from the Western Front, but not everyone shared his unquestioning patriotism and F. R. Barry, who was serving as a chaplain in France and later became Bishop of Southwell, described some of his sermons as 'extraordinary'. Neither did everyone appreciate his hearty back-slapping manner and being addressed as 'My dear old friend'. Dick Sheppard, who had spent some time in France before becoming a pacifist, was not best pleased to be greeted by his bishop outside St Paul's with – 'Hello, old chap. Still keen about peace?' W. R. Inge, describing in his diary a Day of Intercession and Thanksgiving for the War held on 6 January 1918, wrote, 'The Bishop of London preached a most unChristian sermon, which with a few words changed might have been preached by a court chaplain in Berlin.'

Winnington-Ingram, the son of a Worcestershire squarson, was born in 1858 and went from Marlborough College to Keble College, Oxford, where he secured a first in Mods and a second in Greats. During his time at Oxford he was greatly influenced by Edward King, whose lectures on pastoral theology he attended, and also by Charles Gore. He became a curate at St Mary's, Shrewsbury, but after only a year moved to become chaplain to the Bishop of Lichfield. Besides serving the bishop he conducted a number of parish missions which were deemed to have been very successful.

In 1889 he was appointed Head of Oxford House, Bethnal Green, and began his love affair with London's East End. The contrast between his style and that of Hensley Henson, whom he succeeded, could hardly have been greater and he quickly threw himself into social and evangelistic work among some of the poorest of the poor. After only two years, however, he became Bishop of Stepney. He was now 39 and Bishop Mandell Creighton explained, 'I do not ask you because I think you will do it well, but because I do not know anyone who would do it better.' It was a very heavy responsibility for the area of East and North-East London entrusted to his leadership had a population of 2 million, of whom 40,000 lived in single tenement rooms. There were 208 parishes served by about 550 clergy, and Winnington-Ingram, who travelled about his area either on foot or by bus, soon became a well known and much loved figure. He was always available to people in trouble and spent much time visiting the sick. A friend related how

> Dr Ingram was walking along the Mile End Road to a meeting on a very wet night when he saw an old woman sitting in the gutter selling chestnuts. She was ill-clad and much exposed to the rain. The Bishop took off his mackintosh and put it around the shoulders of the old woman and then proceeded on his journey, arriving at the meeting all wet.

At that time there was neither stipend nor housing for a Bishop of Stepney, so the post was combined with a canonry at St Paul's and the cathedral pulpit gave Winnington-Ingram a great opportunity to preach to the multitudes. How many of these were otherwise outside any kind of Christian influence is impossible to tell, but he received 3,000 letters when his appointment as Bishop of London was announced, and a huge crowd assembled outside St Paul's to cheer him following his enthronement.

Winnington-Ingram was not the first choice for London when the diocese fell vacant in 1901. The offer went initially to Randall Davidson who was then at Winchester and was advised, on medical grounds, to turn it down. Dining one day with King Edward VII at Sandringham, Lord Salisbury, the Prime Minister, asked the King, 'Who is the young clergyman sitting at the far end of the table?' 'That is the man you have just nominated as Bishop of London,' came the royal reply. The nominee was then 43 and it was not until he was past his 80th birthday and the country was on the brink of another world war that he actually resigned.

During his 38-year occupancy of the see, which at that time had 620 parishes and almost 2,000 clergymen, there was no semblance of policy and the diocese was run in a chaotic fashion. 'Take one day at a time and trust the Holy Spirit to see you through,' was his motto, and on his retirement he admitted, 'I am much too kind to be a good Bishop.' One of the effects of this was a complete breakdown in clergy discipline in respect of the ordering of worship and an unedifying dispute between the Anglo-Catholic and evangelical factions. His willingness to accept into the diocese clergy who had been suspended by other bishops, and ordination candidates who were some way below the intellectual standard normally required for the priesthood, also created many problems. A good deal of church-building took place during his episcopate and besides 79 new churches another 38 were rebuilt or enlarged. The existence of 49 churches in the City of London troubled him greatly, however, and he believed that many of these should be closed or turned to secular use in order to finance new work in the ever-expanding suburbs. But he ran into considerable opposition to this and in the end only five of the City churches were closed.

His excursions into secular affairs were fairly rare, which many believed to be fortunate. Prime Minister H. H. Asquith said, 'He is so superlatively silly that he can do a great deal of harm. He was a good enough little figure as a curate in an East End parish; the biggest mistake ever made was to put him where he is.' But no-one ever doubted that his heart was in the right place and he supported the suffragettes after some of them had invaded Fulham Palace to make their case. Others who came to Fulham Palace included parish clergy and their families who were invited to stay for a time of rest and renewal, and his accounts for the year ended 30 April 1904, which show that his annual income of £10,000 was overspent by £775 4s 2d, included an item 'Saturday entertainment for working people, average 70 persons'.

His modest expenditure on books reflected the fact that he did little reading, apart from small books on Christian apologetics. He was a keen player of golf, tennis and squash on his days off and an obsessive concern for cleanliness of body as well as of mind and soul led him to have three baths a day. Although strikingly handsome, he never married. His later years were a time of waning influence. His voice weakened, so that it became difficult to hear him from the pulpit. But he continued to be held in great affection and many Londoners could not remember the time when he was not their bishop. In 1934, on the 50th anniversary of his own ordination, the 2,205 men whom he had ordained (25 became bishops) presented him with a book containing their names and describing him as 'A true Father-in-God, whose love never faileth – a man greatly beloved'. Towards the end of his life he told a group of these clergy, 'My brothers, I have been preaching the Gospel for 50 years, and even now I never go up the pulpit stairs without a thrill of eagerness to proclaim the Good News.'

Walter Carey

Another greatly loved bishop deeply committed to evangelism was Walter Carey, who was Bishop of Bloemfontein in South Africa from 1921 to 1935 and on his return to England spent eight years as a public school chaplain before helping to found the Village Evangelists – a simple organization which eventually became a 350-strong company of priests and laity, each devoting ten days each year to village missions. Carey's commitment to the preaching of the gospel in simple, challenging terms began when, as a young priest-librarian of Pusey House, Oxford, he held one-man open-air preaching missions in Kent, and it was reinforced by his experience as a Royal Navy chaplain during the 1914–18 war. He served in the battleship HMS *Warspite* at the Battle of Jutland in 1915 and shortly before sailing with the Fleet from Scapa Flow wrote an article for the *Church Times* under the heading 'The Standard of Revolt'. The main problem, he believed, was that the Church's teaching and for-mularies were too difficult and attempted too much. They were designed as if everyone had the mind of a first-class scholar, thus the Church had no hold at all on the uneducated:

> Are we to meet our returning servicemen with the same heavy teach-ing, the same unilluminating exhortations to a dreary morality, the same hopeless services when they sit semi-animate to monotoned interminable prayers and anthems in which they cannot join? We ask too much, we strain them beyond reason. I have been a priest 15 years, yet I declare that when I go to a cathedral service and hear the priest beginning a series of prayers after the third collect I have a feeling of something like despair. When I take sailors to such a service and hear that terrific succession of admittedly beautiful prayers begin, I feel I could rise and say 'Have mercy on my poor boys; they can't follow all this; shorten it and make it real.' And then, after the service, I see all the Canons and dignitaries filing off to their tea; and my boys look at them with great admiration, as if they were enjoying the spectacle of the Great Mogul, without the inkling of a suspicion that these are *their* bishop, *their* Canons, *their* Fathers-in-God and personal friends. It is piteous, it is ludicrous, it is maddening . . . Let us band together, let us have a programme, let us make trouble.

Carey was born in 1875 in Abington, Northampton, where his father was the Rector. At Bedford School he showed no great academic promise and later confessed, regretfully, that 'at the age of 15 I fell in with a bad lot and spent two unhappy years as a lout and wastrel'. Before this he had been head of school, captain of rugby and a member of the school boat. His admission to Hertford College, Oxford owed everything to his rowing ability, though in the event he chose to play rugby and was a Blue for four years. He also did well in classics and, having had at the end of his school days a religious experience which gave him a new sense of purpose, went to Ely Theological College to prepare for ordination. In 1899 he became a curate at the Church of the Ascension, Clapham Junction, in South London, where for nine years he combined pastoral and social work in a slum parish and preached to large Sunday congregations.

He was then appointed as a librarian of Pusey House, Oxford – a post which, he was always delighted to relate, had nothing to do with books and everything to do with exercising a Catholic pastoral ministry among undergraduates. He now came under the influence of Bishop Charles Gore and Canon Henry Scott Holland, who had moved from St Paul's to Oxford as the Regius Professor of Divinity, and was inspired by Father Stanton, the Vicar of St Alban's, Holborn, and Father Dolling, a slum priest in Portsmouth – the two leading exponents of Catholic social action. Carey sometimes dressed as a tramp and slept in common lodging houses, in order to discover what poverty felt like, and began to speak out about housing and social justice.

He enlisted as a naval chaplain on the outbreak of war in 1914, and after spending nine months on a decrepit guard ship on the Humber joined HMS *Warspite* shortly before the Battle of Jutland. His initial assignment during the battle was, as he put it, 'to loaf about between decks, behind the 6-inch guns "looking brave", as many of the crew were young and it was thought that I would steady them if I wandered about looking unconcerned'. But more than this was soon required of him. A German shell hit one of the casements, causing a fire and killing all but five of the men it housed. Carey helped to extinguish the fire, but when he lifted the survivors their flesh came off in his hands. He administered morphine from his first-aid kit, but two more died. Meanwhile the ship's steering gear had jammed, leaving it to sail directly into a line of German battleships. Eventually it managed to turn but not before it had sustained great damage and the loss of another 50 men.

When the war ended he was invited by Bishop Edward Lee Hicks to become Warden of Lincoln Theological College. This was in many ways a strange appointment which only a bishop as unconventional as Hicks would have made, but with the college full of ex-servicemen he believed that a warden who had shared their experience would be of more use to them than a highly qualified academic. Carey saw his task in characteristically simple terms – 'My principle in trying to manufacture clergy was to make them men first and then clergy. I made them all join the golf club – so useful later on in life . . . St Paul says that the greatest of virtues is charity, but I'm tempted sometimes to think that "the greatest of these is common sense".' This common sense and social commitment took Carey to the chairmanship of the Lincoln Labour Party, to the leadership of a deputation of unemployed men to interview a factory manager and to denunciation of avaricious landlords. Neither before nor since has there been such a head of a theological college.

But it was too good to last, and after only two years Carey received a cable from South Africa informing him that he had been elected Bishop of Bloemfontein. This was a shock but, having enquired if there was a golf course there, he accepted. The diocese, within the Orange Free State, was as large as England and Wales, and among the white population the largest element was Afrikaner. The Africans numbered over half a million. From the outset, Carey – who was a big man physically, large-hearted and extrovert – determined to get to know the Afrikaners. This greatly displeased the British, but his optimism led him to believe that he would be able to show them the error of their apartheid ways and he struck up a strong and lasting friendship with General Hertzog, the Prime Minister, and other leading government figures. But most of his time was devoted to visiting the clergy (40 white, 10 black) at their remote mission stations and he revelled in this. The informality and spontaneity of African village life, and the deep commitment of the African Christians, gave him an experience of so much that was lacking in the English Church.

After fourteen years of strenuous ministry, however, he had a breakdown and soon after returning to England had a heart attack which put him out of action for two years. There was no possibility of his being appointed bishop of an English diocese, so he became chaplain of Eastbourne College where he remained for the next seven years. In spite of his egalitarian ideals, the public school world suited him rather well. By the time of his retirement from it he had preached in all but three of these schools and wrote, 'I wouldn't change the public school system for anything in the world. I want improvement – we all do. But it doesn't want fuss, nor a lot of highbrows to turn them into Bloomsbury boys.' Carey was in fact a curious mixture of the radical and the conservative. He strongly objected to the 1930 Lambeth Conference decision that in some circumstances married couples might use contraceptives, left the Conference in protest, refused to attend its final service in Westminster Abbey and sent a petition to the King. On the other hand, his attitude to race relations in South Africa led to a threat of deportation, even though he believed that Africans were not yet ready for the vote and that the Afrikaners needed to be understood, rather than universally condemned. His views on the value of sport was decidedly quaint:

At games you learn leadership, pluck, decision; you learn how to win happily and lose gracefully. I reckon that if Hitler had been a rowing Blue or a rugger Blue history would have been different. If Stalin had learnt how to captain a cricket team he might captain Russia very differently and much better.

His involvement in rural evangelism began in 1947 when Brother Edward invited him and six other people to join him in three days of prayer. The freelance friar, who had a firm conviction that Christ would soon return to the earth in a special revelation, felt that God was calling him to some special task. Out of the retreat came the idea of the Village Evangelists. Divided into teams of ten or more, those who joined were allocated to a group of rural parishes where they carried out an intensive programme of visiting homes, meetings in pubs and private houses, open-air preaching, and mission services in the main churches. The message was a simple one – 'Something is wrong with England and something is wrong with the souls of men – and the only remedy is to get God back into England and souls, and souls and England back into God.' Carey devoted himself to the work full-time and wherever he went made a considerable impact both by the force of his personality and the style of his preaching which was without any degree of sophistication. 'Tables and chairs don't happen,' he would point out, 'Somebody planned and made them. If so with tables, why not a universe?' The response in terms of numbers attending the events was usually impressive, but Carey recognized that the results depended largely on the quality of the follow-up provided by the parish clergy and their church councils – 'If we find the spiritual temperature of the parish is 40 degrees, we try to leave it at 45; that's worth doing.'

In 1950 Carey went with his wife to live with their son and daughter-in-law in Kenya and was delighted to find what he called 'a door of missionary work' open to him there. 'O how I shall love it,' he exclaimed, 'But God bless old England, too.' He died in 1955 believing that the Church of England was better and stronger than ever before in her history.

Christopher Chavasse

Christopher Chavasse was Bishop of Rochester from 1939 to 1961 – a period when evangelical bishops were rare – and also made his mark as the founder of an Oxford college, the leader of the opposition to the 1928 revision of the Book of Common Prayer, and the chairman of an archbishops' commission on evangelism whose report *Towards the Conversion of England* became an immediate best-seller. His identical twin brother, Noel, won fame as the holder of the VC and Bar – earned for his extraordinary heroism as a medical officer in the 1914–18 war. Christopher, who served as a chaplain, won a Military Cross. The same courage characterized his peacetime ministry in which he was an indomitable fighter for what he believed to be gospel truth. As a bishop there was no possibility of mistaking his evangelical credentials and he had a formidable personality which expressed the kind of dignity and formality associated with Victorian and Edwardian bishops. His friends were always addressed by their surnames, though in an open letter to coalminers in 1947 he so far forgot himself as to address them as 'My dear chums.' No such chumminess was expressed, however, at the consecration of Mervyn Stockwood as Bishop of Southwark in 1959 when, although informality was the new bishop's wish, Chavasse turned up attired in gaiters, episcopal tall hat, suede gloves and Malacca cane.

Yet, in spite of his attachment to tradition, most especially the Protestant tradition of the Church of England, he was often surprisingly open to other insights, the propagation of which sometimes got him into serious trouble with evangelicals of a narrower outlook. Thus at the Islington Conference in 1956 he was bold enough to warn against a fundamentalist approach to the Bible. This brought a storm of protest from his audience and from others who read reports of the conference. When he voted in favour of a revised Canon which permitted the use of Eucharistic vestments by the clergy (he would never have dreamt of wearing them himself) he was accused of betraying the evangelical cause. And his assertion that the Christian ministry of healing was no longer to be thought of in terms of miracles, but rather in terms of antibiotics and modern surgery, was deemed to be deeply shocking. So also was his suggestion – virtually unheard of at the time – that in some circumstances divorced people might attend church for the blessing of their second marriages. On the other hand, he was always strongly opposed to the abolition of capital punishment.

Chavasse, the son of a notable evangelical Bishop of Liverpool, was born in 1884 in Oxford – his father being at that time Rector of St Peter-le-Bailey and soon afterwards Principal of Wycliffe Hall. When the family moved to Liverpool in 1900 Christopher and his twin brother attended Liverpool College, and both represented the United Kingdom in the 1908 Olympic Games. When therefore Noel secured a first in physiology and Christopher failed his finals and had to take some other papers in order to obtain a pass degree the family was deeply shocked. But he was ordained by his father to a curacy in St Helens, where he played rugby for the town, and then became chaplain to his father. The twins both enlisted in the army in August 1914 and, after serving in a military hospital in France, Christopher was with the Royal Artillery at the Battle of Hooge in May 1915, when he was Mentioned in Despatches. A period as senior chaplain on Salisbury Plain was followed by further service in France where he was wounded in the foot, awarded the MC and the French Croix de Guerre, and finally appointed as a Deputy Assistant Chaplain General. The heroic death of Noel in 1917 affected him greatly and one of his two other brothers who served in France was also killed.

On demobilization at the end of 1918 Chavasse became Vicar of St George's, Barrow-in-Furness – a parish which was to experience mass unemployment through the decline of its shipyards. With the assistance of four curates and 62 Sunday School teachers he exercised a dynamic ministry until, after three years, his health broke down and he was obliged to rest for three months. Soon after his return to duty he was appointed Rector of St Aldate's, Oxford, and head of the Oxford Pastorate which offered an evangelical ministry to undergraduates. The church was soon full to capacity and its popular rector also conducted open-air services. During the next six years he was assisted by his father, who had retired to Oxford, and it often seemed that the young rector was still his father's chaplain.

In an address to the Islington Conference Bishop Chavasse appealed for the foundation of a new hall, based on St Peter-le-Bailey, Oxford, which was now linked with St Aldate's. The church would provide the chapel, while the church hall and school would be converted into accommodation for undergraduates. These would usually come from poorer backgrounds and be taught within the evangelical tradition. The conference gave its backing, but soon after the appeal was under way the bishop died and Christopher resigned from St Aldate's in order to concentrate on his father's project. The inevitable financial problems were encountered, but eventually the necessary money was raised from evangelical trusts and private individuals. Unfortunately, not everyone in the university was happy about this development. At a time when church influence in the colleges was still deliberately being reduced, the prospect of a new establishment under militant evangelical auspices and devoted to the lower social orders was unwelcome. Moreover – and this was the chief objection – it was obvious that Chavasse would become the first Master and he, equipped with no more than a pass degree, lacked the calibre expected in the head of an Oxford college. In the end, however, the objections were overcome and in 1928 twelve men went into residence in St Peter's Hall. Four years later the number had risen to 90, with a small but able teaching staff, and in 1961 the hall was made a full college of the university. It was a remarkable twentieth-century achievement and owed everything to Chavasse.

But during the 1920s this project was not his only concern, and the publication of a pamphlet *The New Prayer Book: Can We Accept It?*

soon led to his becoming the unofficial leader of the opposition to the proposed book. There was no beating about the bush on his part:

> I must leave the Church of England, in which I have been born and bred and in which I have ever counted it my highest privilege to serve, if ever, as regards the alternative Prayer of Consecration, I am called upon to declare before my Chief Shepherd and the flock he has committed to my charge that 'I believe the doctrine therein contained to be agreeable to the Word of God'.

The opposition led by him was successful inasmuch as the new book was rejected by Parliament, but unsuccessful inasmuch as the tide of liturgical change could not be halted and many of the new proposals went into use in parish churches with the blessing of the bishops.

It was widely believed that Chavasse's prominent role in the controversy would stymie his chances of following in his father's footsteps and becoming a bishop, but in July 1939, as the storm clouds of war were becoming daily darker, he received a letter from the Prime Minister, Neville Chamberlain, offering him the Bishopric of Rochester – a diocese with a strong evangelical tradition. He had no great difficulty in accepting and his consecration was fixed for 30 November, St Andrew's Day, but while on holiday with his family in County Donegal in August he was involved in a sailing accident which he, and they, were fortunate to survive. He was however kept in hospital with a crushed leg until March of the following year and was eventually consecrated, while still in great pain, on 25 April, St Mark's Day. After some years it was necessary for the leg to be completely amputated.

By the time of his enthronement in May Chavasse was bishop of a diocese in the front line and over which the Battle of Britain soon raged. During the next four years 105 (72 per cent) of its churches were either damaged or destroyed, along with 55 vicarages, 32 church halls and 45 church schools. None of which seemed to trouble him. His 1914–18 war experience stood him in good stead, his evangelical faith enabled him to offer uncompromising leadership, he worked long hours (letters were always responded to by return of post) and he was out and about a great deal in the parishes. But although his patriotism and commitment to the war effort was never in doubt, he deplored the ending of the war in 1945 by means of the atomic bombs dropped on two Japanese cities. He believed that a warning demonstration should have been given in a remote area of Japan, and annoyed Field Marshal Montgomery who, after attending a victory service in Rochester Cathedral at which this view was expressed, left the cathedral declaring, 'I do wish parsons would stick to subjects they understand.' He was more widely criticized for a speech in the House of Lords in which he said that, although there must be burning indignation against the Germans for the grievous wrong and injury they had inflicted on others, revenge and reprisals were entirely ruled out by Christian ethics: 'Instead, we are to have a concern for their welfare – both of the body and the soul.'

Chavasse's life-long concern for evangelism made him the obvious choice for the chairmanship of an archbishops' commission on the subject. This reported in June 1945 and its wide-ranging proposals aroused considerable interest – 'The state of the Christian religion in this country urgently calls for definite action. That definite action is no less than the conversion of England to the Christian faith.' Canon Max Warren, a leading overseas missionary statesman, described *Towards the Conversion of England* as 'one of the most remarkable statements ever authorized for publication by the Church of England', and at this point Chavasse was ready to resign from his bishopric in order to spearhead a movement that would implement the report's recommendations.

But the Church's initial enthusiasm soon evaporated. After long years of war it was too weary to respond to such a challenge and Archbishop Geoffrey Fisher believed that the post-war priority was the revision of canon law. It was also the case that the gulf between the Church and most of the English people was now too wide to be bridged by such things as teaching missions, popular services, Sunday observance and advertising, though Chavasse's protest in the Church Assembly against ever-increasing expenditure on administration at the expense of evangelism deserved more serious consideration than it received.

Whether or not a proposed course of action would further the cause of evangelism was always the yardstick for his decision-making. It was a pity therefore that – mainly because he was so formal in his personal relationships – he retained the image of an uncompromising Protestant who was out of sympathy with the liturgical and other reforming movements of the post-1945 world. There was more to him than that. He died in 1962.

Cuthbert Bardsley

Cuthbert Bardsley, who was Bishop of Croydon from 1947 to 1956, then of Coventry until 1976, was an episcopal evangelist of a decidedly respectable sort. His burning convictions and missionary zeal were tempered by an Eton and Oxford education that would not permit indulgence in anything remotely vulgar. His sermons and mission addresses, which often attracted large numbers without ever rivalling the Billy Graham crusades, were characterized by a simple – over-simple, some thought – gospel message delivered with warmth and enthusiasm by an attractive personality, and reassuring to many in its affirmation of traditional moral values. It was essentially a personal message which brought some to faith and strengthened the existing faith of many more. But although he often talked about social issues and the importance of relating the teaching of Christ to current problems in politics, industry and education, he never seemed quite able to understand the complexity of such problems or to recognize that they were not patient of solution simply by the application of biblical texts and stories. Equally, he was mystified by the theological questioning that began in the 1960s, so he was eventually left with an 'old time' message that made less and less impact on serious enquirers.

Bardsley, born in 1907, came from a remarkable family which, within three generations, produced 29 clergymen, including three diocesan bishops. His father was Rector of Ulveston and when his mother inherited her family's fortune he was sent to an expensive preparatory school in Oxford and on to Eton. There he acquired charm and confidence but not much intellectual skill, and at New College, Oxford, where he obtained only a poor class in philosophy, politics and economics, he was remembered more for his rowing. 'A nice chap but a bit naive' was the verdict of a fellow undergraduate. He was nonetheless an effective president of the Student Christian Movement, then in its heyday, and towards the end of his time at the university joined the Oxford Group Movement, later renamed Moral Rearmament. This led to an intense spiritual experience and later he described his involvement with the group as 'the greatest single adventure of my time in Oxford'. 'Adventure' was a word he often used.

Feeling drawn to Holy Orders, Bardsley now went to Westcott House, Cambridge, for ordination training and in 1934 became a curate at All Hallows Church on London's Tower Hill, where the vicar was the legendary Tubby Clayton, co-founder of Toc H. No church could have suited him better and 'soap box' speaking on Tower Hill provided scope for his evangelistic zeal. His involvement with the Group soon deepened to a point where it seemed right to him to devote himself to its full-time service. A life-long friendship with the founder, Frank Buchman, was established and he spent five years travelling extensively in Britain and abroad, meeting businessmen, trade-unionists and politicians, and on one occasion addressing a packed London Albert Hall. He was an ideal ambassador for such a movement – tall, handsome, always immaculately turned out, a rich voice, and great enthusiasm. But the outbreak of war in 1939 and the power of evil manifested by the German Nazi machine had a devastating effect on Moral Rearmament, as it had now become. Bardsley was filled with doubt and uncertainty and went through a period of ill-health. He recovered from this during a three-months stay with the Community of the Resurrection at Mirfield, which also had the effect of deepening his awareness of the importance of the Church and the sacraments. The Bishop of Southwark thereupon appointed him Rector of Woolwich – one of the largest and most challenging parishes in South London which was now being heavily bombed.

This was a bold move on the bishop's part, and it worked remarkably. Bardsley was in his element and the challenge drew the best out of him. While the bombs were falling he toured the air-raid shelters and afterwards spent much time comforting the dying, the bereaved and those whose homes had been destroyed. Church attendance rapidly increased, outdoor services were held and previously torpid church life became vigorous. The Woolwich Arsenal and a Siemens electrical components factory also attracted his attention and every Wednesday lunchtime he conducted a canteen service, making himself available for an hour afterwards for personal pastoral work. Soon he was the best-known and most admired figure in Woolwich. When therefore a new Provost of Southwark Cathedral was needed in 1944 the bishop recruited Bardsley – at 41 the youngest ever to be appointed. The Woolwich formula was repeated and the life of the cathedral was revitalized. V1 flying bombs and V2 rockets now threatened life and homes and he resumed his air-raid shelter ministry. He also continued to visit the Siemens factory and became a popular broadcaster.

In 1946 Archbishop Fisher asked him to undertake a long tour of the British Army units serving in Germany, and this extended over three months. He treated it as a mission, gave innumerable sermons and addresses, talked with senior officers and ordinary soldiers, encouraged ordination candidates and conducted retreats for chaplains. His style suited many in the army at that time and he made a great impression. News of this reached Fisher and when Bardsley returned to Southwark he invited him to become Bishop of Croydon, then within Canterbury diocese, and also Bishop to the Forces. It was a good choice: Croydon was compact enough for him to make an immediate impression and small enough to enable him to devote a fair amount of time to work among the armed services. The pattern of his German tour was enlarged and extended. He travelled widely, ministering in Korea during the 1950–53 war and in Kenya during the Mau Mau uprising. A popular figure, his influence on individuals was considerable, but after nine years of ceaseless activity his health began to suffer and he was saved by appointment in 1956 to the Bishopric of Coventry.

Again, it was a good choice. Coventry, at that time a boom town with few serious social problems, and conservative Warwickshire appreciated his style. Moreover a new cathedral was rising from the ruins of the

early-fifteenth-century building famously destroyed by wartime bombing. He was enthroned soon after the completion of the new foundations, with the shape of Basil Spence's creation now discernible, and the
sermon was vintage Bardsley:

> I have come among you at a moment of acute tension in the life of our
> nation. The peace of the world is precarious. Racialism, nationalism,
> class-hatred may lead us over the precipice into the total destruction
> of mankind . . . We must choose life and greatness or death through
> littleness.

He went on to speak of the needs of the Church – 'New methods, New
men, New money.' The building of the cathedral greatly excited him
and his chief contribution to its future was the appointment of a very
gifted team of provost and canons. As the time for the consecration of
the completed building approached, a ten-day mission to the diocese was
organized – 'A consecrated cathedral needs a consecrated people.' At
the consecration itself, watched on television by millions world-wide, his
sense of theatre served the occasion well, though the histrionics were too
much for some. It soon became apparent, however, that the innovative
ideas of the cathedral team were leaving the bishop some way behind,
though his chief work was in the diocese where he started a Fellowship
of Prayer, with 350 members, launched a widely read newspaper, and
appointed chaplains to work among immigrants, young people and the
students of the new University of Warwick.

In 1966 Bardsley was one of the few bishops who supported Billy
Graham's Greater London Crusade and he called on a crowd of 100,000
at Wembley Stadium to 'thank God for raising up a man who has shown
us how great are our capacities as a nation to respond to the challenge
to live and work for God and the service of others'. He was himself
already planning a 'Call to Mission' to be held in Coventry in 1968.
Study courses were held in all the parishes of the diocese, 400 counsellors
were trained, and for ten days the mission meetings filled the cathedral
and were relayed by close-circuit television to other churches in the
city. Bardsley was the chief missioner but before his address famous
sportsmen, television personalities, politicians and other celebrities spoke
about their personal faith. On the day following the final meeting an
outdoor Eucharist attracted 15,000 people and the shining of the sun
during an unsettled period was described as 'miraculous'.

Barnsley's diary rarely had empty spaces, apart from his annual
holiday, usually spent painting abroad. He had regular meetings with
Coventry city councillors, representatives of industry and commerce,
and educationalists – these always ended with silence and prayer in

his private chapel. Weekend conferences were held, on an ecumenical basis, for landowners and farmers, industrialists and trade union leaders, and professional people. He was president and an ardent supporter of Coventry City Football Club. At his suggestion, the Archbishops of Canterbury and York formed a Council on Evangelism, with himself as its chairman. This was intended to keep evangelism in the forefront of the mind of the Church, but although it met for several years and at one time had a research and development officer, it achieved little – partly because it did not relate directly to the official structures of the Church, but chiefly because the Church as a whole felt no evangelistic imperative. Bardsley conducted many campaigns based on the Coventry model in various parts of England and also in Canada. He often spoke in the House of Lords and was for many years a prominent Freemason.

In his final message to Coventry diocese on the eve of his retirement, he spoke of the Church's 'Barren lean years of the 1960s when evangelism was a suspect word' and went on, 'I believe that we are moving out of the trough towards the crest of a new wave of the power of the Holy Spirit.' Unfortunately, he was mistaken. But not in his decision when he was 65 to embark upon what proved to be a very happy marriage which extended over 15 years of retirement. He died in 1991.

There is clear, unmistakable evidence that traditional forms of evangelism expressed in mass rallies addressed by powerful preachers make no significant impact on a society in which most people have no identifiable Christian commitment. Those attending such rallies consist almost entirely of existing church members and, although a few of those outside the Church's life who are pursuaded to accompany them may be drawn to faith, their number is nowhere near large enough to have missionary significance. There may, or may not, be other benefits in the strengthening of the commitment of those who attend. Some of those who attended the Billy Graham crusades in the 1960s eventually offered themselves for ordination and are now involved in the current mini-evangelical renewal, but none of this is making Britain more Christian and church attendance continues to decline. The Decade of Evangelism declared in 1990 was, in terms of conversions to the Christian faith, a failure.

All of which was entirely predictable. During the nineteenth century various revivalist movements sought to 'win people to Christ' by means of powerful preaching and hymn-singing but, although some converts were made, it proved impossible to change the hearts and lives of the multitude of the working class who for a hundred years or more had embraced no recognizable religious faith. The failure of latter-day evangelists to learn from that experience is as astonishing as it is depressing. Meanwhile the twentieth century witnessed the middle class leaving the English churches in large numbers as society became more secularist and pluralist, and social pressures to conform were reduced.

This is not the place to attempt an analysis of the forces which have weakened the churches and made their mission more difficult. But the point to be recognized is that the factors are as much sociological as religious and that a more sophisticated approach to mission and evangelism is now essential. During the late 1940s a French priest-sociologist carried out a survey of Mass attendance in France over the previous 100 years and a striking feature of the result of this survey was that in certain regions attendance had remained consistently low throughout the period, and lowest of all in those regions where there were granite quarries. None of which could be explained by the quality of the preaching in French churches.

The truth is that, whereas the overseas missionaries of the nineteenth century, and earlier, crossed geographical frontiers, the home missionaries of the twenty-first century are required to cross sociological frontiers – to penetrate and influence those elements in modern culture that militate against any form of religious belief. This involves inevitably a more serious attempt to express the Christian faith in terms that relate to modern culture and are accessible to those who live under its influence. The issue was raised with crystal clarity by Dietrich Bonhoeffer from his German prison cell in 1944: How do we communicate the meaning of Christianity in a world radically without religion? How do we speak in secular terms of God? How can Christ be Lord even of those without religion? During the last 50 years a number of theologians have attempted to answer these questions, but the Church has tended to be highly critical of their efforts, rather than grateful for them, and there is little sign of Christian preachers being even aware of the questions, much less allowing them to influence their understanding and expression of the gospel. There can be no progress in mission and evangelism without this.

Alongside theological change, structural change is needed. The present diocesan and parochial systems, initiated by Archbishop Theodore of Tarsus in the seventh century and developed over the next five centuries, still have value but they cannot provide the only structures required by a church seeking to exercise its mission in the highly complex societies of the modern industrialized world. If the mission is confined only to those places where people reside it will fail to make an impact on the greater part of their lives and if evangelism is seen only in terms of traditional preaching in church or in Alpha-course homes progress will remain impossible.

The evangelist-bishop has had his day and the need now is for mission bishops who encourage attempts to reinterpret the Christian faith in contemporary terms and who lead the Church in carrying out those organizational changes that are essential if it is to engage fully with the modern, ever-changing world.

13

The odd men out

The cleric is always an odd man out inasmuch as he or she holds a unique office. This involves a commitment to continue in the contemporary world the ministry of Jesus – the odd man out whose life and teaching was eccentric enough to cause him to be publicly executed by the establishment of his day. The priestly office is entered in a religious ceremony of deep solemnity and requires its holder to challenge at many points the beliefs and values of the society in which the Church is called to witness. The priest has also an involvement with individuals at the key, mysterious turning points of human existence – birth, marriage and death – as well as in other times of joy and suffering. No other human being has this particular responsibility and experience and, although the priest is simply expressing in personal terms the mission and ministry that belongs to the Church as a whole, the symbolic, representative role has inevitably the effect of separation. In the days of small railway carriages a clerical collar often guaranteed its wearer an uncrowded journey.

It is also the case that since religious belief and experience belongs to the deep wells of the human psyche it can, and frequently does, lead to unusual attitudes and actions on the part of those for whom it has become a full-time, professional occupation. The stage parson, who is always good for a laugh, is a caricature but always an easily recognizable one and often enough hardly different from the reality. Within the Church of England the difference, the separation, the oddity has been given ample scope, and indeed encouraged, by the high degree of independence accorded to the clergy. Historically, the priest and the bishop have been answerable to no-one, apart from God whose constraints are invisible, and, although recent financial problems and attempts to make the Church more efficient have led to some erosion of clerical independence, the recipients of Holy Orders still have greater freedom in the exercising of their duties than any other profession on earth.

This is something to be applauded and treasured, for although it sometimes leads to embarrassment, and occasionally to harm, the freedom of the clergy is essential to a ministry that is truly personal and challenging. Moreover the wide variety of understanding, style and method provides the Church with a richness of ministry that would be lacking in a body of like-minded, rigidly disciplined ecclesiastical officers.

What is true of the priest is no less so of the bishop whose comparative rarity serves to enhance the sense of difference and to elicit unusual responses from those who find themselves in his company. There is broad recognition that episcopal consecration makes him an odd man out. It is also the case that highly gifted people are often individualists or eccentrics and happily some of these have found their way into the episcopate.

Henry Phillpotts

Henry Phillpotts, Bishop of Exeter 1830–69, played a large part in ensuring that for the greater part of the nineteenth century the bishops, as a body, would be deeply unpopular. A pugnacious man of trenchant speech, he was in many ways an eighteenth-century figure who simply could not cope with the radical changes that gathered pace in Victorian England. He resolutely opposed all attempts to undermine the prosperity of the most privileged members of society and exploited pluralism so that he might himself belong to their number. He ruled his diocese by fear rather than by love, and during his episcopate spent £30,000 (over £800,000 in today's money) on 50 legal actions, largely against his own clergy.

A relentless controversialist and for 30 years one of the most prominent bishops, Phillpotts was essentially a loner. Dr Edgar Gibson, a historian Vicar of Leeds, described him thus:

> The subject of endless stories, always amusing, not always edifying; restlessly active in enforcing discipline; in lawsuits innumerable; a prolific writer of letters and pamphlets; a constant astonishment to onlookers; compelling an unwilling admiration from those who liked him least by the vigour of his utterances and actions; exasperating more often than winning over his friends by utterances which they could scarcely defend, and by his championship of causes which had better been left alone.

After his sustained opposition to the 1832 Reform Bill a mob attacked his Exeter palace and coastguards were enlisted as a defence force. His effigy, with that of Guy Fawkes, was burned on a bonfire in the city on 5 November. Soon after this an outbreak of cholera claimed the lives of

345 people in Exeter, but Phillpotts moved out to a villa at Teignmouth and refused to return to the city until the epidemic ended. Thereafter he was often described as the bishop who ran away, and his heavy-handed style and constant recourse to the law in the enforcement of clergy discipline made him a very unpopular figure in the diocese. In his novel *Maid of Sker*, R. D. Blackmore (better known as the author of *Lorna Doone*) told of a Devon parson who dug a huge hole in his rectory drive which he then filled with bog water and sat back to enjoy the spectacle of the bishop, with his carriage and pair, falling into it when on a parish visitation. The bishop was understood to be Phillpotts.

He was born in Bridgwater in 1778, but four years later his father moved to Gloucester to keep the Bell Inn. Young Henry attended the cathedral school from where, at the age of thirteen, he won a scholarship to Corpus Christi College, Oxford. In the year of his graduation, 1795, he won the Chancellor's prize for an essay on the influence of religious principle and soon afterwards was elected a fellow of Magdalen College. Ordained in 1802, and having married a niece of the Lord Chancellor's wife, he was immediately presented by the Crown to the living of Kilmersdon, near Bath. He never resided there and clung to its income when, after two years, the Crown appointed him Rector of Stainton-le-Street in County Durham. In the same year, now being 26, he declined an invitation to become Principal of Hertford College, Oxford, but he did not have to wait long for further preferment, for in 1806 he became chaplain to Bishop Shute Barrington of Durham and also, again at the bidding of the Crown, Rector of Bishop Middleham in County Durham. He now felt comfortable enough to resign from Kilmersden, in distant Somerset, but retained Stainton and actually resided in Bishop Middleham for a couple of years.

Bishop Barrington then appointed him to the rich Rectory of Gateshead and to an equally lucrative Canonry of Durham. Another two years passed and the Dean and Chapter of Durham, of which of course he was a member, appointed him Rector of St Margaret's, Durham, but although he became a good parish priest there he did not feel under any obligation to resign from Gateshead. While at Durham he served also as a magistrate, which whetted his appetite for litigation, and he once declared that it was good for labourers to have to work long hours as this made them more appreciative of their time off. In 1815 he seized an opportunity to exchange his Durham canonry for an even richer one which he retained until his appointment in 1820 to Stanhope, where the living was worth almost £200,000 per annum in today's money and enabled him to build a palatial rectory. Meanwhile he had established his reputation as a controversialist. A pamphlet supported the action of the magistrates at what became known as the Peterloo massacre when troops were ordered to open fire on a Manchester demonstration in favour of reform, killing eleven and injuring 500 in the crowd. Another pamphlet from his pen attacked a proposal by the Prime Minister, Lord Grey, that Roman Catholics be allowed to hold public office. The editor of the *Edinburgh Review* commented that Phillpotts displayed 'a power of invective equal to, if not exceeding, that of Dean Swift'.

In 1828 he was appointed Dean of Chester, taking care to retain Stanhope, but this was only a brief interlude before the Duke of Wellington made him Bishop of Exeter. From the outset there were problems. The tradition of the diocese was evangelical, whereas Phillpotts was a High Churchman in the Laudian tradition, so the Protestants complained and Lord Grey, now in opposition, challenged the duke's choice. Moreover the new bishop was unhappy about the financial arrangements – the income of the see, £2,700 per annum, was relatively small for the time – and he stipulated that as a condition of acceptance he be allowed to retain Stanhope. The duke agreed to this, but the parishioners of Stanhope, who had experienced several absentee rectors, objected and before the negotiations had been completed the Whigs replaced the Tories in government and Lord Grey, back in power, refused his consent. Phillpotts was furious and threatened to expose Grey's action to the public, so a compromise was reached and he exchanged Stanhope for a Durham canonry. The Bishops of Bristol and Chester also held Durham canonries at that time, while the Bishop of St David's held the deanery.

Soon after Wellington returned to office in 1834 he received two letters from Phillpotts about his spiritual condition, warning him of the dangers of high office and urging him to attend church regularly. In his response the duke explained that he attended church regularly when at Stratfield Saye and Walmer, and sometimes went to the 8.15 am service at St James's, Piccadilly, where he was usually the only member of the congregation and therefore not publicly noticed. In general, however, he found the London churches too cold for his bare head and injured ear. He ended – pointedly it might be thought – 'No doubt we all have room for amendment in our lives.'

The indiscipline of the clergy in Exeter diocese was undoubtedly a serious problem which Phillpotts determined to resolve, but his popularity was not increased when a Devon parson prosecuted by him lost the case and was committed to prison for failing to meet the legal costs. A public subscription organized by the parson's sympathizers secured his release. Another of his legal cases – not in fact initiated by himself – became a nineteenth-century cause célèbre and entered the annals of English church history. George Cornelius Gorham, a distinguished botanist and antiquary, had been instituted by Phillpotts to a Cornish parish without any fuss, but when in 1847 the Lord Chancellor presented him to the living of Brampton Speke, near Exeter, the bishop insisted on examining him about his beliefs. Over the course of eight days and occupying 52 hours, Gorham was required to answer 149 questions in what he described as a penal inquisition. As a result it became apparent that he believed infants did not benefit directly from baptism, since they were unable to receive the sacrament worthily. This view, influenced by a form of Calvinism, was contrary to Church of England doctrine, so Phillpotts refused to institute him to the parish. Gorham appealed to the Court of Arches which upheld the bishop's decision, but at a further appeal to the Judicial Committee of the Privy Council, of which the Archbishops of Canterbury and York were members, this decision was overturned and Phillpotts was ordered to carry out the institution.

This he steadfastly refused to do and instead sent a letter, sealed with his episcopal seal, to the Archbishop of Canterbury in which he declared –

> Any Archbishop or Bishop or official who shall institute the said George Cornelius Gorham will thereby incur the sin of supporting and favouring the said heretical doctrine . . . I hereby renounce and repudiate all Communion with anyone, be he who he may, who shall so institute the said George Cornelius Gorham.

The Archbishop of Canterbury, John Sumner, was not greatly troubled by this and, after further legal wrangling, instituted Gorham himself. Once this had been accomplished Phillpotts bore the new incumbent no ill-will and later sent him a donation towards the restoration of his church. But at the national level the controversy was fuelled by the publication of some 60 pamphlets and books – concerned chiefly with the state's jurisdiction over a doctrinal issue – and the Archdeacon of Chichester left the Church of England to become a Roman Catholic and a cardinal. A foreign visitor congratulated England on having suffered no greater a revolution than that provoked by 'le père Gorham'.

Phillpotts continued to do everything in his power to prevent any kind of revolution. Mention of Robert Owen and his socialism never failed to raise his blood pressure, and besides the Reform Bill, which came early in his episcopate, he went on to oppose the setting up of the Ecclesiastical Commission, the Ecclesiastical Discipline Bill, the commutation of tithes, the abolition of pluralities (naturally), the establishing of a bishopric in Jerusalem, the Dissenters Chapel Bill and an act for the registration of marriages. He played a leading part in the opposition to the appointment of R. D. Hampden to the Bishopric of Hereford, while a proposal in 1850 that a commission should examine the possibility of reforming Oxford and Cambridge drew from him what A. C. Tait, a future Archbishop of Canterbury, described as 'a thundering letter'. Neither was he a friend of the poor, being the only bishop to oppose an amendment to the Poor Law which until 1854 consigned unmarried mothers and their children to the workhouse.

Yet, although Phillpotts was deeply conservative in so many ways and fortunately, as it may seem, an inveterate backer of lost causes, he was strikingly ahead of his time in the matter of church reform. As early as 1833 he was suggesting the setting up of a college for the training of clergy. This did not materialize until 1861, when he gave £10,000 for its financing, and it survived for only six years, by which time theological colleges were springing up in many other cathedral cities. He recognized the need for a separate diocese for Cornwall and laid the foundations for the creation of the Diocese of Truro in 1877. He saw the need for more clergy and new churches in the expanding towns and, in the teeth of fierce opposition, facilitated the revival of women's religious communities in the Church of England through his support of Priscilla Lydia Sellon's Devonport Sisters. The Diocesan Synod of Clergy which he convened in 1851 was the first to be held in the Church of England for a very long time and, although concerned primarily to call the clergy to doctrinal order in the wake of the Gorham case, he took the opportunity also to advocate a diocesan training college for teachers, more work among young people, more frequent church services and the wider observance of holy days. Other innovations included the ordination of non-academic men to the permanent diaconate but an earlier attempt to enforce the wearing of surplices by clergy when preaching had to be withdrawn after 'surplice riots' in Exeter.

In old age Phillpotts mellowed somewhat and failing health caused him to live in seclusion from 1863 onwards. Bishop Samuel Wilberforce, visiting him in 1867, found him still 'in full force intellectually' and added, 'It is very striking to see the taming of the Old Lion.' Two years later, when an act empowering bishops to resign from their sees was passed, Phillpotts indicated his readiness to go, but he died before the necessary legal documents were ready for signature. He had fourteen children.

T. B. Strong

When F. R. Barry, who later became Bishop of Southwell, was vicar of Oxford's university church in the late 1920s he wrote to his bishop, T. B. Strong, seeking advice about a relatively minor pastoral problem. To his great surprise he was summoned to the Bishop's Palace at Cuddesdon and even more surprised when, the matter having being dealt with in a few minutes, he was engaged in general conversation and invited to stay for lunch. The talk continued well into the afternoon and, as Barry got up to go, he apologized for taking so much of the bishop's time. 'But, my dear boy,' came the reply, 'I am so grateful to you. I find it so hard to occupy my time here.' That was in a diocese which covered three counties, with over 600 parishes, 750 clergy and many schools, colleges and religious communities.

The sad truth was that Strong (Bishop of Ripon 1920–25, Bishop of Oxford 1925–37) had already virtually given up on what was widely recognized as an impossible job. In any case, it is doubtful that it was his vocation to be a bishop. Before his appointment to Ripon he had spent 41 years at Christ Church, Oxford – nineteen of these as a highly effective dean. He was not a scholar of the first rank, as his books clearly demonstrate, but he had unusual administrative gifts which were fully displayed during his time as vice-chancellor of the university. He had also chaired a small wartime committee which selected university men for army commissions – as many as 2,000 being interviewed in August and September 1914. He was rewarded for his energy and skill by appointment in 1918 as a Knight Grand Cross of the Order of the British Empire (GBE) – one of the highest orders of chivalry and a unique honour for a clergyman.

At this point he let it be known that he would welcome a change from university work and the opportunity to serve the Church as a bishop. This led to a sharp disagreement between the Archbishop of Canterbury, Randall Davidson, and the Prime Minister, Lloyd George. In 1920 the Bishopric of Durham became vacant and Davidson, firmly supported by Archbishop Lang of York, pressed the claims of Strong, arguing that he was a scholar and, as a former examining chaplain to Bishops Lightfoot and Westcott, knew the diocese well. But Lloyd George doubted if Strong's academic background would impress Durham's miners and insisted on translating Hensley Henson, a recent Dean of Durham, from Hereford. Davidson protested in vain, but in the end Lloyd George agreed to appoint Strong to Ripon which also chanced to be vacant.

He was bitterly disappointed to miss Durham but set about Ripon with a will and for the relatively short time he was there enjoyed the work, especially in Leeds and other urban areas. He also used his administrative skills to implement with great efficiency the provisions of the 1919 Enabling Act which prescribed parochial church councils and other participatory bodies. But although a devout man, endowed with an optimistic and sweet-tempered nature, he soon began to display some surprising tendencies in a bishop. He disliked public occasions and did not seem over-fond of church services. He was a poor speaker and preacher, and his special gifts as a musician made him particularly sensitive to the limitations of village organists and choirs. Of one choir he said, 'The noise it made was such as to twist the intestines of a hyena.'

Sometimes he would consent to preach in a village church only if he were allowed to play the organ for the service. Problems over music in worship extended to ceremonial. 'I dislike symbolism,' he once declared, and when an anxious vicar enquired, 'May I ask, my Lord, where your pastoral staff is?' he replied, 'Well, I'm not really sure, but I hope it is lost.'

Tommy Strong, as he was generally known, was born in Brompton, London, in 1861 and throughout his life remained very much a townsman. He went from Westminster School to Christ Church, Oxford, where, even in that society, his ungainly figure, crowned by a shock of red hair and attended by strange mannerisms, caused some comment. He took a first in Mods but only a second in Greats, having devoted rather too much time to the Oxford Musical Society. He was a highly competent organist and played for Evensong at Christ Church on Thursdays when Dr Corfe, the organist, was out hunting and could not get back in time. After taking his degree he became a lecturer at Christ Church, was ordained in 1885 and elected a student (fellow) in the following year. He was a High Churchman, on the liberal wing of the Tractarian Movement, and among his colleagues were Edward King and Henry Parry Liddon, as well as Charles Dodgson, otherwise Lewis Carroll of *Alice in Wonderland* fame. His Bampton Lectures in 1895 were devoted to Christian ethics but, since they advanced little further than ancient Greece and first-century Judaism, and ignored contemporary issues, they aroused little interest. Nonetheless he was a very popular member of Christ Church. Retiring and shy, and unable to express his feelings, he made an impact through his presence and the scintillating quality of his conversation. He expressed himself best through music and was happiest with the undergraduates, among whom was William Walton, the future composer, who benefited from his financial help. Women frightened him. He became Dean in 1901 and during his tenure of the deanery did much to rid the college of its reputation for snobbery.

His translation from the Bishopric of Ripon to that of Oxford in 1925 was a tragic mistake. Now aged 64, his sight and general health were already in decline. Yet he remained in office for thirteen years and in the words of his sympathetic biographer, Harold Anson, who knew him for over sixty years, 'endeared himself to individuals, but to the majority of his vast flock was an incomprehensible and aloof figure, out of touch with the increasing love of ceremonial occasions and multitudinous services which marked the ecclesiastic work of his day'. On one occasion, when visiting a parish to institute a new vicar, he chose to put on his robes in his car so that he would not have to meet the assembled clergy in the church vestry. Asked what hymns he would like, he replied, 'No hymns.' And, having conducted the service at breakneck speed, he shook hands with the vicar, said, 'I hope you will be happy,' and drove speedily off. Confirmations conducted by him were invariably disappointing and were hardly improved when he called out 'Faster, faster' to the clergy who were marshalling their candidates.

On the other hand, he gave a great deal of time to the students at Cuddesdon Theological College, near his home, and they provided him with some sort of family, for he never married. As Clerk of the Closet, he often stayed with King George V whom he described as the best type of Pass man, and he admired the Prince of Wales (the future King Edward VIII) whom he had come to know as an Oxford undergraduate and whose signed portrait always stood on his desk. The central administrative affairs of the Church were of not the slightest interest to him and when a lady asked him if he had been to see *Much Ado About Nothing*, then being played in Oxford, he replied, 'Yes, I have just spent a week at the Church Assembly.' Music was always his greatest love and one of his chaplains reported that during the evening he would often be found with the score of a Wagner opera or a Mozart concerto on his knee, enjoying the music in his head.

During his final years in Oxford diocese, which he always believed should have been divided into three, his memory lapses were serious enough to indicate some form of dementia. Failure to arrive for a confirmation at Eton led to an emergency call to one of the suffragan bishops who came with all haste while the congregation waited. Another confirmation, in a village church, was notable for the presence of three bishops. Strong, having decided two days earlier that the weather was too inclement for him to make the journey, asked each of the suffragans to take his place, then at the last minute went himself without informing either of them. His retirement was spent in London where he lived with his sister and, in spite of the wartime bombing, arrived at the Athenaeum at precisely 10 o'clock every morning. On Sundays he attended Westminster Abbey where he felt very much at home. Invited to lunch at the Inner Temple one day a neighbour asked who had succeeded him as Bishop of Oxford. 'I am afraid that I haven't the slightest idea,' came the reply. He died in 1944.

Mervyn Stockwood

Mervyn Stockwood, Bishop of Southwark, 1959–80, was one of the twentieth century's most colourful bishops, and also one of its most enigmatic personalities. Arriving at Southwark to a fanfare of trumpets, after hugely successful ministries as a parish priest in the East End of Bristol and as vicar of the university church at Cambridge, he was seen by many

as a beacon of hope in the renewal of the Church of England. Throughout the radical 1960s 'South Bank religion' became shorthand for things
new in theology, ethics and parish life. Under Stockwood's leadership
some of the most able clergy of the post-war era tackled the long-
standing problem of the Church's alienation from all but a tiny per-
centage of London's population. A lot of noise was made and some
developments of permanent worth achieved, but when, after 21 years,
Stockwood retired, the number of people in the diocese attending church
was fewer than ever before and he had spent the final years of his episcopate in debilitating depression.

The failure to arrest decline was certainly not his fault, and it served
to demonstrate beyond dispute that the Church's inner-city problems
could not be solved simply by recruiting gifted and dedicated clerics.
Stockwood was both, and for the greater part of his time at Southwark
his leadership was inspiring. Yet those who observed him closely were
aware of strange inconsistencies. Unmarried, he craved affection but was
a demanding and sometimes ruthless friend whom it was not always easy
to love. He made no secret of his socialism, but neither did he of the
fact that he employed a liveried servant and a cordon bleu cook. He was
genuinely concerned for the poor, and spoke up for them in the House
of Lords, but he was more often in the company of the titled rich, among
whom he was at various times pleased to number the Duke and Duch-
ess of Windsor, Princess Margaret and the Prince of Wales. He hated
fascism, but was a close friend of Sir Oswald Mosley who had been the
leader of the British fascists in the 1930s. In church matters he was the
enfant terrible of the Establishment, which probably stood in the way
of his translation to the Archbishopric of York when this fell vacant
in 1975, but in his personal faith and devotion he was traditional and
sometimes exhibited the worst feature of prelacy. Michael De-la-Noy
subtitled his biography of Stockwood 'A Lonely Life' and there was
broad agreement among those nearest to him that his disciplined homosexuality precluded the establishing of a permanent, sustaining relationship which might have brought him happiness and fulfilment at the
deepest level.

He was born in Bridgend, Somerset, in 1913, but following the death
of his solicitor father in the Battle of the Somme in 1916 the family
moved to Bristol. He was brought up by his mother who, until her death
in 1967, played a large part in his emotional life. At Kelly College, Tavis-
tock, he was remembered as a loner, but as a small child felt drawn to the
priesthood and in Bristol was much influenced by the Anglo-Catholicism
of All Saints Church, Clifton. Owing to financial problems a university
education could not be afforded so he taught for a time in a preparatory
school until he had enough money to go to Christ's College, Cambridge.

There he came under the liberal influence of the Master, C. E. Raven, and having taken seconds in history and theology went to Westcott House to prepare for Holy Orders. He now established a lasting friendship with John Collins, the future controversial Canon of St Paul's, and said later that he arrived at Westcott House as a Tory and left as a Socialist. This led in 1936 to a curacy at St Matthew's, Moorfields – a large parish in the poorest part of Bristol – where he exercised a remarkable ministry for the next nineteen years. He had intended to move to a Sheffield parish in 1941 but the first heavy bombing raids on Bristol coincided with the departure of the Vicar of St Matthew's and he was persuaded to stay on in his place. The bombing continued, causing great damage in the parish, and Stockwood exercised an heroic ministry amid much danger and distress. In this situation he recognized the need for all the churches to work together and was instrumental in founding the Redcliffe United Front – a pioneering ecumenical venture.

After attending a pre-war meeting addressed by the local MP, Sir Stafford Cripps, Stockwood had joined the Labour Party and become a close friend of the future Chancellor of the Exchequer. So much so that when Cripps was expelled from the Labour Party in 1938 Stockwood was among the local supporters who went with him, and it was not until 1944 that he rejoined. Two years later he was elected to Bristol City Council and became chairman of its health committee, causing some controversy by setting up a birth control clinic in one of the poorer areas of the city. He also had a number of central church appointments and on his visits to London often stayed with Sir Stafford Cripps at No. 11 Downing Street – a privilege he greatly enjoyed.

In 1955 he moved to Cambridge as Vicar of Great St Mary's and over the next five years completely transformed the life of the university church. When he arrived it was poorly attended and generally in low water, but by the time he left as many as 1,000 people were attending the Sunday evening service and his own impact on both town and university was considerable. The time was ripe for his kind of ministry. In the aftermath of war there was a mini-boom in religious interest and during the 1950s the college chapels were attracting large numbers of enquiring, idealistic undergraduates. The dynamic Stockwood, whose pastoral gifts were accompanied by openness to new ideas and the flair of an impresario, was able to meet that need. Some of the most famous preachers and speakers on the national and international circuits were enticed to Cambridge on Sunday evenings and, after they had addressed one of the key issues of the day, conducted question and answer sessions. It was an exciting time and Stockwood continued his own political work as a member of the town council, though being part of a Labour minority restricted his influence.

Archbishop Geoffrey Fisher then pressed for Stockwood's appointment to Southwark in 1959 and managed to persuade the Conservative Prime Minister, Harold Macmillan, that his nominee's political views were not a serious obstacle. Stockwood was however soon to find it much more difficult to persuade Fisher that John Robinson, who had been one of his Bristol curates and was now Dean of Clare College, Cambridge, should become Suffragan Bishop of Woolwich. But in the end he got his way, though his relations with Fisher went into decline. 'You are doing a great job,' Fisher wrote to him, 'though very often in the wrong way.' Later they fell out when Stockwood refused Freemasons the use of a church in the diocese.

During the furore that followed the publication of *Honest to God* in 1963 John Robinson was strongly supported by his diocesan bishop, though Stockwood himself did not feel the need for such a radical questioning of traditional statements of belief. The two bishops collaborated closely over the pioneering Southwark Ordination Scheme, designed to train men, and later women, for the priesthood while remaining in their secular occupations. Stockwood always made interesting choices for his suffragan bishoprics, most of whom went on to become outstandingly good diocesan bishops.

The pastoral care of the clergy was a high priority for him, though he quarrelled badly with some and at one time had the inconvenient habit of summoning men for interview at midnight. He was also a demanding guest if invited to stay at a vicarage overnight – sending advance instructions about his requirements, which included a hot-water bottle and a glass of whisky by his bedside. Rose-water was requested for episcopal finger-washing at the Eucharist. In 1961 he attracted wide publicity through his handling of the case of an adulterous vicar who, having been found guilty by a consistory court, was unfrocked by the bishop in a grotesque ceremony in Southwark Cathedral. In this he was undoubtedly badly advised by his chancellor, who was a close friend, but the dramatic aspects of the whole affair were not unattractive to him. Later he fell out with the chancellor on the grounds that he was being unduly legalistic in his dealings with applications for faculties for church alterations and he took over the chancellor's role, dealing himself with such submissions.

Stockwood spoke frequently in the House of Lords on a wide range of subjects, including homosexual law reform, divorce, apartheid, capital punishment and housing. He always took a liberal position and in a debate on Rhodesia shortly before Christmas suggested that the racist Smith regime in that colony should take tins of whitewash and change the colour of the kings at the crib. His views were often expressed in colourful language (Enoch Powell's notorious 'rivers of blood' speech on immigration was described as an 'evil fart') and he enjoyed the consequent publicity. The Church Assembly and its successor the General Synod bored him greatly and he made no secret of his frustration with its lack of vision and courage. More to his liking were visits to Romania and Russia, though the lavish hospitality heaped upon him on these occasions led to some unwise statements about the supposed benefits of communism.

He also greatly enjoyed entertaining in style at Bishop's House in Streatham and guests were sometimes surprised when the aperitifs were interrupted by the arrival of a servant of Middle Eastern origin, clad in a smart livery, who announced, 'Lunch is served, my Lord.' Those who had made their journey by car needed to exercise the greatest discipline, since the flow of fine wines, then of liqueurs, was constant. Sometimes his own speech became slurred, though his chaplains all testified to the fact that he was not an alcoholic. Equally, it was agreed that the long sequence of close friendships with young men never went beyond the boundaries of sexual propriety.

Depression, accompanied by boils and eczema, struck him in 1975 and for the next five years, until his retirement, he was a sad figure. He had been left at Southwark far too long, for he was essentially an innovator rather than a sustainer and needed the stimulus of excitement and success. At his final service in Southwark Cathedral he was presented, among other things, with a Jeroboam of champagne which he acknowledged to be an appropriate gift since 'I have attempted to bring a little fizz into the diocese.' In retirement in Bath he recovered some of his former zest and took part, controversially, in the ordination of an Englishwoman to the priesthood in the United States. He died in 1995 and his funeral requiem was followed by a champagne reception.

Douglas Feaver

Douglas Feaver's appointment to the Bishopric of Peterborough, which he occupied from 1972 to 1984, occasioned some surprise, not least to himself. He had reached the age of 58 and, believing himself to be generally out of tune with the times, both in church and society, was contemplating early retirement. He was at that time Vicar of St Mary's, Nottingham, where he had been for the past fourteen years, but when he arrived at Peterborough all thoughts of retirement had been vanquished: 'Well, here we are,' he announced to his first diocesan synod, 'I won't say with Wolsey that I have come to lay my bones among you, but I have no intention of moving again: the undertakers can be my next removers and the Church Commissioners can pay.' He did not keep this promise, which was just as well.

Feaver had a fine intellect and was an arresting preacher, though his ringing, alliterative style was not to everyone's taste. He cared deeply for the Church of England and believed that the Authorized Version of the Bible and the Book of Common Prayer remained the primary sources of its spirituality. Those drawn to the 1980 Alternative Service Book were advised to 'taste it and spit it out' and when celebrating Holy Communion in reordered sanctuaries he would order the altar to be returned to its former place against the east wall. 'One of the present feckless follies is to try and throw away the experience, tradition and redeemed realities of the past,' was his response to proposals for liturgical change. He also strove to maintain the traditional parochial system, with a priest to every parish, long after this was practically feasible, and he exemplified the concept of the bishop as a leader of independent mind whose authority lay beyond challenge.

This deeply conservative outlook was accompanied and expressed by a barbed tongue which often stood in the way of effective pastoral ministry. During a confirmation service he turned to the boy candidates and asked, 'Do you know the sort of girl you would like to marry?' Then, pointing his crozier in the direction of three elderly women candidates, he added, 'Mind you, there's not much choice here tonight.' It was intended as a joke, but it was hardly the most sensitive way to prepare these ladies for confirmation. His remark that the women members of the General Synod had 'seething bosoms but nothing above' was also as offensive as it was untrue and aroused the ire of a number of women whose intellect was not inferior to his own. On the day of his consecration as a bishop the notably wise and charitable Dean of Westminster, Eric Abbott, who knew him well, told a friend, 'I do hope the Holy Spirit has worked. He'll need it, because he is the rudest man in the Church of England.' The dean and others were due to be disappointed, for the habit was too deeply ingrained.

One explanation of his rudeness and apparent delight in hurting was that he was permanently scarred by a traumatic experience when, as a young RAF chaplain, he was serving in Egypt and became critically ill. He heard his grave being dug outside the hospital ward where he was lying and, although he recovered and was left only with a permanent limp, the psychological damage may well have remained. Undoubtedly he was, beneath his formidable exterior, a deeply shy man – he always refused to shake hands – and his brusque insensitivity on public occasions when he was the centre of attention may perhaps have been a defence against the intense interior strain which these occasions caused him. He would himself have quickly dismissed any such attempted explanations of his behaviour, preferring something more robust, such as 'original sin'.

Feaver was born in Bristol in 1914 and went from the city's grammar school to Keble College, Oxford, where he carried all before him, taking firsts in modern history and theology and winning the Liddon Studentship. Rejecting the suggestion of an academic career, he prepared for Holy Orders at Wells Theological College and in 1938 became a curate of St Albans Abbey. He was in the RAF from 1942 to 1945 and on demobilization returned to St Albans where, although only 32, he was made a canon and the Sub-Dean. During the next twelve years he became more widely known in the Church and was influential through his work as chief book reviewer for the *Church Times*. He was an editor's dream contributor, with an ability to get to the heart of a big book quickly and then produce – never late – a review of exactly the right length, penned in lucid and elegant prose. His sermons suited the abbey's intelligent congregations and those who found his personality difficult had other members of the chapter to whom they could turn for pastoral care.

By the time he had reached his mid-forties there was every reason to suppose that Feaver would be appointed to a deanery or even to a bishopric, but his inability to work with others and his rudeness were now well known and seemed to constitute an insuperable obstacle to high office in an increasingly insecure Church that looked for collaboration and kindness in its leaders. In the end Bishop F. R. Barry of Southwell, who appreciated intellectuals, came to the rescue and appointed him Vicar and Rural Dean of Nottingham. This was never going to be an easy job, for St Mary's was geographically off-centre and had not become established as the focal point of the city's religious life. Nor was Feaver ever likely to make it so, for he was not the kind of priest ever to become involved in a wide range of community activity.

The Book of Common Prayer, with good music and fine preaching, was his ideal for any parish church, and this was greatly valued by those – a declining number – who appreciated traditional Anglicanism at its best. He demanded high standards of those entrusted with reading Lessons and once ordered a curate who was struggling with a difficult passage at a crowded Mothers' Union festival service to 'come down and stop that rubbish'. The young man had been asked to read only a few moments before the service started. Problems eventually and inevitably arose over Feaver's relations with his bishop. This was partly a matter of personal chemistry, but mainly due to a clash between Barry's liberal mind and Feaver's militant conservatism. At one never-to-be-forgotten diocesan conference, when Feaver stood to speak, Barry – who was now very deaf – enquired of a neighbour on the platform, 'Is that Feaver speaking?' On being told that it was, he ostentatiously switched off his antiquated hearing aid and said in a loud voice, 'Tell me when he's finished.'

Feaver's appointment to Peterborough made sense inasmuch as he would preside over one of the Church of England's most conservative dioceses and he was certainly no more backward-looking than his predecessor, Cyril Eastaugh, had been. The Archbishop of Canterbury (Michael Ramsey) and the Prime Minister (Edward Heath) were united in believing that he would add intellectual weight to the bench. Within the diocese he proved to be, in spite of all his rudeness, an exemplary pastor to the clergy, while the leading lay people came to appreciate his astringent style. He believed that the clergy should be left free to get on with the running of their parishes without episcopal interference, though he was always on hand if a crisis arose. He refused to have a suffragan bishop to assist him, claiming that they were no more than 'consecrated nannies to look after the clergy'.

National and international meetings that took a bishop away from his diocese were an anathema to Feaver and his *Who's Who* entry included under Hobbies – 'Conferences not attended'. Of the General Synod, which as a bishop he was obliged to attend, he said 'I wonder when I am sitting there why Church people should be asked for money to pay to keep this cuckoo growing.' The prospect of spending nearly a month at the 1978 Lambeth Conference filled him with horror and at the end of it he told his diocese, 'Nothing much came of it, but then nothing much was put in.' In 1982 he was one of the eleven bishops who voted against a scheme for uniting the Church of England with the Methodist, United Reformed and Moravian Churches under a Covenant, and in the following year wrote to his diocese, 'The next step towards the reunion of Christendom must be Romewards and must be pursued not by attack and counter-attack but by exploring tradition and history and becoming thereby a little wiser and a little more full of hope.' He retired in 1984 and at his farewell the vice-chairman of the diocesan synod said, 'He has been his own man. How refreshing to have had a leader who never worried about being liked.' He died in 1997.

It is none too easy for today's bishop to be his own man and, sadly, the day of colourful personality on the bench seems to have passed – only temporarily one hopes. The chief obstacle to episcopal independence is undoubtedly the advent of synodical government and a new understanding of the bishop's role.

Twentieth-century insights led to important and welcome recovery of the corporate character of the Church. No longer is the Church seen simply in terms of the clergy. Rather is it a body in which, in the words of the Good Friday collect, 'every member of the same in his vocation and ministry may truly serve God'. The implications of this have yet to be fully worked out, but the laity now play a much greater part in the Church's ministry and in decision-making. Another consequence is that bishops have lost most of their previous independence and are expected to consult, and to submit to democratic procedures when decisions are required. The concept has arisen of authority being exercised by the bishop-in-synod.

The recognition of the Church's corporate character has brought many benefits, not least in places where lack of clergy has given scope for lay leadership. But the synodical system adopted by the Church of England is not popular. The General Synod commands little respect. Diocesan synods are poorly attended, often by fewer than 50 per cent of their members, and, since deanery synods are little more than talking shops, the representatives of the parishes usually have to be dragooned into accepting election. Important legislation must pass through these different levels of government before returning to the General Synod for final acceptance and implementation – a process that often takes a year or more. Modest reforms have made little difference to any of this and a more radical approach will be needed if the Church is to become a dynamic instrument of mission in which bold decisions can be made quickly.

A bishop of strong personality can sometimes secure synodical agreement to policies which he believes to be right for his diocese, but even in the most favourable circumstances it is a laborious task. Many have to face frequent disappointment. Part of the reason for this is simply lack of trust engendered by a partisan spirit which accords priority to factional interests and hampers effective leadership. This is exacerbated when, as now, money is tight and decisions about expenditure of funds are made by structural fundamentalists who are without a vision of what the Christian mission now requires and are apparently deaf to the prompting of the Holy Spirit.

Yet the Church of England remains an episcopal church in which the bishops are at their consecration entrusted with a heavy responsibility of leadership. They are not intended to be the elected chairmen of a series of elected committees. It is essential that their responsibility should be shared, only so it can be properly discharged. But it is also essential that they should be trusted (hardly an outrageous suggestion in a Christian community) and given freedom to make unusual and unexpected proposals as well as support in their implementation. Only so will the Christian mission be advanced.

Christian ministry in all its aspects is exercised through the personality of the minister – lay person, deacon, priest or bishop – as indeed it was through the personality of him who came 'not to be ministered unto, but to minister and to give his life for many'. This requires space for the expression of personality, for distinctive style, for the sharing of insight and for the making of mistakes. Virtually every bishop portrayed in this volume was free to be his own man and the result was rich variety. Only the most recent – Mervyn Stockwood and Douglas Feaver – felt the constraints of synodical pressure and they rebelled against it. Archbishop Michael Ramsey, while presiding over a particularly serious General Synod debate, burst into loud laughter. Asked later about the reason for his mirth, he explained that his mind had been far removed from the subject of the debate – 'Yes, yes, I was far, far away.' The episcopate will be grievously diminished if there is no longer room for the Odd Man Out and the bench is permanently reduced to worthy but dull uniformity.

14

The pioneers – looking ahead

The Church of England, in common with all the major churches of Western Europe, is experiencing an unprecedented decline in numerical support and influence. Church attendance fell throughout the twentieth century and the point has now been reached when fewer than one million people attend English parish churches on Sunday. In 1970 this figure was 1.5 million, while in the same year the number of Christmas communicants was over 1.6 million and Easter communicants totalled 1.8 million. By 1999 the number of communicants at both Christmas and Easter had fallen to about 1.2 million, though in that year, as in 1970, the total church attendance on these major festivals was significantly higher. More serious for a Church which has always valued its links with those who are not regular worshippers, only one in five babies are now baptized at its fonts, only one in four marriages are solemnized at its altars, and in urban areas most funerals are now conducted in crematorium chapels, often without a Christian ceremony. Shortage of money is making it increasingly difficult for a full-time stipendiary ministry to be maintained even at the reduced level caused by the decline in vocations to the priesthood. In this serious situation, whatever the reason for it may be, the need for visionary leadership and bold mission strategy is desperately urgent – and generally lacking. Hence the importance of reconsidering, in the light of historical development, the origin and nature of the episcopal office through which the leadership of the Church is chiefly exercised.

The long-standing belief that bishops have a lineage that goes back in unbroken succession to the Apostles chosen and sent out on mission by Jesus is no longer tenable. There is no evidence that he intended the Apostles to appoint successors and every indication that their missionary function was to be exercised by the whole of the Christian community, of which they were the nucleus. The earliest years of Christianity were characterized, as might be expected, by a variety of forms of organization and leadership, with presbyters or elders most commonly presiding at the Eucharist. The expansion of the Church during the second century required however a more widely recognized and unifying form of leadership and this was entrusted to certain of the presbyters who would exercise a ministry that could appropriately be described as apostolic. They were to be guardians of the original gospel, as this had been taught by Jesus to the Apostles, and they were also to be leaders of the Church's mission in the world. The title Bishop – in Greek *episcopos*, literally an overseer – indicated their additional role of pastoral oversight, and they were commissioned by the laying-on of hands with prayer – a sacramental act, a means of grace, to sustain them in the carrying out of their sacred duties. Their office was not however sacerdotal, but always representative and exercised on behalf of, and with the authority of, the whole Church.

The exercising of the bishop's pioneering missionary role was later modified as the Church continued to grow and the new Christian communities required more and more pastoral oversight, together with a more developed organization. The importance of the bishop as a focus of unity also became more significant and division over matters of belief required recognized arbiters of orthodoxy. By the time of Cyprian (Bishop of Carthage 248–58) episcopacy was ceasing to be seen in corporate terms. Cyprian, himself a reluctant recruit to the episcopate, believed and taught that it was of divine origin, and for him the authenticity of a Church's life and ministry required evidence of validly ordained bishops in a succession allegedly traceable back to the Apostles. This distorted development of doctrine and practice was destined to hold the field for many centuries and is still accepted by the Roman and Orthodox Churches, and in some parts of the Church of England. Unsurprisingly, belief that bishops were appointed by God, inspired by God, and responsible only to God soon elevated their status and power, and led to an increasingly wide distance between the holders of the office and the rest of the Church.

The rapid growth of the Church in the Mediterranean world following the Emperor Constantine's Edict of Milan in 313, and its new relationship with the state, led to a further distortion of the earlier pattern of episcopal ministry. Pastoral oversight eclipsed any remaining missionary role, while involvement in the hierarchical Roman world encouraged some leaders of the Church to view their own organization in even more hierarchical terms. This led to the Church being regarded, both internally and externally, primarily as the clergy, with bishops elevated to the rank of princes and the laity reduced to the role of supporters. The consequence of this loss of apostolic vision and pioneering spirit by the Church's leaders was a disastrous misunderstanding of the Church's calling which has been a grievous hindrance to the Christian mission in most parts of the world ever since.

But not everywhere. The conversion of England in the seventh century was largely carried out by pioneering missionary bishops. In the following century Boniface – probably the most successful missionary who has ever lived – went from England to become a pioneering bishop in Germany and was largely responsible for the conversion of the German people from paganism to Christianity. He travelled on foot, preached the Gospel in the open air and baptized converts in streams and rivers. A similar pattern characterized the missionary movement that took the Christian faith from England to Africa, Asia, Australasia and most other parts of the English-speaking world during the nineteenth century. In the grandeur of Westminster Abbey or the intimacy of the chapel of Lambeth Palace, courageous young men were consecrated as bishops to undertake pioneering missionary work in territories where the Christian faith was unknown, and to establish churches and dioceses. Their expression of the apostolic, pioneering character of the Church is as inspiring and as challenging as any in Church history and the lives of a few of them have been portrayed in Chapter 11.

The mission of the Church of England today cannot be exercised in ways that seemed appropriate in previous eras, and in some ways the task is more difficult inasmuch as the division between belief and unbelief is much less clear-cut. In his illuminating Gifford Lectures, published in 1975 as *The Secularization of the European Mind in the Nineteenth Century*, Owen Chadwick analysed some of the causes of this process – new machinery, the growth of large cities, a cheap press, the organization of the working class, the impact of Marx, the problems posed by evolutionary science, the development of democracy. At the end of his study he confessed, however, that it was still far from clear why all these movements had come together during a relatively brief period of history and what the long-term consequences were likely to be. Nonetheless, the effect on religious belief and church attendance is all too plain, even though some residual, ill-defined religious faith remains. In times of social trauma church attendance increases for a short time, and the Church of England still has substantial resources of buildings, clergy and money, but there is every sign that the secularization process will continue.

In these circumstances the Church has only two options. It can continue more or less along the traditional pattern of life it has inherited from the Middle Ages, with minor reforms here and there, and in the hope that the decline of membership will eventually bottom out, and that one day a new age of faith will dawn. More people will then recognize the truth of the Christian faith and return to regular worship in their parish churches. This is evidently the policy of the Church of England today, which if not stated in so many words is implied by almost every element in its organization and activity.

The alternative option, which this book is concerned to promote, involves recognition of the fact that the Church is now in an unprecedented missionary situation in which the methods and systems appropriate to a Europe which had so completely embraced the Christian faith that it could be described as Christendom are no longer effective. Blomfield, Wilberforce and other activist Victorian bishops came to see that the new urban masses were far removed from Christian faith, but the only tools they used to remedy this situation were those they had inherited from a stable, agrarian past – church buildings in the Gothic style, geographical parishes and gentlemen clergy. The impact was negligible, yet – with far less excuse – these same tools continued to be used throughout the deteriorating years of the twentieth century, and modest experiments in new forms of mission were abandoned when money became tight.

At the beginning of a new century, fraught with danger to civilization, the old tools still await modification and augmentation – a neglect that can be explained only in terms of lack of vision and inspired leadership. In such a situation it may seem futile to suggest radical change and, at a time when war is being waged against global terrorism, it may seem scandalously trivial to recommend, yet again, the reorganization of the internal life of the Church. Yet if religion is as important as the present world crisis indicates it to be, and if the Church of England is to make any significant contribution to the maintaining of Christian belief and values, and to the promoting of inter-faith and inter-cultural harmony in these islands, it is hard to see how change can be avoided or even further delayed. The same is true of all the other churches but precise knowledge and space is lacking for the scope of this volume to be enlarged.

Fortunately, those who are concerned for the recovery of the Church's mission in England do not have to start thinking and planning from scratch. Much work on mission theology and its implications in the modern world has already been undertaken and awaits serious consideration. This contains no exact blueprints but provides enough material to point in the general direction of radical change and enough suggestions to stimulate further thought and bold action in places where movement is urgent.

In 1961 the Third Assembly of the World Council of Churches authorized an ecumenical study of the Missionary Structure of the Congregation. This turned out to be a largely Western European project which involved some of the most able theological, sociological and missionary minds of the region. Over a period of several years extensive consultations were held, some in England; research papers were evaluated and published, experiments were encouraged. A well-attended conference in Birmingham aroused much interest and enthusiasm. But the project failed to make an impression on the Church of England's bishops who became distracted by church unity proposals and items of reform which, while not in themselves unimportant, failed to address the broader and more fundamental question of how the Church might restructure its life for mission. It is fair to assume that a new generation of bishops is unaware of the project and the fruit of its labours.

It was obvious to all who took part in it that mission today has little if anything to do with open-air preaching designed to win individual converts. For 150 years and more this has proved to be ineffective, simply because it takes little account of the other influences at work in an individual's life. On the other hand, there remains an important place for thoughtful, intelligent preaching and teaching of the Christian faith in contemporary terms during acts of worship in church, and in groups, meetings and publications. There is a gap here that urgently needs to be filled. More pressing however is the conversion of the local congregations from their attachment to maintenance to the embracing of mission. The consequent reorientation of church life will lead to new openness, so that through group activity and personal witness in service the wider community, of which the Church is a part, will be infiltrated and improved. This is a long-term approach, which will not yield immediate results in the form of larger congregations, but aims to inject by a variety of means Christian values into society. At the same time it should provide clues as to the future shape of the pioneering missionary Church. There is already a great deal of experience of Christian involvement in social and community work at certain levels and this needs to be expanded to meet unfulfilled need. Recent suggestions that parish churches might provide facilities for rural post offices and banks are another pointer in the right direction.

Movement from maintenance to mission does however raise an important question regarding size. It is impossible for very small congregations to offer dynamic acts of worship in large, mainly empty, church buildings. It is also unrealistic to expect small congregations, struggling to maintain a large, probably mediaeval, building and some semblance of traditional church life, to launch out into extensive mission activity in their parishes. Larger, and therefore in the present circumstances fewer, units of church life are required in order that resources can be concentrated and used strategically to meet the needs of mission in areas larger than the traditional parish. This need not necessarily involve the closure of many churches – in villages and other definable communities this is always undesirable – and they can be kept open for prayer, occasional acts of worship and inspection by visitors. The locking of churches during the hours of daylight should be forbidden.

A missionary Church cannot however base its work solely on units, large or small, that are serving only residential communities. Until the great movement from rural areas to the new industrial towns in the eighteenth and nineteenth centuries most people spent the whole of their lives – home, work, leisure – in a small, closely-knit community, with the church at the centre and the parson, if resident, running a mini-welfare state for the needy. This is no longer the case. Most people are now involved in several different communities – for work, education, leisure, shopping – in a highly complex social network, and the Church, mainly through its laity but not without strategy, needs to be in touch with these communities, serving and influencing them. This requires very much larger units of church life that embrace a zone or region and enable the mission to encompass every aspect of social activity. Closely related to this is the need to be in regular contact with society's influencers and decision-makers, for it is no longer at neighbourhood or even town levels that the decisions affecting the quality of community life are made. If the Church is not to retreat, or allow itself to be pushed, to the margins of society it will need to be organized to make a significant contribution at the highest levels – contributions which are at the moment by no means unwelcome if informed by recognizable expertise. Industrial Mission at its best provided, and where it survives continues to provide, an important example of this, and the concept could be enlarged to take in other spheres of corporate social and economic life.

Such a change of direction raises the issue of the deployment of the Church's clerical resources, nearly all of which are engaged in parish work in residential communities. This cannot continue if a pioneering Church is to carry out its mission by serving and influencing wider fields of human endeavour. It is also the case that the present parish-based ministry is in most places a long way from dynamic or even satisfactory. The uniting of several rural parishes under one, itinerant, rector, has – in spite of all that is said and done about lay leadership – caused only a weakening of church life in all of them. In towns and cities the haphazard deployment of the clergy often reflects only a makeshift strategy and creates frustration, stress and exhaustion among those charged with the leadership of unnatural and non-viable parishes.

This was clearly discerned in 1983 by Canon John Tiller and discussed in a report to the Advisory Council for the Church's Ministry entitled *A Strategy for the Church's Ministry*. He was nearing the end of his five years as chief secretary to the council, during which time he had been involved in many discussions about the training and deployment of the clergy and spent eighteen months gathering information from all parts of the country in order to make, at the request of the council, a personal report. The resulting 175-page book is as comprehensive and as acute a survey of the early-1980s situation as could be wished for, followed by a series of bold proposals concerning the future. Stated briefly, these envisaged two sorts of priest – local, unpaid priests who, in collaboration with a lay eldership, would be primarily responsible for the leadership of the Church in residential communities, and diocesan stipendiary priests whose primary responsibilities would be missionary and educational. These would be employed in areas wider than a parish and engage in preaching and teaching the faith, in counselling and spiritual direction, in training courses and as consultants to local churches. Many would be involved in specialist work in industry, commerce, education, the health service, leisure-time pursuits and other frontier ministry. Large urban parishes and cathedrals would continue to have clergy on the diocesan payroll. Both diocesan and local priests would undertake a ministry of prayer, help to equip the laity for their ministry in the world, and act as representatives of the Church wherever they might be ministering. Canon Tiller, unaware of the financial problems that were to loom ever larger in the 1990s, did not envisage any reduction in the number of stipendiary priests, but rather the recruitment of many more local, unpaid clergy. He recognized that most of the diocesan priests would require further training. His report was debated by the General Synod but, eighteen years later, still awaits implementation.

There could not be firmer evidence that the revival of the Christian mission in England now requires church leaders of wider vision and who are courageous enough to adopt bold strategies. This points clearly to the need for a recovery of the primitive understanding of the role of the bishop as the pioneering leader of a pioneering Church, though not now in the sense of one who engages in direct missionary activity – at least, not often. In the more complex world of our time the bishop is the one who sees more clearly than most the essential truths of the Christian faith and has a vision of how these truths might be expressed in the life of the Church and in the wider community. These related tasks require generous amounts of time for prayer, study, analysis and reflection, as well as the opportunity to consult his senior colleagues, theological advisers and specialists in secular disciplines. The determining of priorities and the deployment of resources must, as in all strategic thinking, be the aim.

None of which is inconsistent with the spiritual character of the bishop's office, powerfully expressed by a godly bishop of Truro, Edmund Morgan, in 1961:

It is to the Ascended Christ that the Bishop must direct his gaze, to him that he must be attached and responsible, with him that he must be clothed; and above all it is to the Ascended Christ as he presents himself to the Father, for it is by the Bishop's Godward life that his ministry will bear fruit and be controlled. In order to guard against overwork, to counteract the snare of activism, to curb his concern for his reputation, to overcome the temptation to love the praise of men more than the glory of God, his life must be a continual Sursum corda; he must be ever groping, fighting, leaping Godwards. He must in fact give priority to spirituality, abiding in the certainty that God, and not merely 'the things of God', is central in life, personal, ministerial and social. It is God's world, God's Church, God's diocese, God's parish. From the Bishop's Godward apostolate there will flow the energy of divine love. By his self-offering in union with the Ascended Christ he will hold the door open for God to take possession.

The Ascension marked the starting point of the Church's mission and the spread of the Christian faith throughout the Roman world owed everything to the strategic sense of the God-possessed St Paul.

A vital part of the modern bishop's role, once priorities of mission have been determined, will be the deployment of the diocesan priests who are involved in specialist ministries. Their work and new experiments in mission will need to be regularly monitored and evaluated. Quick results are not to be expected, though work which turns out to be clearly unproductive must be abandoned in order that new initiatives may be sustained. The bishop himself, like most of the episcopate today, will be in touch with leaders in other walks of life and in other churches and faiths.

Unlike his predecessors, however, he will be much more deeply involved in his diocese's financial affairs – with the raising and the spending of money. Although many of the Victorian bishops were very active, and successful, fund-raisers – for the building of churches, schools and vicarages, as well as for the stipends of clergy in the new inner-city parishes – their twentieth-century successors tended to steer clear of money, believing this to be best handled by the laity. When the amounts of money required were relatively small this was perhaps excusable, but not so today when very large sums are needed to sustain essential existing work and to finance new enterprises. In this, as in other important matters, the leaders of the Church must lead. If the bishop does not believe fund-raising to be important enough to require his involvement, why should anyone else? Equally, the bishop needs to be influentially involved in decision-making related to major expenditure in order to ensure that the right priorities are established and the right balance struck between maintenance and mission.

The workload of the new- yet really old-style pioneering missionary bishop is already increasing alarmingly and if its burden is to be carried effectively he will need to be liberated from most, if not all, of the present pastoral and administrative work required for maintaining the Church's corporate life. Some of this can be achieved by decentralization and devolution of authority. The deaneries should become budget-holders and decide all matters relating to the deployment of the clergy allocated to them, the support of church schools in their area, social work projects and lay training, including youth and children's work. Where the organization of a diocese, including its synodical structures, stands in the way of reform this should be altered to meet the new requirements.

Any suggestion that smaller dioceses are called for should immediately be rejected, since these would increase establishment costs as well as make it more difficult for the Church to relate to large secular institutions that take no account of diocesan boundaries in the ordering of their affairs. Collaboration between dioceses when these institutions overlap their boundaries will obviously be necessary, and some specialist bishops will be needed to oversee the Church's mission to national bodies such as the railways, the postal and telecommunications services, the universities and the National Health Service.

The greater part of the pastoral and related administrative work of the diocesan bishop must be delegated to area bishops who are chosen for their ability to combine these twin episcopal functions. This will enhance their role and provide them with a sphere of authority and distinctive ministry. As members of the episcopal team they will be in close touch with the diocesan bishop, keeping him well acquainted with the broad trends in parochial life and bringing to him opportunities and problems requiring joint decision-making.

The diocesan bishops required for a renewed pioneering role will need to be strategic thinkers and therefore men and women of considerable ability. Some of the existing bishops will qualify and, released from their present entanglements, the gifts of these will have greater scope. John V. Taylor, who was Bishop of Winchester from 1975 to 1985, went to this senior see when he was aged 60, having spent 30 years in missionary service, first in Uganda, then as Africa and subsequently General Secretary of the Church Missionary Society. A considerable theologian and a man of vision, he played an important role in the transfer of authority in the African dioceses during the 1960s when Britain's former colonies were obtaining their independence. He also had great gifts as a preacher, an actor and a poet, and during his time at Winchester wrote and produced an acclaimed Passion Play which was broadcast on television. The missionary spirit never left him, and he would have been a much more useful bishop had the day-to-day demands of running Winchester diocese been left to the two suffragan bishops, thus allowing his vision and strategic gifts to be devoted to pioneering mission work.

Bishops of the calibre of John Taylor are uncommon but in the longer term it is reasonable to hope that a changed episcopal role will prove to be attractive to the most able priests and to some professional theologians. Tampering with the method of appointment along the lines proposed in the General Synod report *Working With the Spirit* (2001) will not solve the more fundamental problem which is that of an acute shortage of able and willing candidates. The opening of the episcopate to women in England will also greatly increase the size of the field of choice and it may be anticipated that women bishops will have their own particular feminine sights and styles, though the limited experience of women bishops in New Zealand, the USA and Canada suggests that they too are as trapped in the traditional role as are their male counterparts.

During the last two centuries the episcopate of the Church of England has included, as I have sought to illustrate in this book, a rich variety of men of deep spirituality, immense intellectual gifts and no little courage. If this tradition is to be recovered and developed in the centuries to come, the original pioneering role of the bishop will need to be recovered quickly, while there is still time. The Church now has to adopt and experiment with new forms of mission and needs leaders who will point the way and themselves travel along it as men and women sent out by God to proclaim his Kingdom and help establish it.

Bibliography

No-one attempting to write sensibly and accurately about the Church of England in the nineteenth century can afford to be without Owen Chadwick's two-volume classic *The Victorian Church*. Likewise David L. Edwards's *Leaders of the Church of England, 1828–1978* is essential reading for those who are interested in the influence of the Church's leaders, and not only bishops, during both the nineteenth and twentieth centuries. A. C. Benson's *The Leaves of the Tree*, published in 1911, is a delightful volume of portraits of some leading nineteenth-century figures, including several bishops, whom he knew first-hand through their visits to his father, Archbishop Edward White Benson. More recently, Bernard Palmer's *High and Mitred* offers, with scholarship and wit, much information about the way in which Prime Ministers have exercised their responsibility for nominating bishops, while his *A Class of their Own* tells the remarkable tale of how no fewer than six of the eight Archbishops of Canterbury who reigned between 1862 and 1961 were former public school headmasters.

The following list of biographies, and a few autobiographies, is not intended to be exhaustive but is provided for the guidance of readers who may wish to know more about some of those whose lives have been outlined in this present volume. The perceived importance of the nineteenth-century bishop is demonstrated clearly by the large number of episcopal biographies, sometimes in two or even three volumes. Many of these are now to be found – at modest prices – in second-hand booksellers and the Internet is miraculously capable of finding any of them published after about 1870. Try www.abebooks.com.

Cuthbert Bardsley by Donald Coggan, 1989
Ahead of His Age (E. W. Barnes) by John Barnes, 1979
George Bell by R. C. D. Jasper, 1967
Joost de Blank: Scourge of Apartheid by John Peart-Binns, 1987
Charles James Blomfield, 2 vols, by A. Blomfield, 1893
Goodbye to my Generation (autobiography) by Walter Carey, 1951

The Later Cecils (chapter 5: Lord William Cecil) by Kenneth Rose, 1975

The Chavasse Twins by Selwyn Gummer, 1963

John William Colenso, 2 vols, by G. W. Cox, 1888, and a modern study by P. B. Hinchliffe, 1964

Life and Letters of Mandell Creighton by Louise Creighton, 1913

Randall Davidson, 2 vols, by G. K. A. Bell, 1935

The Bishops of Peterborough (chapter on Douglas Feaver) by Geoffrey Carnell, 1993

Archbishop Fisher: His Life and Times by Edward Carpenter, 1991

Friends for Life: A Portrait of Launcelot Fleming by Donald Lindsay, 1981

James Fraser: Life by Thomas Hughes, 1887

The Life of Charles Gore by G. L. Prestige, 1935

Neville Gorton: Reminiscences edited by Frank W. Mayle, 1957

Hensley Henson by Owen Chadwick, 1983; see also *Retrospective of an Unimportant Life* (autobiography) and two volumes of Letters edited by E. F. Braley, 1950–1954

Edward Lee Hicks: Life and Letters edited by J. H. Fowler, 1922; see also *Radical Churchman: Edward Lee Hicks and the New Liberalism* by Graham Neville, 1998

Memoir of William Walsham How by F. D. How

Strategist for the Spirit (Leslie Hunter) edited by Gordon Hewitt, 1985

The Mind and Work of Edward King by B. W. Randolph and J. W. Townroe, 1918; a modern study *Search for a Saint: Edward King* by J. A. Newton, 1977

Kenneth Kirk: Life and Letters by E. W. Kemp, 1959

Cosmo Gordon Lang by J. G. Lockhart, 1949

Joseph Barber Lightfoot: Memoirs and Appreciations edited by G. R. Eden and F. C. Macdonald, 1932

Charles Mackenzie: Memoir by Harvey Goodwin, 1865

John Percival by William Temple, 1921

Henry Phillpotts by G. C. B. Davies, 1954

Ian Ramsey: A Memoir by David L. Edwards, 1973

George Ridding: Schoolmaster and Bishop by Laura Ridding, 1908

John A. T. Robinson by Eric James, 1987

George Augustus Selwyn, 2 vols, by H. W. Tucker, 1879

Edward and Catherine Stanley: Memoirs by A. P. Stanley, 1879

Mervyn Stockwood: A Lonely Life by Michael De-la-Noy, 1996; see also *Chanctonbury Ring* (autobiography)

T. B. Strong by Harold Anson, 1949

Charles Sumner by G. H. Sumner, 1876

Archibald Campbell Tait, 2 vols, by R. T. Davidson and W. Benham,

1891; see also *The Victorian Church in Decline: Archbishop Tait and the Church of England 1868–1882* by P. T. Marsh, 1969

Edward Stuart Talbot: Life by G. Stephenson, 1936

Frederick Temple by P. B. Hinchliffe, 1997

William Temple by F. A. Iremonger, 1948; also by John Kent, 1993

Connop Thirlwall by J. C. Thirlwall, 1936

Brooke Foss Westcott, 2 vols, by A. Westcott, 1903

Bishop of Zanzibar (Frank Weston) by H. Maynard Smith, 1926

E. R. Wickham – for ideas and work see his own *Church and People in an Industrial City*, 1957; also *The Church Beyond the Church: Sheffield Industrial Mission 1944–94* by Paul Bagshaw, 1994

Samuel Wilberforce, 3 vols, by A. R. Ashwell and R. G. Wilberforce, 1980–82

Winnington-Ingram by S. C. Carpenter, 1949

Edward Woods by Oliver Tomkins, 1957

Robin Woods an autobiography, 1986

Index